PARLIAMENTARY REFORM

A Survey of Recent Proposals for the Commons

PARLIAMENTARY
REFORM

A SURVEY OF RECENT PROPOSALS FOR THE COMMONS

PUBLISHED FOR
THE HANSARD SOCIETY BY
CASSELL · LONDON

CASSELL & COMPANY LTD

35 Red Lion Square . London WC1

MELBOURNE · SYDNEY · TORONTO

JOHANNESBURG · AUCKLAND

———

First edition 1961
Second (revised) edition 1967

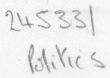
304 92565 9

Printed by J. W. Arrowsmith Ltd., Bristol
1067

CONTENTS

CONTENTS

FOREWORD TO SECOND EDITION

In 1958 the Council of the Hansard Society for Parliamentary Government decided to investigate a question which in a sense has been topical since the establishment of Parliament. In general terms it is the question whether, at any given period in our history, the current arrangements and methods whereby the British Parliament transacts its business enable it adequately to carry out its responsibilities. The flexibility of the British Parliamentary system is one of its glories and Parliamentary history is a record of continuous change.

During the past sixty years, social, technical and economic changes have been so widespread and rapid (and this has been especially true since 1945), that the question outlined above has been under continuous discussion. A very large number of suggestions have been made for changes, great and small, in the Parliamentary set-up.

To acquaint himself with these proposals the student had to search in many publications, including of course the voluminous records of Hansard. It was therefore decided to publish a book which would contain a representative collection of these proposals arranged under appropriate headings and linked together by objective comment. This work was undertaken by two Officers of the House of Commons—Mr. David Pring, a Deputy Principal Clerk, and Dr. David Menhennet, Deputy Librarian. The result of their labours was published in 1961 and played, we believe, a valuable part in the movement for reform which resulted in the changes of 1964–7.

With those changes, and the lapse of time, it is felt that a new edition of the work might be useful. This has again been prepared by the original research team.

Perhaps the most important difference between this edition and its predecessor relates to the House of Lords. In order to avoid the impression that our Parliament has only one Chamber, an

Appendix dealing with some of the proposals for reforming the Lords was included in the 1961 edition. It is now felt, however, that there are obvious disadvantages in including in a book of this character an Appendix treating similar material in a less thorough-going manner. It has accordingly been omitted from this edition, which is therefore confined to proposals for reform of the House of Commons.

Because Parliament is a living body no book on the subject can be completely up to date, and this volume, published at a time when new suggestions for reform of the procedure of the House of Commons are being made almost daily, is no exception to this generally accepted fact. The present survey therefore should be regarded as complete to about the end of 1966.

While the period originally covered extended roughly over the previous thirty years, occasional references to major proposals for reform prior to that time were not excluded. But such retro-spective references as now remain are rare and brief, as it is felt that maximum usefulness can be attained only if the subject is kept within manageable proportions.

As the titles to the Chapters show, the terms of reference have been discussed under certain broad subject headings. Within these headings, a limited amount of overlapping was inevitable; the question of political parties, for example, occurs on several occa-sions outside the main chapter devoted to the subject. The book should in consequence be read as a whole, not as a series of self-contained essays.

No attempt has been made to comment in any way upon the virtues or weaknesses of the various criticisms and proposals studied. The aim has been to provide a classified and indexed survey of the facts, with copious references at the end of each chapter, which will serve as a basis for further comment and discussion. The various 'conclusions' within and at the end of each chapter are therefore nothing more than an attempt to clarify, analyse and sum up the opinions of others. Similarly, those pro-posals put forward from an extremely partisan point of view and which would appear to be little more than propaganda for some particular body or interest have either been ignored or mentioned only in passing.

The starting-point, and the subject to which the work returns, is the House of Commons. Such factors as local government, external pressure groups and the Civil Service have been mentioned briefly if and when their respective influences have appeared to have a direct bearing on our subject—the reform of the Commons.

The vital theme of criticisms voiced and remedies suggested has been: how can the present system be strengthened and improved, so that it may long continue as the centre of British constitutional democracy? The more recent suggestions for answering that question—differing greatly in type and scope—are collated here.

EDWARD FELLOWES
Chairman of the Hansard Society
Formerly Clerk of the House of Commons

ABBREVIATIONS

THE following abbreviations are frequently used in footnotes to the text:

H.C. Deb.	House of Commons Debates
H.L. Deb.	House of Lords Debates
H.C.	House of Commons Paper
Cmd. or Cmnd.	Command Paper

I

Elections and Representation

(*a*) INTRODUCTION: FRANCHISE AND CONSTITUENCIES

A British General Election is regarded nowadays as an eminently serious matter. Not only does the average elector appreciate the importance of the occasion, but the psephologists and sociologists have won possession of Eatanswill. Farce is out, facts are in: since the last war, Nuffield College has sponsored inquiries into each General Election, and there have been many other serious studies in the same or related fields. Press and sound-radio give full coverage of elections. Further, the tremendously increased importance of 'television politics' now makes a very considerable impact on the electorate, to such an extent, in fact, that very few homes in the country could remain in ignorance of, or indifference to, the major issues at stake in recent General Elections.[1]

The potential significance of those proposals for electoral reform which are still open to consideration scarcely needs emphasizing, therefore. In the nineteenth century and the earlier years of the present century the focus for reforming activity in the matter of representation was, of course, the franchise. The principal goals of reform have now been reached in that respect, and the arguments advanced about a hundred years ago—both for and against an extended franchise—make strange reading today.[2] Yet the chapter is not completely closed. Just prior to the 1959 General Election, a committee reporting for the Labour Party on 'The Younger Generation' brought up anew the question of reducing the qualifying age for the franchise from twenty-one to eighteen.[3] Support for the idea was expressed at a meeting of the Labour Party's National Executive Committee in January 1960, and Emrys Hughes subsequently attempted, unsuccessfully, to make eighteen the

For Notes and References see pages 25–28

minimum statutory age for parliamentary franchise.[4] People called up for military service, he argued, should be entitled to vote; moreover, 'at the age of eighteen the young people of today are citizens', and therefore entitled to the full benefits of citizenship. Anthony Wedgwood Benn, in support of the Bill, suggested that such an extension would help convince the young folk that Parliament was no mere ceremonial sword, but rather an instrument they might use for their own purpose. Alan Thompson hoped that the Bill, on becoming an Act, would mark a further landmark in the progress towards *full* democracy.[5] In the event, the Bill was not passed, but support for the idea seems if anything to have increased since then, and it is no longer confined to one party. This is a point on which the current Speaker's Conference on Electoral Law has been asked to opine.

In 1953, it was being suggested that, with regard to the franchise, the one really contentious issue likely to arise concerned university representation.[6] Winston Churchill said in 1952 that it remained the declared intention of the Government to legislate on the subject, and already in their election programmes of 1950 and 1951 the Conservatives had promised the restoration of the university franchise.[7] The question slumbered however, although Sir Alan Herbert briefly revived the matter in his 1958 election address to East Harrow. If it is raised again, D. E. Butler's prophecy of 'contention' will undoubtedly be realized. As he points out, the closeness of recent election results would certainly add to the vehemence of Labour opposition to any move to re-establish the university seats.

The question of constituency boundaries would appear to have been largely settled—temporarily, at least—by the acceptance of permanent bodies known as Boundary Commissioners, who undertake periodic, impartial reviews of boundaries.[8] Nevertheless, there had been some explosive comment and discussion prior to the 1958 Act—not only from Members who feared (sometimes correctly) that redistribution would mean the loss of their seats, but from local authorities who felt that the Commissioners' changes had not taken local opinion sufficiently into consideration. Under the 1958 Act, if 100 electors or an interested organization object to a proposed change, an inquiry must be held, unless there was an inquiry prior to the actual announcement of the proposal. But, as Peter Richards has said, there is still no means of appeal against the suggestion of the Commissioners except to the Home Secretary or to Parliament—where the Government has in any case the power of its parliamentary majority to enforce its wishes. Dr. Richards continues: 'Should the decisions of the Commissions be open to review and, if so, by what kind of body?' Then again, if redistribution is completed shortly before a General Election (as in 1955), is this fair to Members and their local supporters who have to face, unprepared, a changed electorate? To minimize such inconvenience, the suggestion has been put forward that redistribution should not be too frequent (the 1958 Act went some way towards meeting this demand) and that the Commissioners should begin their work immediately after a General Election. There is fairly widespread agreement that all constituencies cannot consist of exactly equal electorates (numerically speaking), if natural and local authority boundaries are not to be completely ignored; and also that Scotland, Wales and rural areas must have a smaller quota of electors than the rest of the country.[9] This acquiescence in the numerical inequalities of electorates is challenged only by those who, associating the latter with the existence of single-member constituencies, use those same inequalities as another argument in favour of electoral reform. Thus, J. F. S. Ross writes that 'the single-member constituency is a rigid unit that is quite conspicuously unsuited to the immense variety of conditions, urban and rural, to be found in any modern country, and . . . is, in practice, incompatible with the principles of equal electorates. Where all constituencies are confined to the return of a solitary Member each, you *cannot* secure equal electorates . . . unless you are prepared to draw constituency boundaries with a ruthless disregard alike for common sense and local feeling'.[10] Ross goes on to argue the merits of a five-member constituency under proportional representation.

A subject which has been considered is that of colonial Members. A scheme for Malta was agreed upon which would involve the presence of Maltese representatives at Westminster, and on 7th December 1949, Harold Davies suggested to the Commons that all colonies should send Members direct to Westminster. The suggestion was rejected, partly for the strong reason that the colonies were in any case more interested in self-government.[11]

(b) THE PROGRESS OF ELECTORAL REFORM

The progress in the present century of electoral reform has been described, *inter alia*, by J. F. S. Ross, by R. W. G. Mackay and by D. E. Butler.[12] Most of the recommendations of the earlier Speaker's Conferences on electoral reform (in 1916–17, 1929–30 and 1944 respectively) have now passed into law. But certain of the issues raised are still outstanding. A skeleton summary of the course of events regarding these live issues—notably proportional representation (P.R.) and the alternative vote (A.V.)—follows.

The first Speaker's Conference proposed, among other things, the adoption of proportional representation by the single transferable vote (that is, preferential voting and quota counting) for elections in all boroughs returning three or more Members each, including London outside the City, and the adoption of the alternative vote for elections in single-member constituencies contested by two or more candidates.[13] These 'bold and even startling innovations' (in Ross's words) were recommended by the Conference; but when in 1917–18 the Government put through the Representation of the People Bill that embodied the recommendations of the Conference, the clauses concerning proportional representation and the alternative vote were left to free votes of the House. After lengthy parliamentary battles involving both Houses, the clauses were defeated, P.R. remaining only for the two- and three-membered University constituencies.

The first Speaker's Conference produced an impressive series of unanimous recommendations; the second was largely sterile. It was set up in 1929 by Ramsay MacDonald when he held office with Liberal support. The General Election of May 1929 had proved disastrous for the Liberals and it was not surprising that they pressed MacDonald for a measure of electoral reform as the price of their support. However, in the second Speaker's Conference, the participants were apparently entirely lacking in 'the admirable temper and conciliatory disposition' which the Speaker had found in 1917;[14] no agreement was reached on the issues (which included P.R. and the A.V.) before the Conference. In spite of the lack of agreement the Government announced, in the King's Speech on 28th October 1930, ' a measure of Electoral Reform'. This appears to have been promised to the Liberals in return for

4

their support in the House of Commons.[15] On 17th January 1931, the text of a bill was published, the main feature of which was the introduction of the alternative vote. Labour support for the latter system was only half-hearted: *The Times* commented, on 4th February 1931, that the Second Reading debate made it clear that 'no party except the Liberal party really wants any change in the electoral system at all'. In a debate on electoral reform held on 6th December 1933, Mr. Attlee said that although he had voted for the alternative vote in the debates on the bill, he had disapproved of it and only voted for it because of the 'bargain' with the Liberals.[16] However, in spite of some adverse votes and abstentions by Labour Members, the bill passed the House of Commons, only to be rejected by the Lords. The Government intended to push through the bill under the provisions of the Parliament Act, but in August the Government fell and the bill proceeded no further.

For a long time thereafter the electoral system excited little interest in Parliament. However, during the last war, it was apparent that there would be urgent problems arising at the end of hostilities, particularly concerning the need for redistribution of seats. A third Speaker's Conference was therefore set up in 1944. It passed a great many agreed resolutions which have subsequently been enacted, but resolutions concerning proportional representation and the alternative vote were decisively defeated: a resolution to introduce P.R. generally by twenty-five votes to four, a resolution to introduce P.R. experimentally by twenty-four votes to five, and a resolution in favour of the A.V. by twenty votes to five. The minority consisted of the Liberal and Independent members, whilst some Labour Members abstained on the vote concerning the alternative vote.

In spite of their defeat in 1945 the Conservatives' faith in the electoral system was in no way shaken—they were willing, as D. E. Butler said, 'to await the day when they once again would benefit by its natural exaggerations'.[17] The Representation of the People Act 1948 excited great party bitterness because it went beyond the recommendations of the Speaker's Conference by abolishing University seats and the business vote, but its results now appear to be accepted, temporarily at least.

Some other proceedings regarding electoral reform—Sir Winston

Churchill's speech of 1950 and the canvassing of the alternative vote system—will be discussed below in the section on *The Prospects for Electoral Reform*. The convening in 1965 of a new Speaker's Conference on Electoral Law brought the subject of electoral reform back into prominence, and its report is awaited with interest.

(c) PROPORTIONAL REPRESENTATION

The fundamental question in electoral reform today is that of the voting system used, and although the story of the 'progress' of reform in this century shows a steady movement away from proportional representation and the alternative vote (unanimously recommended by the first Speaker's Conference), the latter systems still have their devoted, active advocates.

The general position taken up by protagonists of reform is stated by J. F. S. Ross as follows:

> Systems of voting and of counting votes are the mechanism by means of which the country records and measures its reactions to the political issues of the day. As with all recording and measuring devices, therefore, it is important that these systems should be as accurate, as reliable, and as impartial as we can make them. To tamper with them—or to tolerate the continuance of their known defects—in the interests of a particular party or policy should be regarded as one of the things that are simply not done: it is on a par with using false weights and measures.[18]

The premise on which all argument for electoral reform rests is that Members should be returned more exactly in proportion to the votes cast than under the present system in this country.[19] It has been frequently demonstrated that the present system is unfair in that Members may be elected on minority votes, and that the number of seats obtained in the House is seldom in exact proportion to the percentage of votes received in the country.[20] Gilbert Murray once said that it was a condition of our keeping the Parliamentary system that the voting system should be fair—not ideally fair, but decently fair. Only proportional representation could meet this need; the alternative vote would not be adequate: 'We want

6

a system which will give an assurance to the average citizen that he will have a chance of voting for a representative of whom he really approves, and that, if outvoted, he will be outvoted by a real majority.'[21] As might be expected, the Liberal party, the worst sufferers from the inequalities of the present system, also uses the argument of 'fairness'. The Liberals are not tied to definite proposals, but have suggested proportional representation by the single transferable vote, with the alternative vote in rural areas, as 'the fairest way out'.[22] At Speaker's Conferences the Liberals have, of course, consistently supported P.R. or, as a second-best, the A.V. Ross argues that proportional representation, as well as being less clumsy and capricious in its action than the present 'first-past-the-post' system, would give more scope for the elector to exercise actively his choice and shrewdness, and would result in a better-balanced, more gifted House of Commons.[23] The use of P.R. would avoid foregone conclusions, would afford the elector a choice of persons as well as of parties (because in multi-member constituencies each party would run more than one candidate), would abolish caucus-controlled safe seats, and would tend to eliminate inferior candidates.[24]

Lakeman and Lambert add that the Member would himself be given a greater degree of independence. They also deal at length with the familiar criticisms of the technical aspects of P.R., since some of those who support the reform in theory are doubtful as to whether it would work in practice. Lakeman and Lambert argue that it is not too difficult for the voters to understand, that it does not take too long to carry out the count, that it is not excessively costly, and that it is possible to overcome the difficulties of by-elections when one Member retires or dies in a multi-member constituency. Far from encouraging abstentions on account of its supposed difficulties (the authors claim), P.R. would in practice lead to fewer abstainers: voters would not feel that the result was a foregone conclusion, and would be pleased at the wider choice of candidates offered them on the ballot paper.[25]

L. S. Amery, following the recommendations of the first Speaker's Conference, favoured the use of P.R. in the larger cities.[26] Churchill also, in 1935, spoke in favour of P.R. in the larger cities. R. Muir advocated the system with the single transferable vote in constituencies returning from three to seven members.[27] Another argument sometimes used in favour of P.R. is that when, as in 1945 or 1931, one party receives far more than its share of seats, the opposition is seriously weakened and is liable to be ineffective.[28] Most supporters of P.R. point out that a system which leads to such 'inequitable' results as that of 1945 undermines the prestige of Parliament. A Parliament in which the Government, though it has a large majority in the House of Commons, has the support of only a minority of the electorate cannot properly claim to have the nation's confidence or accurately reflect its views.

(*d*) CRITICISMS OF PROPORTIONAL REPRESENTATION

Critics of P.R. attack the very basis of the arguments of its supporters. Ross recognizes this: 'The crucial divergence is between those who think it vital that representation shall be a living reality, and those who think it of little importance so long as we get what they call "strong government". This is a clash of opinion that threatens the stability of the whole electoral system.'[29] Some examples of these criticisms of the whole aim of P.R. follow. The *Economist*, commenting on the report of the 1944 Speaker's Conference, said that the rejection of P.R. was right: the chief strength of the British system of government was that Cabinets could usually rely on the assured support of a majority in the House of Commons. The purpose of elections was not to secure an exactly representative House, but to put into power the Government the electors like most or dislike least.[30]

J. P. Mayer, in a review of Ross's *Parliamentary Representation*, doubted whether P.R. would work in a modern mass state.[31] The author, Mayer contends, is clearly antagonistic towards parties: but without firmly organized political parties it is difficult to see how the modern mass electorate can be transformed into manageable units. It is more profitable to think of ways in which an adequate representation of the electorate might be achieved *within* the party machines. Mayer also discounts the argument that the present system, with its exaggerations of majorities, leads to a weak opposition: he points out that, in fact, an 'exaggerated' or 'false' majority cannot disregard a strong minority, nor a majority of votes against the Government in the country. Arithmetically the voters are disenfranchised, but actually they do count. There is also, according to Mayer, no doubt that the two-party system is 'the unwritten law underlying the new parliamentary order of things in England' (G. M. Trevelyan in his Romanes lecture of 1926), and if proportional representation upset this system it could also upset the Constitution. The view of supporters of P.R. and of many other writers on the electoral system, that the main object of the House of Commons is 'to reflect the views expressed by the electorate' (a dictum of the second Speaker's Conference), is also not universally accepted. It is argued that this view ignores the rôle of the House of Commons as an organ for the *formulation* of the social will. Whereas proportional representation sets out to mirror, or 'photograph', the undecided mind of the electorate, what general elections should result in are definite and decisive majorities.[32] Similarly Harold Nicolson, while admitting that the present voting system and the two-party system are logically indefensible, claims that they are the best means of running representative institutions.[33] Harold Laski, as a 'strong believer in a stable executive',[34] also criticized proportional representation, and he did not admit that Parliament should mirror national opinion. He believed that P.R., with its probable multiplication of parties, would lead to excessive compromise. This argument is developed by other writers, for instance Michael Stewart, who wrote: 'Under proportional representation the elector would know that, whatever party he voted for, there would be little likelihood of its policy being carried out; for the Government would be a coalition whose nature and working would be unpredictable.'[35] Ivor Bulmer-Thomas also argues that P.R. would make for weak Government and tend to substitute 'backstairs intrigue' for open debate; it would, moreover, weaken the link between the Member and his constituency.[36] The same writer concedes, however, that P.R. might be tried experimentally. M. R. Curtis also reasons against the system, on the grounds that the government would be produced by party bargaining over which the elector had no control.[37] Finally, not a few impartial observers of the campaigns for and against the system of proportional representation hesitate to accept the evidence of its success in other countries as conclusive proof that it would function well here. What is good for Tasmania is not necessarily good for the United Kingdom—and vice-versa.

Lakeman and Lambert endeavour to counter criticisms of

proportional representation in Chapter VIII of their *Voting in Democracies*. They argue that the system does not itself create a multiplicity of parties, but rather secures fair representation for the parties that exist for other reasons. Tasmania still has only two parties and some Independents after half a century of P.R. On the other hand, the French voters tend to divide among the parties, and the use of a majority system has never checked this tendency. Lakeman and Lambert favour the spirit of compromise that P.R. might tend to produce, as in Scandinavian countries; they are prepared for coalition: 'a coalition backed by a majority of voters is preferable to a single-party government supported only by a minority'.[38] In answer to the critics who point to the ineffective minority Governments of 1924 and 1929, they refer to three periods when government without an assured Parliamentary majority worked well: 1846–52, 1886–92, and 1910–15.[39]

(*e*) THE ALTERNATIVE VOTE[40]

The adoption of proportional representation would be a thorough-going reform of the electoral system involving a complete re-drawing of constituency boundaries, and it would probably have far-reaching effects on our political life. The alternative vote system, on the other hand, could be applied within the existing electoral framework, and its effects would probably be less drastic than those of P.R. The alternative vote would improve the prospects of 'fair' electoral results without offering the more exact relationship between seats and votes obtained by proportional representation. The former system has been put forward as a compromise solution (in the Labour Government's Bill of 1931); was recommended in certain areas by the first Speaker's Conference; and has been canvassed from time to time up to the present day. Its distinction is that it has been suggested not only by the Liberals or by writers on political matters (as Ross, for example, advocates P.R.), but also, at various times, by some members of both major parties.

An article in the *Economist* of 10th June 1944, though approving of the third Speaker's Conference's rejection of P.R., said that if three-cornered contests resulting in the election of M.P.s by a minority vote became common, the case for the A.V. would be a strong one. The *Manchester Guardian* (now the *Guardian*) recommended the adoption of the alternative vote, and referred to the bill introduced by Ramsay MacDonald's Government in 1931.[41] The *Economist* returned to the subject in 1952, and again in 1958, arguing its thesis thus: 'The case for the alternative vote is that it would make policies more important in politics without disrupting the two-party system, as full proportional representation admittedly might do. It would provide the elector in the middle with an opportunity ... to show that ... he is not voting for extreme party measures.'[42]

The question of the A.V. was raised again (in 1958) as the result of improved Liberal votes at by-elections. After the 1958 Torrington by-election, in which the Liberals won the seat from the Conservatives, Christopher Hollis contributed an article to the *Manchester Guardian* entitled 'Now the alternative vote'.[43] He argued that the Torrington result made an unanswerable case for electoral reform. Whereas it had seemed that the electorate *wanted* the two-party system, it now appeared that it wanted the end of the two-party system. Without electoral reform it was possible that the Liberals would win one fifth or even one quarter of the votes, yet still receive no more seats than today. Such an unfair result would have a deplorable effect on the prestige which Parliament holds. Hollis also pointed out that the alternative vote provided the remedy for the excessive power of the caucus within a political party. In the situation which developed at Bournemouth East, when Nigel Nicolson declined his local executive's invitation to resign, both Nicolson and the local party executive candidate could have stood as Conservative candidates under the alternative vote system. Conservative electors could then express their preference between them without the risk of letting the seat go to Labour.[44] Hollis similarly referred to disagreements within the Labour Party: the proposed new system would enable the electors to decide between rival Labour candidates (and policies) instead of leaving the matter in the hands of the party 'caucus'.[45] The subject was also ventilated about the same time in correspondence to *The Times*. G. Beyfus pointed out that recent by-elections showed many electors wished to vote for a third party. The alternative vote would enable them to vote for the candidate of their choice without fear that by so doing they would merely help a candidate they

opposed.[46] In a leading article which concluded ensuing correspondence, *The Times* refused to be committed beyond the opinion
that 'it is fair to probe for defects in a system of election (i.e., the
present one) which produces admittedly distorted ratios between
seats and votes'.[47]

(f) CRITICISMS OF THE ALTERNATIVE VOTE

In the first place, the system is criticized as inadequate by supporters of proportional representation. Lakeman and Lambert voice
a number of objections.[48] It means that the major parties must
angle for the second preferences of those groups that have least
support in the electorate. (For this reason Sir Winston Churchill,
during a debate on 2nd June 1931, described the A.V. as 'the worst
of all possible plans .... The decision is to be determined by the
most worthless votes given for the most worthless candidates'.)[49] Nor,
it is said, is the system of the alternative vote much better than the
present 'first-past-the-post' system as regards faithful reflection of
the nation's wishes, or as regards the absence of uncertainty in
the result. Further, it does not provide any cure for the failure of
personal merit to carry weight in elections, except in such hypo-
thetical cases as might arise if two opposed candidates of the same
party contested the same seat (as might have happened at Bournemouth East in 1959). Lakeman and Lambert agree that the great
merit of the alternative vote is that, although it may do nothing to
improve the relation between the votes cast and the result, it could
improve the relation between the votes cast and real wishes of
those casting them. In other words, it does away with the 'wasted
vote' bogey. Before the 1950 election the Gallup Poll asked:
'Would you vote Liberal if you thought the Liberals could win?'
To this question 38 per cent replied 'Yes'—28 per cent more than
those who then intended to vote Liberal, and 29 per cent more
than those who actually did so at the election. That is to say, the
votes of more than one quarter of the electorate were determined
less by what they themselves wanted than by what they guessed
most of the other electors would want.

(g) THE PROSPECTS FOR ELECTORAL REFORM

The introduction of proportional representation would be as great a leap in the dark as any nineteenth-century measure of reform, while the adoption of the alternative vote would lead to results which are also impossible to calculate. Lakeman and Lambert have shown how varied could be the consequences of the latter proposed reform. They point out that in 1950 most Liberal candidates were third on the poll: in this position they would be immediately eliminated under the A.V. system and therefore would not profit by it. The A.V. gives no chance to the candidate who is everyone's second choice. On the other hand, if all Conservatives gave their second choice to a Liberal, and all Labour supporters did the same, and provided the Liberals had sufficient first preferences to be in the second position on the poll, then they would be able to win every seat in the country if they acquired only just one-third of the electorate's first preferences![50] D. E. Butler has published a table showing the probable result of each general election from 1922 to 1959 if it had been held under a system of proportional representation.[51] The table reveals that only two elections in the series would have been likely to return a party with a clear working majority (namely, those of 1931 and 1935). Thus the fears of the critics of P.R.—that strong majority government would disappear—would have been realized. It is admitted, on the other hand, that the unbalanced Houses of Commons with overwhelming majorities, which were characteristic of the period, would have been averted. The necessity of coalition could, moreover, have made the House of Commons a more genuinely deliberative body. The same writer's calculations regarding the probable effects of the alternative vote bring out that the method would in no case have changed a decisive result into an indecisive one—the majority might have been reduced but would have remained adequate.[52] The majority of 1945 might have been still further exaggerated.[53] Where the results of the election were close, however, the alternative vote might have changed the situation: the narrow Labour majority of 1950 would probably have been transformed into a minority. The system would not prevent a party which won less than 50 per cent of the votes from obtaining a parliamentary majority, and it would be as likely to multiply as to reduce protests at the 'injustice' of the electoral system. D. E. Butler thinks that, in all General Elections since 1923, the Liberals would have had a 'more proportionate' representation under the alternative vote. Max Beloff has suggested that electoral reform of this type would help a third party indirectly as well as directly. With 'wasted' votes wasted no longer, it is likely that people who had abandoned the third party, or never joined it, because support for it would have been ineffective or because they felt obliged to choose the 'lesser evil', would be drawn to it.[54] At the same time, 'both major parties might find that, given electoral reform, and an alternative home for some of their dissidents, unsuspected fissiparous tendencies would develop'. Beloff postulates that this possibility, as much as any calculation of seats to be lost and won immediately, makes electoral reform distasteful to both the main party machines.

However incalculable the results of electoral reform may be, there is general agreement that both major parties would suffer; in their own eyes if not in the opinion of their critics. For this reason, the prospects for reform are slight. The possibility was raised at a high level by Sir Winston Churchill in the Debate on the Address on 7th March 1950.[55] He said, after a General Election which had produced near stalemate, that 'we must not be blind to the anomaly which has brought to this House of Commons 186 representatives who are returned only by a minority of those who voted in their constituencies. Nor can we ... overlook the constitutional injustice done to 2,600,000 voters who ... have been able to return only nine Members. ... I therefore ... [propose] that we should set up a Select Committee to inquire into the whole question of electoral reform. ... I am well aware that it has several times been examined before, but we have never examined it in the light of a practical situation of major importance such as has now been brought about.' However, the proposal was not taken up by other Conservatives, nor was it pressed by Churchill, and it was rejected by the Government. In 1953 there were Liberal–Conservative talks on electoral reform, but these produced no concrete results. When in 1964 an Independent Conservative sought leave of the House to legislate on the Single Transferable Vote, he was defeated in a free vote by 137 to 20.[56]

On 1st May 1954, a letter was published in *The Times* appealing to the Government to appoint a Royal Commission on Voting. This would collect the facts regarding various voting methods so that advantage could be taken 'of this vast body of experience to reconsider our own practices' and also to help and guide countries such as Malaya or Nigeria—countries which had acquired or were then approaching self-government. The letter was signed by Anthony Greenwood, W. J. Brown, D. L. Savory, Dingle Foot and other 'Sponsors of the Committee for a Royal Commission on Voting'. However, on 27th July of that same year, the Prime Minister (Sir Winston Churchill) rejected a request to set up such a Royal Commission.[57] The 'practical situation' to which Churchill referred in 1950 has disappeared; the subject as a whole has receded into the background again, although exponents of reform are by no means completely disheartened.

It seems most unlikely that one major party will attempt to impose electoral reform without the agreement of the other (though the *Economist* recommended this step in its article of 8th March 1958), or without seeking a specific mandate. Meanwhile both large parties know that they benefit from the inequalities of the present system and will hesitate to upset it. Both have kept silent in recent discussions of the alternative vote. They are concerned less with logic and fairness than with the struggle for power. The situation might change if the Liberals recovered sufficient force to make their voice heard: but will the present 'first-past-the-post' method allow a substantial Liberal recovery? The last word rests with the opponents of electoral reform.

(h) FUNCTIONAL REPRESENTATION

Representation according to people's occupations has been suggested from time to time: either as the sole form of representation, or as the method to be used for a subsidiary legislature under a scheme of devolution. Functional representation was part of the scheme of the Fascist Corporative State. It has been advocated by Sir Oswald Mosley; the latter suggested that if Parliament were elected on an occupational franchise it would be a practical rather than a political assembly, and would become more 'serious'. Hollis's third Chamber, the House of Industry, would be elected

15

by people engaged in industry voting in 'occupational constituencies'.[58] The idea has also been supported by Amery as the system of election for his House of Industry or sub-Parliament.[59] Stewart, on the other hand, argues that functional representation might well aggravate the sectional spirit and would encourage selfishness; representatives would be expected by their constituents to press the interests of their particular 'industries' regardless of the national interest. Fascists countered this sort of objection by saying that the Government would see that each group in the Assembly remembered the over-riding interests of the State. But if the Government controls the Assembly, then the Assembly cannot control the Government: and this was the case in Fascist Italy.[60]

(*i*) THE REFERENDUM AND MANDATE

Occasionally, the use of referenda in this country is suggested as a means of obtaining the expression of public opinion on specific issues. But, as C. S. Emden puts it, recent experience indicates that this method is generally regarded not only as impracticable, but also as un-English.[61]

After years of trial and debate, the doctrine of the people's mandate is still not clearly formulated. Emden thinks that it could be organized by inter-party agreement, however, in such a way that the people would be able to comment effectively on the broad outlines of projected policy at election time. Otherwise, democracy may receive a serious set-back, for the public must feel they are playing a real part in parliamentary government.[62] This line of argument, of course, assumes that 'the people' *ought* to contribute positively in such matters; many reputable supporters of democracy regard effective participation of this kind as impossible.

(*j*) MORE MEMBERS?

J. F. S. Ross suggested that the number of Members should be increased to 'say 700'. Apart from enabling Scotland and Wales to keep their present representation, whilst removing their present unfair weighting, the increase would have other advantages: it would ease the task of redistribution of seats; it would restore the proportion of private Members in the House to a healthier figure; it would spread the burden of committee work; and it would

16

decrease the burden of a Member's work in relation to his constituents.[63] The *Economist* has agreed that there are arguments for a larger number of Members—it would encourage closer contact between the Member and his constituents, and, as suggested by Ross, it would be the only way to restore the balance between private Members and office-holders, so distorted by the multiplication of Under-Secretaries, Parliamentary Secretaries, and Parliamentary Private Secretaries. The *Economist* suggested an electoral quota of about 50,000.[64]

On the other hand, supporters of some form of devolution argue that the Parliament at Westminster needs to be *reduced* in size. Hollis has said that Parliament is far too large as it is, and its number should be drastically reduced.[65] In *Has Parliament a Future?* he suggests that the maximum number of M.P.s should not much exceed a hundred. In an issue of the *Director* in July 1966, Desmond Donnelly has argued that the Commons could do with 400 fewer Members.

Adams also expected that, after devolution, Parliament would be smaller.[66] The general consensus of opinion at present is against any numerical increase on the scale advocated by Ross.

(*k*) THE PERSONNEL OF PARLIAMENT

The question of the personnel of Parliament—the qualities of Members and of candidates—is a difficult (not to say invidious) topic on which to put forward concrete, specific suggestions for reform. It is, rather, the subject for generalization. It seems that, like *Punch*, Parliament is never as good as it used to be, and from time to time a lament goes up for the giants of yesteryear. The real or supposed shortcomings of Members are ascribed to a number of causes: the one relevant point is the criticism of the way in which parliamentary candidates are chosen and elected. A detailed study of the selection of candidates has been made by Austin Ranney in *Pathways to Parliament* (1965): the following paragraphs do no more than touch very briefly on a complex, delicate topic.

Advocates of proportional representation believe, of course, that their multi-member constituencies would improve the quality of Members by enabling electors to express preferences between different candidates *of the same party*, whereas in single-member constituencies a Conservative voter, say, generally votes for the Conservative candidate—however much he disapproves of him personally—for fear of letting the seat go to a rival party.

Roger Fulford has noted that the powers of constituency associations have increased enormously, and that in safe seats the constituency association virtually chooses the Member: the election is a foregone conclusion.[67] This point is developed by Nigel Nicolson in his *People and Parliament* (1958): a book which arose from the author's experience of being 'disowned' by his constituency association. Those who 'elect' the Member for, say, Bournemouth or Barnsley, are not the electors but the members of the 'caucus' of the local Conservative or Labour association. These nominate their official candidate; the latter is then automatically elected to Parliament. On the subject of a local association's right to choose its own candidate, Nicolson suggests that there is no need for revolutionary reform. The Party Headquarters should perhaps encourage selection on 'a wider basis' and over 'a longer period'. No one should be able to win the official candidature by an adroit twenty-minute interview (the method, apparently, by which he was himself chosen at Bournemouth). He also suggests a sort of 'primary' election, where two prospective candidates might 'run in harness for a year' and so work for their official candidacy.[68] Bulmer-Thomas has similarly commented on the 'tyranny' of the local party organization.[69] A group of Conservative Members and others, reporting in 1946, felt that Headquarters should not recognize a local association unless its subscribing membership represented a reasonable proportion of the Conservative electors.[70]

At heart, it must be confessed, these are largely internal matters for the party machines. It would be difficult to frame legislation to prevent what happened following the Suez operations (to Stanley Evans at Wednesbury, Sir Frank Medlicott in Norfolk, Anthony Nutting at Melton or Nigel Nicolson at Bournemouth) from occurring again—however much there is general agreement that a Member is a representative and not a delegate, and that a local association is acting tyrannically if it withdraws support from a Member who does not always see eye to eye with it.

J. F. S. Ross has made suggestions about the procedures of candidacy and elections which could be implemented by legislation, though some of them might seem to be beyond the realm of practical politics. He begins by attacking the deposit of £150 required of every candidate. It presents a real barrier to poor candidates without any organizational backing; moreover, a financial barrier is not effective in preventing 'frivolous' candidatures. Not all 'freaks' are poor—nor are all rich men models of wisdom. Ross suggests, pending the abolition of the deposit, that it should be reduced to £50 and that it should be forfeited only if the candidate gains less than one-tenth of the votes, instead of the present fraction of one-eighth.[71]

In his address to the electors of East Harrow (8th December 1958), Sir Alan Herbert wanted to see the deposit abolished. Calling it an undemocratic device, he said that the deposit system often frightened away genuine Independents, rather than freaks. A candidate who has sought—albeit unsuccessfully—to serve his country should not be obliged to lose his £150 if he does not get enough votes. It was like an umpire saying to an unhappy batsman: 'You are out, sir. May I add that you are out for a duck? And now you will be hit on the head with a bat.'

Ross further claims that the deposit system could be abolished safely if the system of nomination were tightened up. It is at present very easy to become a candidate—apart from the deposit, one only need present a nomination paper subscribed by the signatures of ten electors with their electoral numbers. In place of this extremely cursory procedure, what is needed is a nomination system carefully designed, not merely to discourage the frivolous, but to eliminate as far as may be possible candidates personally unsuitable for membership. A deposit can never do this: integrity and ability cannot be measured by any financial device. Electors might be given more say in the choice of a candidate by a requirement that the nomination should be supported by the signatures of 500 or 1,000 electors. Such a form of nomination would serve many useful purposes. The old bogy of the 'freak' or 'frivolous' candidate would be dealt with. The genuine candidate would have no difficulty in securing the signatures, and these would show that he had real local backing. The necessity of obtaining the larger number of signatures would make the inner ring of the party more sensitive to the desirability of choosing not only a 'sound party man' but someone who is acceptable to the general run of electors.[72]

Ross also maintains that a candidate ought to be obliged to give the electors reasonably full and authentic information about himself. The returning officer should issue, on the basis of information required to be supplied by the candidate, a concise and standardized statement setting forth the essential facts about each candidate.[73] In his earlier book, *Parliamentary Representation*, Ross went further and suggested that candidates should submit voluntarily to a series of 'psychological, intelligence and aptitude tests' such as those developed by the National Institute of Industrial Psychology. The results could be published for the benefit of electors.[74] He also endorsed Laski's proposal (made in *A Grammar of Politics*) that candidates should be required to have three years' service on some local body.

However extreme some of these suggestions may seem, Ross puts them forward with the aim in mind of 'the urgent necessity' of a much higher standard of members. The danger is, of course, that any attempt to improve standards might exclude a person of real ability who has followed unorthodox paths. Would the young Winston Churchill—or the young Aneurin Bevan or Ernest Bevin —have passed Ross's tests of suitability for membership of the House of Commons?

(*l*) ELECTION EXPENSES

Criticisms of the deposit system have already been discussed. In their *Proposals for Constitutional Reform*, the group of Conservatives mentioned above went some way towards summarizing other aims of reformers in the field of election expenses. The Group (which included Viscountess Davidson, [Sir] Kenneth Pickthorn and Viscount Ridley) suggested that candidates should be forbidden by law from subscribing to the funds of their local political associations; further, that the State should refund election expenses on an approved scale, related to the area of the constituency and the size of the electorate; and that it should be illegal to exceed this amount.[75] (The limit on such expenses, incidentally, has remained unchanged since 1948, thus inhibiting election activities in an increasing degree, or else inviting evasion of the law. In January 1966, the Speaker's Conference recommended, in a letter to the Prime Minister [Cmnd. 2880], that the legal maximum should be raised by £300.)

Ross, in Chapter 17 of his *Elections and Electors*, pointed out that the average election costs of successful candidates were £763 in 1950 and £752 in 1951. The mean value of these two figures is £758. The average duration of the eight Parliaments between 1918 and 1951 (excluding that of 1935–45) was two years, ten and three-quarter months. Thus, if one assumes an expenditure of £758 every two years, ten and three-quarter months, the average election costs of Members amount to a continuous charge, year in year out, of five pounds a week. Further, these large sums may have to be found at short notice, and they are only *election* costs, not covering normal constituency outgoings or the routine expenses of parliamentary life. In these circumstances, it is inevitable that the scales are still biased in favour of the candidate who can shoulder a large part of the burden of election expenses himself, or can find a trade union or other body to do so. Thus, it is argued that entry to the House of Commons is still governed to a considerable extent by finance rather than merit. The potential candidate who has financial backing stands a better chance than a rival who lacks that advantage. Further, a man who has to depend on the backing of a trade union or a comparable body is to that extent hampered in his freedom of action and independence of judgement. He must consider the interests and prejudices of those who meet his election bill. Legal control of maximum election expenses can do no more than prevent corrupt or over-lavish expenditure by exceptionally well-off candidates. It cannot alter the fact that a modern election contest is necessarily an expensive affair.[76]

To meet this situation Ross puts forward a scheme first suggested by him in his earlier book, *Parliamentary Representation*. He argues that the community should recognize that *bona fide* candidates perform a public service by offering themselves for election, and they should be helped to meet the high cost of so doing. What he suggests is that the State should contribute towards each candidate's costs a sum calculated on the basis of the number of valid votes recorded for that candidate. This scheme would ensure that the expenses of 'freak' candidates would not be paid. Ross records that he put forward this plan in a memorandum to the 1944 Speaker's Conference, but that the Conference stated in its Report, without giving any reasons, that it had 'agreed not to accept a proposal that the State should afford direct financial assistance to candidates'. The writer admits that the exact form of a State grant and what proportion of the total cost it should cover would need careful study. It might be enacted that the grant should not exceed, say, two-thirds of the expenses incurred.[77]

(m) ELECTION LAW MISCELLANEA

Some miscellaneous proposals for reform arising out of the state of the existing electoral law are mentioned briefly below.

(i) *Getting to the Poll*: Under Section 88 of the 1949 Representation of the People Act, it was forbidden to offer organized conveyance to the place of voting except in a limited number of registered party cars. The Conservative Government repealed Section 88 in 1958. There was considerable Labour opposition to this piece of legislation during an animated discussion in the House of Commons on 5th November of that year. One speaker said that the Government, if they felt compelled to amend existing law in this way, should not have dealt with one section in isolation. They should have combined their proposed amendment with 'other things to help to get the voters more easily to the polls'—for example, the provision of more polling stations, including mobile polling stations in country districts, and the strengthening of Section 63 of the main Act dealing with election expenses.[78] A leading article in *The Times* of 30th October 1958, had suggested that the principal effect of the repeal of Section 88 would not lie in the availability or otherwise of cars to take electors to the polls, for it could not be doubted that, in general, there would be plenty of cars for voters of all main parties. But, the article continued, much greater significance would be henceforth attached to the efficiency of party organization in constituencies: the freely permitted use of cars would entail careful planning to ensure that all potential voters for a particular party were conveyed to the polling booths. This increased influence of party organization would not be regarded by all as an unmixed blessing. D. E. Butler and R. Rose subsequently mentioned that extra Conservative votes may have been gained in Reading in October 1959 by the device of sending cars equipped with loudspeakers to greet every returning train of com-muters.[79] According to Butler and King in their study of *The British General Election of 1966*, cars were 'more plentiful than ever' (p. 201).

(ii) *Postal Voting*: Just over 2 per cent of votes cast in October 1959 were registered by post, and Butler and Rose noted some 'chronic grievances' about the state of existing legislation which ensued.[80] Persons on holiday could not avail themselves of the postal vote—was it fair that they should have to choose between their holiday and their right to vote? The privilege of postal voting was extended only to those who had moved from one election registration district to another. Butler and Rose cited the example of people who, having migrated some fifteen miles *within* the city boundaries of Glasgow or Birmingham, were not eligible; on the other hand, people who had moved 'a few hundred yards over a district council boundary' were permitted a postal vote. Other voices were raised in protest against this anomaly, and it was referred to by the Labour Party's opening spokesman in the debate of 21st July 1960 on Political Expenditure (Control). A Bill to enable people to vote despite their absence from the consti-tuency on polling day was talked out in 1964;[81] a similar Bill was debated, then withdrawn, in June 1966.

(iii) *Broadcasting and Television*: The significance of sound broad-casting and of television in recent General Elections has been mentioned above, and has been ably dealt with by Butler, Rose, and others.[82] That significance will almost surely increase. Hence, the case for reviewing electoral law to cope properly with the advent of these new forces will also grow stronger.[83] It is significant that the terms of reference of the Speaker's Conference require it to investigate the use made of broadcasting.

(iv) *Opinion Polls during an Election*: Opinion polls attained an altogether new level of prominence during the 1959–64 Parliament, said Butler and King in their book on the 1964 election, and they had an unquestionable impact on the style in which the 1964 election was fought and on the morale of the protagonists.[84] The authors ascribe this new importance of the polls to two factors—

the transformation of the political scene due to the changes in public opinion which were then taking place, and the arrival on the scene of a second major polling organization. The publicity given to the polls has led to intermittent suggestions that they should be banned, lest people should be led to vote for a particular party because it was sure to win or to abstain from voting in the belief that their party was bound to be defeated. There is however, say Butler and King, no evidence whatever that opinion polls have ever induced 'bandwagon voting';[85] and Richard Rose argues that people tend to select from the mass media only those items which are in harmony with their already established partisan predispositions.[86] In any case, there is some doubt as to the value of polls during an election—a value which Rose believes to have been overrated. Butler and King agree; they say that polls are excellent indicators of opinions and voting intentions to within a narrow margin of error—but it is that margin which decides elections.[87]

Conclusions

The most important, persistent questions of reform in the field of elections and representation have for a long time been those of the voting system, the selection of candidates, and election expenses. Another problem which, whilst by no means new, has become increasingly urgent over recent years is that of the relationship between a Member and his constituents—and especially his local association. The exercise of his independent judgement by a Member has to be balanced by his consciousness of the views of those whom he represents. The relationship may become an impossible one without give-and-take on both sides. A Member can no longer expect the support of those who elected him if he departs frequently and seriously from their views; at the same time, the electors may be called upon to recognize that a Member has not only the interests and opinions of his constituents to consider, but also his judgement of the national interest and the dictates of his conscience. The problem is not made any simpler by the difficulty, or even the impossibility, of framing precise remedies. The 'give-and-take on both sides' referred to above seems the one practical answer.

It is Bernard Crick's thesis that the General Election is a continuous campaign, beginning on the first day of each new Parliament.[88] Certainly, elections are the threshold to the whole mansion of parliamentary activity proper. Proposals for reform in this latter domain now fall to be considered.

NOTES AND REFERENCES

[1] D. E. Butler and R. Rose: *The British General Election of 1959*, Chap. VII: Television and Radio.

[2] Lord Eustace Cecil's objections to the 1867 Reform Bill are a good example. He is reported as saying that 'the Bill would perpetuate bribery and lead to an extension of the influence of wealth, *and eventually lead to manhood suffrage and electoral districts*'. (Parl. Deb. 3rd Series, Vol. CLXXXVIII, c. 595.)

[3] A reduction to eighteen had already been rejected (though not unanimously) by the 1944 Speaker's Conference. Lord Altrincham has suggested that the minimum age should be sixteen (*Manchester Guardian*, 27th October 1958, p. 12).

[4] Representation of the People Act, 1949 (Amendment) Bill. Second Reading, H.C. Deb. 617, cs. 1607–73, 19th February 1960.

[5] H.C. Deb. 617, c. 1634.

[6] Butler: *The Electoral System in Britain 1918–51*, 1953, p. 139.

[7] H.C. Deb. 507, c. 1861.

[8] Established under the House of Commons (Redistribution of Seats) Act of 1944, these Commissions have had their statutory duties subsequently amended in 1946 and 1948, consolidated in 1949, and further amended under the House of Commons (Redistribution of Seats) Act, 1958. For details of this whole question see: (i) Butler: *op. cit.*, and an article by that writer on 'The Redistribution of Seats', in *Public Administration*, Vol. 33, pp. 125–47; (ii) Richards: *Honourable Members: A Study of the British Backbencher*, pp. 45–9.

[9] Thus, the electorate of Caithness and Sutherland at the 1959 General Election totalled 26,716—compared with electorates of (for example) 72,441 and 68,209 at Hull East and Bournemouth West respectively.

[10] *Elections and Electors: Studies in Democratic Representation*, 1955, pp. 104–5.

[11] H.C. Deb. 470, cs. 1873–4. Mr. Davies wanted a Royal Commission to be set up to investigate the possibilities of colonial representation at Westminster.

[12] Ross: *op. cit.* Part V, Chaps. 18–22.
Mackay: *Coupon or Free?*, 1943, pp. 54–86.
Butler: *op. cit.* Part I.

[13] Ross, pp. 305–6.

[14] *ibid.* p. 321.

[15] Butler in *op. cit.* pp. 62–8 discusses the 'bargain' made with the Liberals.

[16] H.C. Deb. 283, c. 1746.

[17] *Op. cit.* p. 102. (Labour's victory in 1945 was secured with only 48% of the votes.)

[18] Preface to *Voting in Democracies* by E. Lakeman and J. D. Lambert, 1955, p. 9.

[19] The present system of a simple majority in single-member constituencies is described by Ross and by Lakeman and Lambert, where its failings and inequalities are noted at length.

[20] cf. the example cited by Richards, p. 35, of the 1929 General Election result at Northwich: Lord C. Crichton-Stuart (C.) 15,477 (Elected); Mrs. B. A. Gould (Lab.) 15,473; J. D. Barlow (Lib.) 14,161.

[21] *The Contemporary Review*, Vol. CXLI, March 1932, pp. 296–308.

[22] cf. Grimond: *The New Liberal Democracy*, 1958, pp. 4–5; and G. Watson: *The Unservile State: Essays in Liberty and Welfare*, 1957, pp. 50–1.

[23] There are frequent remarks to that effect in the writer's *Elections and Electors*.

[24] Ross: *The Achievements of Representative Democracy*, 1952, p. 19.

[25] Lakeman and Lambert, pp. 132–48; also J. H. Humphreys: *Objections to P.R. Answered*, P.R. Society Pamphlet, No. 83.

[26] Amery: *Thoughts on the Constitution*, 1947, p. 55.

[27] Muir: *How Britain is Governed: A Critical Analysis of Modern Developments in the British System of Government*, 2nd ed. 1930, p. 181.

[28] cf. S. R. Brett in the *Quarterly Review*, Vol. 284, 1946, pp. 457–68.

[29] See: Preface to Lakeman and Lambert, p. 10. The question of the need or otherwise for 'strong government' crops up in a great many aspects of parliamentary reform: cf. Chaps. IV & V.

[30] The *Economist*, 10th June 1944, pp. 773–4.

[31] *Political Quarterly*, Vol. XV, 1944, pp. 113–23.

[32] cf. Harley in *Fortnightly Review*, September 1930, pp. 307–18.

[33] *The Independent Member of Parliament*, Hansard Society Pamphlet No. 2, 1946, p. 18.

[34] Laski, p. 53.

[35] Stewart: *The British Approach to Politics*, revised 3rd ed. 1955, p. 132.

[36] Bulmer-Thomas: *The Party System in Great Britain*, 1953, pp. 103–4. This latter objection is not admitted by Lakeman and Lambert: *op. cit.* pp. 132–4.

[37] Curtis: *Central Government: An Introduction*, 1956, p. 17.

[38] Lakeman and Lambert, p. 156.

[39] *ibid.* p. 156. No attempt has been made to describe methods of proportional representation: these are discussed at length in Ross's books and in Lakeman and Lambert. Neither has the present brief summary of the arguments for and against proportional representation any claim to completeness. Readers wishing to study this very complex problem are referred to *Voting in Democracies*, and to the works by Mackay and Ross listed in the bibliography of this book.

[40] Very briefly, this system would ensure that the successful candidate in a single-member constituency had a majority of the votes polled. Candidates are placed by the voter in order of preference: if an absolute majority does not accrue to any candidate following the count of first preferences, the first preferences given for the lowest candidate are ignored and the second preferences of those voters are then distributed amongst the remaining candidates.

[41] *Manchester Guardian*, 8th March 1950, p. 6.

[42] The *Economist*, 6th December 1952, pp. 663–4. Another article appeared in the issue of 8th March 1958, pp. 824–5.

[43] At the 1959 General Election, the Conservatives regained the Torrington seat.

[44] Lakeman and Lambert also refer to this feature of the A.V. in *op. cit.* p. 65. Nigel Nicolson did not stand as a candidate at the 1959 General Election.

[45] *Manchester Guardian*, 31st March 1958, p. 6.

[46] *The Times*, 22nd May 1958, p. 11.

[47] *The Times*, 9th June 1958, p. 11.

[48] Lakeman and Lambert, *op. cit.* pp. 62–7.

[49] H.C. Deb. 253, c. 106.

[50] Lakeman and Lambert, pp. 66–7.

[51] Butler: *The Electoral System in Britain since 1918*, p. 191, Table 39.

[52] *ibid.* pp. 192–4.

[53] *ibid.* p. 193.

[54] Article in *The Times*, 27th January 1953, p. 9.

[55] H.C. Deb. 472, cs. 143–4.

[56] H. C. Deb. 696, cs. 247–54.

[57] H.C. Deb. 531, c. 233.

[58] Hollis: *Can Parliament Survive?* 1949, p. 120.

[59] Amery, pp. 64–7; and H.C. Deb. 249, cs. 656 ff.

[60] Stewart, pp. 133–4. 'Functional Devolution' is discussed in section (*b*) of the following chapter.

[61] *The People and the Constitution*, 1956, pp. 297–302.

[62] *ibid.*, pp. 302–4; pp. 315–6; Gordon, pp. 163–4.

[63] *ibid.* p. 123.

[64] The *Economist*, 10th June 1944, pp. 773–4.

[65] *Encounter*, February 1955, pp. 12–20.

[66] *Listener*, 17th February 1932, pp. 236–7.

[67] 'The Member and His Constituency', Ramsay Muir Memorial Lecture, 1957.

[68] N. Nicolson, p. 43.

[69] Bulmer-Thomas, pp. 204 ff.

[70] *Some Proposals for Constitutional Reform*: *being the recommendations of a Group of Conservatives*, 1946, p. 39.

[71] *op. cit.* pp. 203 ff.

[72] *ibid.* pp. 228–31. (William Gallacher urged the abolition of the deposit, and its replacement by nomination papers carrying 150 signatures, in a debate on 1st February 1944: H.C. Deb. 396, c. 1333.)

[73] *op. cit.* pp. 231–3.

[74] *Parliamentary Representation*, 1948, 2nd (enlarged) edition, pp. 230–1.

[75] See note 70 above. The third Speaker's Conference expressed disapproval of direct or indirect payment of substantial sums to party organizations with a view to influencing such organizations in the choice of candidates.

[76] In a letter to *The Times* of 13th May 1958, J. A. Gillison stated that 'a union frequently pays 80 per cent of its candidate's election expenses and also some hundreds a year into the local party so long as its candidate remains the representative .... If Parliamentary government is to be respected, or, possibly, to survive, objective examination of this system of "tied" M.P.s is an urgent task'.

[77] *Elections and Electors*, pp. 290–1. The much broader question of the control of political expenditure, by parties and other interested organizations, is discussed in Chap. IV.

[78] H.C. Deb. 594, c. 967 (P. Gordon Walker). During this debate, the wider questions of political expenditure and of the publication of political parties' accounts were raised: refer, in this matter to Chapter IV.

[79] *The British General Election of 1959*, p. 141.

[80] *ibid.* pp. 142–3.

[81] Representation of the People Act 1949 (Amendment) Bill: H. C. Deb. 692, cs. 1474–98.

[82] *op. cit.* Chap. VII.

[83] cf. 'The Hand of the Law', in Granada TV's report on its *Election Marathon, 1959*, pp. 9ff., for an idea of the complex, confusing issues involved.

[84] Butler and King, *The British General Election of 1964*, p. 204.

[85] *ibid.* p. 207.

[86] 'Political Decision Making and the Polls' in *Parliamentary Affairs*, Spring 1962.

[87] *op. cit.* p. 211.

[88] *The Reform of Parliament*, p. 43.

II

Devolution

(*a*) THE CASE FOR DEVOLUTION

It is a commonplace of criticism of Parliament that the House of Commons tries to do too much. Congestion follows, and, as a result, it is said that the Cabinet is taxed beyond its capacity for thinking and taking decisive action, that Ministers rely on their officials more and more, and that the outcome is the growth of bureaucracy. In addition, the House of Commons cannot deal with a tenth of the subjects which enthusiastic Members wish to raise, and the Members consequently become demoralized.[1] Critics of this state of affairs all seek for a way in which Parliament can be relieved of the distracting multiplicity of minor matters; the answer some of them suggest is a devolution of certain of Parliament's powers.[2]

Other people approach the idea of devolution from a different direction. Muir thought it could be argued that there was at present an excessive centralization of government, and that for this reason there should be some devolution;[3] only by setting up subsidiary Parliaments, said Lady Megan Lloyd George,[4] can the national affairs of Wales, Scotland and England be properly handled. Devolution of this kind would clearly help to foster national sentiment within the United Kingdom, said Laski.[5] Sometimes this latter plea for national devolution is coupled with the argument that it would make the central Parliament more capable of doing its work efficiently; but it is also sometimes advanced as being strong enough to stand on its own. Thus Ramsay MacDonald said he favoured devolution to subordinate national bodies, not on the ground of saving time in the House of Commons, but as a point of principle.[6]

For Notes and References see pages 42–43

29

A different reason for devolution was advanced by Christopher Hollis.[7] He believed it was the essence of democracy that everyone should do a little politics, and no one should do very much; the political butter, as it were, should be spread more thinly. Members of Parliament should do less political work than they do now, while the man whose only political action is to mark a ballot paper every five years or so, should do more. To achieve this end, much more work should be delegated from Westminster to subsidiary democratic bodies.

It is also frequently said that, with the increasing work on technical subjects that is nowadays undertaken by Parliament, there is a great deal of discussion on matters which many Members today cannot fully understand.[8] One answer to this could be that the discussion of such matters should devolve upon bodies of technical experts.

The supporters of devolution are able to cite the success it has achieved in various foreign countries and especially—as is most relevant—in the Northern Ireland Parliament.[9] Others point out that the powers given to the Church Assembly to initiate legislation have worked excellently.[10] These examples show the kind of thing that can be achieved by devolution, and suggest that Parliament can solve its problems by giving away some limited powers to bodies other than itself.

From the reasons advanced in favour of devolution, it can be seen that its proponents tend to fall into two schools: those who think that subordinate bodies should be created in order to range over a certain area of national administration—such as agriculture, or industry—and those who believe that devolution should start geographically, that certain areas should be allowed their own super-local government. These two types of devolution—'Functional' and 'Regional'—now fall to be considered.

(b) FUNCTIONAL DEVOLUTION

Sir Richard Acland suggested that the House of Commons should be divided into two halves—one, the 'Supreme Council of State', to deal with the more important matters, and the other, the 'Council for Minor Matters', which would deal with the rest.

Members should be allowed to have deputies, and it would be the deputies who would normally sit in the second Council.[11]

The creation of subordinate assemblies, which could bring expert opinion to bear on proposed new legislation, has been put forward at various times. The idea has, of course, affinities with other schemes which suggest the creation of specialist Committees of Members of Parliament for this purpose. But these other schemes—which are based on the existing framework of Parliament —are discussed elsewhere.[12]

Lord Eustace Percy suggested in 1931 that an advisory Assembly of interested parties could usefully be created in order to assist in preparing legislation dealing with economic matters, and legislation affecting local authorities. If such an Assembly were to register its agreement to a proposed new bill, the House would then be able to deal summarily with it.[13]

Something along these lines was also suggested by R. D. Denman, who was more specific about the legislative procedure to be used. Specialist assemblies should be set up to initiate legislation, which would then proceed in the same manner as Church Assembly Measures.[14] He suggested that agriculture, transport, social insurance and housing could all devolve in this way upon subordinate assemblies; perhaps transport would be the best beginning—it was a technical subject, it needed more attention than the House could give it, and (writing in 1933) he said it excited no strong party animus.[15] As a result, he suggested on another occasion, 'a specialist Assembly, given work by this House or originating work of their own, rationed as to finance by this House, submitting to us their conclusions for acceptance or rejection, would make once more possible that this House should be an efficient legislative machine.'[16]

W. G. S. Adams suggested that the great departments of state— such as the Board of Trade and the Ministry of Agriculture— should set up councils representative of the interests which they administer; such councils would initiate much of our social and economic legislation. Parliament would then to some extent be relieved of the need to discuss such measures—for they would already have been discussed publicly—and could concentrate its attention on the effects of the measures on the community at large, and on the financial obligations involved.[17]

The various Assemblies and Councils considered above have been concerned entirely with the legislative side of Parliament's function. Other, broader, proposals have been made to create Assemblies which, while including legislation among their duties, have wider powers—powers which, in some respects, can rival those of either House of Parliament. The three most considered schemes of this kind are those put forward by the Webbs (in 1920), by Winston Churchill (1930), and by Christopher Hollis (1949).

Political and Social Co-Parliaments

The Webbs' plan to divide Parliament's functions into two, and to have a social Parliament co-existing with a political one, was published in 1920.[18] It was re-stated by Mrs. Webb in an article in 1931,[19] and has been so discussed by later writers that it can usefully be reconsidered here.

A new National Assembly, of about 300 members from England and Wales, and fifty from Scotland, would be directly elected on the same franchise as the House of Commons, for a fixed period —say three years. Groups of statutes would be referred to the Assembly, which would be allowed to make regulations under them (much as Ministers now make statutory instruments). The services which would in this way devolve upon the Assembly would be health, education, labour, agriculture and fisheries, transport, mines, works, and some of those which are at present administered by the Home Office and the Board of Trade. Private Bill legislation would also fall to the Assembly.

Finance, as Mrs. Webb admitted in her article of 1931, is the biggest puzzle in any scheme of devolution. The National Assembly should have its own revenue; but on the whole it would be more of a supervising than a spending authority, and the House of Commons would continue to be responsible for the national debt, defence, war pensions, the Post Office, justice, prisons and the colonies. Revenue for those services controlled by the Assembly would come from the devolution of existing taxes, or by precepts to local authorities, or by new forms of taxation. The Assembly's procedure would be based, not on that of the House of Commons, but on that of local authorities. The system of administration by

Committees would enable all members to participate in government, and would ensure closer control.

There would be plenty of work left to the House of Commons —in fact 'all the functions of government known to Pitt and Canning, to Peel and Palmerston, and even to Gladstone and Disraeli prior to the seventies'.[20]

Summing up, Mrs. Webb said that her scheme recognized a clear distinction in the functions of government. On the one hand, there were sovereignty, foreign affairs, defence, law, justice—all functions based on the exercise of power; on the other there were the social services in all their forms—subjects for organized co-operation among citizens. To mix the issues arising out of these two functions was illogical and confusing, for an elector might be an internationalist and pacifist in foreign affairs *and* a believer in private enterprise in social affairs; he may believe in a national health service *and* be an imperialist.

Mrs. Webb's scheme could, she said, be adapted for regional devolution as well; there might be Assemblies for England, Scotland and Wales, which would administer common services by a series of joint committees, or by joint meetings of all the Assemblies. But, preferably, the one Assembly would cover the whole of Great Britain.

The Economic Sub-Parliament

In the Romanes lecture of 1930, Winston Churchill said that the great change that had come over Parliament since the first world war was its new preoccupation with economics; and this presented a dangerous new challenge to its survival. As a remedy, he suggested the creation of an economic sub-Parliament of non-political, non-partisan experts, about a fifth of the size of the present Commons and chosen by it.[21]

These general proposals were elaborated and modified by Churchill in the evidence he gave before the Select Committee on Procedure.[22] The sub-Parliament would, he said, consist of forty M.P.s and eighty others—twenty of them peers, the rest being businessmen, Trades Union representatives and economic experts. They would all be chosen to reflect party strengths in the House of Commons, and would serve a three-year period of membership (which period would not be affected by a general election).

All trade and industry bills would be referred to this body, unless the House of Commons decided otherwise. Other bills—or parts of other bills—could, if the House so resolved, also be sent for its consideration. These bills would eventually be returned to the House of Commons with the criticisms and recommendations of the sub-Parliament. The Economic sub-Parliament could also, if it so wished, initiate inquiries into questions of economic importance, and report its findings to both Houses of Parliament. The expected effect of this arrangement would be to provide a forum where important economic questions could be discussed in a dispassionate non-party atmosphere.

This plan excited considerable interest and controversy, and is still considered from time to time. In 1931, Samuel thought it impracticable,[23] but as re-stated by L. S. Amery (who stressed that the Commons would remain the dominant element in the legislature),[24] it has been advocated by Harold Macmillan.[25]

Industrial Legislatures

J. H. Harley, in 1930, suggested that proposed industrial legislation should be allotted to a functional Parliament, at least for preliminary consideration. This Parliament—modelled on the German Supreme Economic Council of the time—would remain subordinate to the national Parliament, which would continue to regulate the industrial policy of the future; but this policy itself could only succeed if it was prefaced by mutual discussion and agreement between the organized bodies of masters and men.[26] Other people have advocated industrial parliaments along the same lines; thus Kenworthy, in 1931, favoured the setting up of such a Parliament, which would consist of representatives of employers and employees.[27]

But the scheme of this kind which has attracted most attention in the recent past has been that put forward by Hollis in 1949.[28] This proposed a third parliamentary chamber, the 'House of Industry', consisting of Members elected, not—as in Churchill's suggestion—by the political Parliament, but by direct election from 'occupational constituencies' of industrial workers.[29]

This new House would have definite legislative responsibilities, modelled on those of the Church Assembly; it '. . . should play in industrial affairs the part which the Church Assembly plays in ecclesiastical affairs'. It would pass legislation on technical matters and submit it for the approval or otherwise of the House of Commons. Hollis's views have been echoed more recently by Sir Harry Legge-Bourke, who believed that the creation of an Industrial House would result in a closer examination of the great annual sums of money spent on the nationalised industries.[30]

(c) CRITICISMS OF FUNCTIONAL DEVOLUTION

The Webbs' proposal has aroused a certain amount of opposition; Muir called it 'unworkable'—a frequent epithet for schemes of devolution—and Laski thought it would prove difficult in practice to decide into which category, political or social, a particular matter fell.[31] Furthermore, the Webbs' proposal—like Churchill's—could lead to a state of affairs in which the two parliaments were of different political complexions.[32] Jennings said that a government must have unified control over affairs; yet, since foreign affairs and trade policy fell to be decided by different parliaments, the electorate might be able to vote for foreign and economic policies which were quite incompatible.[33]

Laski criticized Hollis's proposal on the ground that the basis of industrial representation had not been sufficiently explained. Were Labour and Capital interests to be weighted equally? Was the housewife to be represented? It was probable that some distinctive industries might prove too small to warrant a constituency of their own; would they have to be joined together? And how was the consumers' interest to be safeguarded?[34]

M. R. Curtis, agreeing that functional devolution would result in a better representation of industrial and similar 'occupational' interests, in a more experienced appraisal of matters of that kind, and in an avoidance of the hampering discipline of the political parties, listed six points of weakness or danger in such a system.[35] These were: (1) There was the possibility of conflict between the two Parliaments. This could only be avoided by making the new Parliament purely advisory: and in that case the supreme Parliament could always ignore its proposals. (2) If it was attempted to make the new Parliament powerful, the present Parliament could always override it by virtue of its ultimate financial control. (3) The division of functions between the two parliamentary bodies would prove difficult to define. (4) The method of election of Members for the new body would present difficulties. (5) Experts could not be expected to show expertise over all the subjects which the new body would discuss; in part of the discussions, they would only be able to put forward the views of an amateur. (6) The experience of continental countries, possessing similar Councils, showed that it was very difficult to avoid party alignments.

On the other hand Lord Campion, in considering the suggested ways of increasing Parliament's effectiveness, thought that functional devolution might do this. He believed Churchill's sub-Parliament to be more promising than the Webbs' co-Parliament.[36]

(d) REGIONAL DEVOLUTION

The demands for devolution of this kind are not always put forward as an alternative to schemes of functional devolution; the two are often proposed together. As mentioned above, Mrs. Webb, in her scheme for a social co-Parliament, went to some length to show it could be adopted to meet the demands of those who wanted a measure of regional autonomy; Churchill, while he was putting forward his scheme of an economic sub-Parliament, also favoured 'very considerable changes in the direction of devolution to local bodies much larger in scale than any that exist, or almost any that exist, in the country at the present time'.[37]

Regional devolution is advocated for a mixture of reasons; partly it is proposed as a more efficient system of government, partly as a way of relieving Parliament of its present great load of business, and partly as a means of satisfying or fostering local loyalties.

Lord Samuel started from the premise that Parliament was giving inadequate attention to many of the subjects under its control; and the only thorough remedy for this was the devolution of business to subordinate legislatures and ministries.[38] Devolution should be geographical, not functional; in addition to the examples provided by many foreign and commonwealth countries, Northern

Ireland showed how it could work. The obvious next steps were to provide Assemblies for Scotland and Wales, followed possibly by Northern and Southern England Assemblies. In an article in *Cross bow*, W. G. S. Adams has pointed to a malaise in Scottish public life, caused by dissatisfaction at the way the Scottish Office deals with Scottish affairs. The suggested answer to this situation was to set up a second House of Lords in Edinburgh, where Scottish peers would perform the functions *vis-à-vis* Scottish legislation, etc. which the Upper House at present performs at Westminster. Adams also thought that the Parliament at Westminster should be relieved of the domestic affairs of the different countries in the United Kingdom; devolution of this kind was essential.[39] The central parliament could then be reduced in size.

Muir thought that Parliament was not only under too much strain, but that government was also over-centralized. He was inclined to believe that regional devolution provided the answer, and suggested the setting-up of regional authorities for Scotland, Wales, and seven areas in England.[40]

The demands for Scottish and Welsh Home Rule seem to spring from grounds of national pride, rather than from the intention of making the present Parliament more effective: though occasionally the two reasons are coupled together, as when Lady Megan Lloyd George advanced them both to favour Parliaments of Wales and Scotland on the Northern Ireland model.[41] Powers to be transferred to the regional Parliaments would include agriculture, fisheries, forestry, education, health and housing. Reserved for the central Parliament would be its powers in connexion with the Crown, foreign and commonwealth affairs, defence, customs and tariffs. Powers relating to coinage, postal services, docks, harbours and electoral law would be shared.

This system, as far as Wales was concerned, had been set out in a pamphlet published in 1953,[42] and was to be repeated in an unsuccessful Private Member's Bill that came before the House of Commons in 1955.[43] It is too early yet to say what long-term effects the creation of a Secretary of State for Wales may have on the demands for Welsh autonomy; but judging from the Carmarthen by-election in 1966, it does not seem that those demands have been stilled.[44]

Lady Megan's father had been a supporter of regional devolution, thinking it especially relevant to the needs of a community as big as London.[45] The Liberal Party has continued to advocate it;[46] a manifesto issued at the time of the 1959 General Election offered Scottish and Welsh Parliaments on the lines advocated by Lady Megan.[47] The principles and proposed methods of implementing a form of regional government remain live issues today; Victor Wiseman has attributed the recent resurgence of interest in regionalism to the publication in 1963 of plans for the regional development of the North-East and Scotland, and of the Buchanan Report on 'Traffic in Towns'.[48] In general it seems that the increased emphasis placed by recent governments on regional plans has not gone far enough for the more fervent Celtic nationalists.

(e) CRITICISMS OF REGIONAL DEVOLUTION

Sir Ivor Jennings thought that Muir, in favouring regional devolution, had omitted to consider two problems: what were the subjects to be devolved, and what were to be the financial relations between the central and regional parliaments? In any case, the relief to Parliament would not be great: England was a single economic unit, and the co-ordinating legislation—which would thus be necessary in respect of each devolved subject—would take up all the 'saved' time. Even if powers were devolved only to Scotland and Wales, the time saved would not be worth the cost and complication involved.[49]

R. J. Lawrence attacked the very citadel of regional devolution on two fronts by saying that, in any area other than Northern Ireland, a separate legislature would aggravate rather than mollify social conflict; and that the supposed benefits of devolution to Northern Ireland had not been as great as generally believed.[50] The problem was basically a financial and economic one. Devolution presumed that the United Kingdom was to remain united, and it follows from this that certain conditions must govern the relations between the constituent countries: no area must be able to discriminate against the others, and all areas must share the benefits and contribute to the cost of the common services. Hence, fiscal policies must be uniform, and taxation as well as social services must be substantially uniform, in order to prevent the flow of persons, goods and capital from one area to another. There would, consequently, be almost no scope for independent action in administration or policy; it would be both difficult and unwise for a subordinate parliament to act independently, except in a few minor matters.

Lawrence supported his argument by an examination of the relationship between Northern Ireland and the rest of the United Kingdom; most Northern Ireland legislation simply re-enacted that passed at Westminster. Devolution was accordingly unlikely to confer on Scotland and Wales advantages that could not be secured in simpler ways, and might well create new difficulties in those areas by stirring up rivalries and conflicts.

These arguments were countered by A. H. Birch, who argued that Lawrence was wrong in basing his arguments against devolution on the experience of Northern Ireland, because that country had never done what the advocates of devolution had wanted her to—namely, initiate legislation that differed from the British Acts.[51] There was no reason why Parliaments for Scotland and Wales should not do this. But they would need greater financial powers so that they could finance some services by local taxation; their level of services would depend on how much revenue they could raise without injuring their economic position. It was not true to say that differences in tax rates would harm the whole nation's economy; it had not done so in America. Federalism was generally stimulating to the economy precisely because it promoted mobility of capital and labour, and the consequent location of resources in the area in which their productivity was greatest.

But perhaps Laski and Hollis have expressed most succinctly the practical views of the critics of regional devolution—Laski, when he said that the basic economic unity of Great Britain prevented any effective devolution,[52] and Hollis when he claimed that Home Rule for Scotland and Wales would not noticeably reduce the burden on the central government, since they were all so much part of the British industrial system.[53] So far as Scotland alone is concerned, the last word may be sought in the Royal Commission which reported in 1954. Much of the pressure for Home Rule came, they thought, from an ignorance of the extent to which devolution of Scottish affairs had already taken place.[54]

(f) OTHER KINDS OF DEVOLUTION

Jennings mentions the possibility of granting more legislative powers direct to Ministers as a sort of devolution; but he adds that this is not a form which generally commends itself to the advocates of devolution.[55] He suggests, however, one way in which it might be considered: all private bills could be controlled directly by Departments, rather than, as at present, having to go through the legislative procedure of both Houses.

Other critics have suggested that the sphere of action of local authorities could usefully be enlarged;[56] Salter, for instance, believed that more actual responsibility for policy should be given to them.[57] But Jennings thought that the time Parliament could save by this means would be 'almost infinitesimal', and that there was, in any case, very little that could be devolved in this way.[58]

Finally, in the arguments about the effect on British sovereignty of entry into the Common Market, it has been pointed out that this would transfer certain subjects to the European Parliament, and so ease the pressure at Westminster, without having recourse to regional devolution in this country.

Conclusion

Each new proposed scheme of devolution has to face two questions—will it work, and will it help?

The practicability of each new scheme is always attacked. Perhaps it is for this reason that the believers in devolution tend to be content with broad general statements of their aims, rather than give details which may be vulnerable and unpopular. By doing so, they leave themselves open to the rebuke of the 1931/2 Select Committee on Procedure: 'These proposals seem ... to have been inadequately considered.'[59] However, the fact that devolution is, in some forms and in some circumstances, practicable, can be inferred from its existing successes in Northern Ireland and in the Church Assembly.

The second question—Will it help?—is apt to draw different answers from different people, since they are considering different ends; some think devolution should aim to help Parliament, while others believe its purpose should be to help those regions (or interests) on whom the powers devolve. It is this mixture of motives which clouds the glass. If the question means, 'Will devolution help the natural aspirations of the regions within Great Britain?' the answer is clearly 'Yes, if such aspirations exist'; but regionalization has its drawbacks, as *Passport to Pimlico* showed. If the question means, 'Will devolution help Parliament?' the answer is in doubt; it seems superficially probable, but Stanley Baldwin said it would create more work in the long run, and several writers have agreed with him.[60] If, finally, it is asked, 'Will devolution help the country at large by bringing together a body who can give expert appraisal to technical matters in a national, non-political way?' the answer would seem to be that it is a consummation devoutly to be wished; but that the practical difficulties of creating such a body, and defining both its powers and its relationship to the House of Commons, are formidable.

The strength of the regionalizers' case seems to be admitted, in part at least, by the steps taken by recent governments to set up regional advisory bodies. But it seems certain that, if regional devolution comes, it will come only as a result of a spontaneous and widespread demand for it from the regions concerned.[61] It will come from below, and not from on top; for, as Denman pointed out, devolution is seldom popular among M.P.s, who prefer to try to handle everything themselves.[62]

However, with the mounting complexity and increasing congestion of parliamentary life, Parliament has already taken a half-step towards devolution by setting up committees of Members who will specialize in certain areas of administration, and keep the House informed of what they find out. In this respect, the creation of a Welsh Grand Committee and the extended functions of the Scottish Grand Committee (both of which now hold general debates on the problems of their countries) could also be significant. Further changes along these lines would not, of course, be devolution. Parliament would be retaining all its powers, but would be using them in a different way—and proposals of this kind are considered in Chapter III. However, being either regional or functional, such committees might to some small extent fulfil the expectations which advocates of devolution claim for their own schemes. If one then went on to allow for joint meetings of two or more of these committees, one would perhaps be advancing towards 'that subsidiary or collateral assembly' which is the goal of devolution.[63]

NOTES AND REFERENCES

[1] e.g. Mrs. Sidney Webb: 'A Reform Bill for 1932' in *Political Quarterly*, Vol. II, 1931, pp. 1–22.

[2] R. D. Denman: *Nineteenth Century and After*, Vol. 113, January 1933, pp. 74–9.

[3] Muir: *How Britain is Governed*, 2nd ed. 1930, p. 282.

[4] *Parliamentary Affairs*, Vol. VIII, 1954–5.

[5] Laski, p. 46.

[6] H.C. 161 of 1930/1, Q. 14–5.

[7] *Manchester Guardian*, 13th November 1952.

[8] e.g. H.C. Deb. 510 cs. 564–5.

[9] see Sir Herbert Samuel: *Political Quarterly*, Vol. II, 1931, pp. 309–12.

[10] Denman, *art. cit.*, pp. 76–7.

[11] Acland: *What It Will be Like in the New Britain*, 1942, p. 170.

[12] See the following chapter on Procedure.

[13] H.C. 161 of 1930/1, Q. 1964.

[14] Under the Church of England Assembly (Powers) Act, 1919, the Church Assembly can propose legislation 'touching matters concerning the Church of England'. Such 'Measures' are considered by the Ecclesiastical Committee (a Joint Committee of fifteen members from each House, chosen by the Lord Chancellor and the Speaker). This Committee cannot amend the Measure, but makes a report stating the effect of it, and its views on its expediency. Each House considers this report and votes to accept or reject the Measure (without amendment). On a single affirmative decision from each House, the Measure is presented for the Royal Assent, and becomes law.

[15] Denman: *art. cit.*

[16] H.C. Deb. 260, cs. 2162–3.

[17] *Listener*, 17th February 1933, p. 236.

[18] *A Constitution for the Socialist Commonwealth of Great Britain.*

[19] *Political Quarterly*, Vol. II, 1931, pp. 1–22.

[20] Mrs. Sidney Webb: *art. cit.* p. 20.

[21] Romanes lecture, 19th June 1930. O.U.P. 1930.

[22] H.C. 161 of 1930/1, Q. 3750 ff.

[23] He was arguing in favour of regional devolution: *art. cit.* p. 310.

[24] Amery: *Thoughts on the Constitution*, 1947, p. 67.

[25] In a speech at Brighton, 5th March 1949.

[26] *Fortnightly Review*, Vol. 128, New Series, September 1930.

[27] H.C. 161 of 1930/1, Q. 3139.

[28] Hollis: *Can Parliament Survive?*, Chap. IX.

[29] 'Functional representation' (see section (*h*) of Chap. I) had been called for by Amery, p. 65, who had suggested applying it to Churchill's scheme for an Economic sub-Parliament.

[30] H.C. Deb. 619, cs. 1356–7.

[31] Muir, p. 296.

[32] Laski, p. 48.

[33] Jennings: *Parliamentary Reform*, 1934, pp. 53–5.

[34] Laski, pp. 48–9.

[35] Curtis, pp. 45 ff.

[36] Lord Campion and others: *Parliament: A Survey*, 1952, p. 32.

[37] H.C. 161 of 1930/1, Q. 1513.

[38] *art. cit.* p. 309.
[39] Adams: *Crossbow*, Vol. 4, No. 10, p. 8.
[40] Muir, Chapter VIII.
[41] *Parliamentary Affairs*, Vol. VIII, No. 4, 1955.
[42] *Parliament for Wales*, Aberystwyth 1953.
[43] H.C. Bill 21 of 1955: H.C. Deb., 537, cs. 2439–527.
[44] On 14th July 1966.
[45] H.C. 161 of 1930/1, Q. 459.
[46] See Motion, 15th December 1952; and *The Unservile State: Essays in Liberty and Welfare*, edited by G. Watson, 1957, pp. 51–2.
[47] *People Count*, published by the Liberal Party, 1959.
[48] *Parliamentary Affairs*, Vol. XIX, No. 1.
[49] Jennings, *op. cit.*, pp. 45–7.
[50] 'Devolution Reconsidered' in *Political Studies*, Vol. IV, 1956, pp. 1–17.
[51] *Political Studies*, Vol. IV, 1956, pp. 310–11.
[52] Laski, pp. 46–7.
[53] Hollis, p. 79.
[54] Cmd. 9212, para 30.
[55] Jennings, *op. cit.*, pp. 37, 40.
[56] Adams: *art. cit.*
[57] In Lord Campion and others, Chap. V.
[58] Jennings, *op. cit.*, p. 41.
[59] H.C. 129 of 1931/2, para. 4.
[60] H.C. 161 of 1930/1, Q. 212.
[61] Lord Samuel: *art. cit.* p. 312.
[62] Denman: *art. cit.*
[63] Lord Campion and others, Chap. XIII.

III

Procedure

'Procedure is all the constitution the poor Briton has.' This observation by Sir Kenneth Pickthorn, during the debate on Procedure of 8th February 1960, underlines the importance of a subject which may not at first sight appear to afford much general interest.[1] A study of the subject must indeed start with the nature of Parliament itself, and, in the same debate, Lord Butler gave his views on this: Parliament, to be healthy, must not only be a legislative assembly, and the arena in which the struggle for power takes place; it must also be a place that captures the popular imagination.[2]

Various writers have listed the functions which Parliament exists to perform; and these can be separated under the general headings of legislation, finance and deliberation. Parliamentary procedure, which can be defined as the internal arrangements each House makes for the carrying out of these functions, may in its turn be considered under those same headings—but with the general proviso that, just as the 'deliberative' function is to some extent implicit within both the others, that category will contain some procedural items (such as 'Divisions') which are common to all three.

This chapter will, then, discuss proposals for procedural reform of the House of Commons under the three headings—Financial Control; Legislative Control; and General Procedural Reforms, which will take in proposed reforms within the 'deliberative' functioning of the House of Commons, together with some other reforms which affect the performance of all its functions. Before considering these, however, we must look at certain suggestions

For Notes and References see pages 97–105

44

which, in their entirety, would come nearest to providing a total reform of the House's procedure: we must examine the suggestions made for transforming the House's Committee system.

(*a*) THE SYSTEM OF COMMITTEES

In considering the many detailed schemes that have been put forward for parliamentary reform since about 1930, it is astonishing to find how widespread has been the belief that the House of Commons ought to set up specialized Committees of Members who would act as some form of link between the House and individual Departments of State. The reasons that are advanced in support of these Committees vary, as do the forms which it is suggested they should take; but it is clear that any scheme which, in general outline, has commanded support from such names as Acland, Amery, Campion, Cripps, Fellowes, Grimond, Hollis, Jennings, Laski, Muir, Salter, and G. M. Young—and the Study of Parliament Group, among many others—is worthy of the closest attention.

The proposal to use specialized parliamentary Committees of this kind was much in the air in the 1920s and 1930s; there was considerable argument, especially within the Labour Party, on the point.[3] These arguments rather worked themselves to a standstill, but interest in the subject revived later, and it was one of the major reforms considered by the Select Committees on Procedure in 1958/9 and 1964/5.

The reason for proposing these new committees is not the usual one that it would save parliamentary time; there is first the feeling that the whole question of Parliament's control over the Executive, the whole relationship between Whitehall and Westminster, needs to be re-appraised.[4] Underlying this is the belief that Members of Parliament are no longer capable collectively of exercising control over some aspects of administration; in order to be able to do so, they should know more about a Department's working and the Minister's reasoning. Thus, in the early 1930s, Lord Ponsonby was complaining that Parliament no longer had any say in foreign affairs; only a Foreign Affairs Committee, which would provide close contact between the Foreign Secretary and Members, could re-establish the greatest safeguard for peace—which was parliamentary control of the Executive.[5] Specialized Committees were necessary, said Lloyd George in 1931, in order that Members should be able to get hold of all the information that was available to Ministers; the Committees would publish reports, which would be debated, and the House would be better informed.[6] Greaves thought that realistic and effective discussion of departmental activities would follow, if the House had the aid of these specialized Committees.[7] Lord Cottenham said that the whole principle of the Executive's responsibility to Parliament was in danger, and that the remedy was an impartial supervision of each Department's work by a Committee of M.P.s.[8] K. C. Wheare believed that informal, all-party Committees, covering the whole range of administrative activity, able to keep in touch with Ministers and to discuss matters with the Department concerned, would be the best way of controlling bureaucracy.[9] Peering into the future, G. M. Young thought the main function of Parliament was going to lie in the control it exercised over the Executive, and that the easiest way of making this control effective lay in regular conferences between the Minister and his officials on the one hand, and Members of Parliament on the other.[10]

A system of this kind would clearly be objected to by Ministers, said Lloyd George, but he believed that it would do them and their officials good.[11] H. R. G. Greaves felt that the activities of a Committee of this kind would enhance the reputation of a good administrator.[12] Amery, speaking from his experience of office, thought such a Committee would actually have been a help to him.[13]

Lord Campion pointed out that advisory Committees of this kind need not controvert the basic tenet of the House's Committee system, which was that Committees should remain subordinate to the House.[14] Nor, said Brogan, need they upset the basis of our parliamentary government—that is, Cabinet control.[15] Both Lord Eustace Percy[16] and Lord Cottenham[17] thought that Parliament could, through a use of these Committees, act on that historic principle which had rather lost its effectiveness: 'the redress of grievances should precede supply.'

One great virtue of Committees like this was that policy and administration could be looked at in a dispassionate 'super-party' spirit, inside Parliament; both Lloyd George[18] and Lord Campion[19] underlined this point. Grimond said that it was difficult to deal with some major matters in the full blaze of political controversy, and that a use of Committees could obviate this. One of the most disturbing aspects of the Suez affray was that the Opposition was not consulted, and the House felt it was being kept deliberately and unnecessarily in the dark. Enlightenment could have been given in an all-party Committee, had one existed.[20] It has similarly been argued that the only way in which the welfare of a Colony can be considered by the House before an emergency there demands action (which might come too late), is by the existence of a specialist Committee which would meet regularly and keep the affairs of all Colonies constantly in mind.[21]

Adoption of this kind of Committee system would, it is said, make a great difference in the effectiveness of each individual Member's work in Parliament. Members would gain real knowledge of certain subjects,[22] and become truly effective in those spheres.[23] A former Speaker has said that 'departmental' Committees would certainly enable Members to acquire a better knowledge of how public money was spent,[24] and this would clearly be an advantage to them. Brogan argued that, from the examples of France and America, it could be seen that these Committees also gave Members greater experience of 'real'—that is, 'executive'—legislation.[25]

These Committees would, it was thought, provide a useful and important job for back-bench members who so often have little useful to do.[26] Members would feel that they were sharing in the effective work of Parliament,[27] and they could do so without— as at present—sitting all day in the Chamber waiting to 'get in' with a speech.[28] Thus the role of Members would have restored to it not only reality, but also influence, said Salter;[29] and Jennings believed that if ever private Members were to do anything more than walk through the lobbies, a development of the Committee system and the process of specialization was essential.[30]

When the practicability of the scheme was called in question, its apologists had three answers: it worked in foreign countries, it had to some minor extent already been successfully employed here, and it could not be less efficient than the system it was designed to replace.

Comparing the British with American and French systems, Brogan averred (in 1952) that in those other countries there is more 'parliamentary government' than with us.[31] Taking a broader view, Lord Campion pointed out that most legislative bodies have recognized the need to organize themselves in this way, in order to cope with the complexities of modern state business: the House of Commons itself relied for leadership on its Select Committees in the seventeenth century.[32]

One British Committee which is cited as an example of how the system has already, to a small degree, been worked successfully here, is the Select Committee on National Expenditure which was set up during the war. The reports of this Committee, said R. S. W. Pollard,[33] show the sort of useful thing that can be expected from a specialized Committee.[34]

In 1932, Adams was citing the Estimates Committee as the progenitor of the kind of committee he wanted.[35] Sir Edward Fellowes thought that the sort of Committee that could emerge might resemble the Public Accounts Committee;[36] but a direct precedent was the Joint Committee on Indian Affairs that had done useful work in 1921 and 1922, when it had had wide general terms of reference.[37] A resemblance to the Scottish Grand Committee has also been pointed out.[38]

The aspect of the present parliamentary system which, it is claimed, could not fail to be improved by the adoption of the new system, is the work done now by Committees of the Whole House. Hollis has said that everyone agrees it to be a farce that a committee of over 600 members should control the nation's business.[39] In the proposals he put before the Select Committee on Procedure in 1931, Jowett said that the House must completely abandon the practice of going into Committee of the Whole House, and leave the work to 'departmental' Committees instead.[40] Referring only to finance, Jennings thought that the Committees of Supply and Ways and Means were not competent to deal with points of detail, and should be superseded by a small Committee of Members who would soon become quasi-expert.[41]

Against the weight of all these arguments, the opposition was more rare than might have been expected and, on the whole, more guarded. It was said that the successful working of these Committees in foreign countries was not relevant to the situation in Great Britain, since their legislatures are founded on the doctrine of the separation of powers between the legislature and the executive; Muir said that the American or French system could not be transplanted as it stood.[42] It was for this reason that Laski thought the U.S. Senate Committee on Foreign Relations was not an appropriate model for the Parliament at Westminster (though he went on to describe the kind of Committee which he thought could be useful),[43] and Campion was very careful to point out that the French system of '*commissions permanentes*', which he was advocating, would need to be modified if it was to be adopted at Westminster.[44] The Select Committee on Procedure in 1958/59, rejecting by a small majority a proposal along these lines, described it as 'a radical constitutional innovation'.[45] Strachey and Joad protested against the proposed new system, because it would lead, they thought, to a complete fusion of Parliament and the Executive.[46] Lord Butler said it would get in the way of administration and blur ministerial responsibility.[47]

Of the other words said in criticism or qualification of the proposed change, Fitzroy pointed out that it would not, he thought, save any parliamentary time,[48] and Samuel was on the whole not convinced by the arguments put forward.[49] Lees-Smith went further. He believed that the existence of these Committees would kill the prospect of a Government with any driving power; Ministers would be driven to placate them and to compromise.[50]

But the most formidable of critics in the forties and fifties was Herbert (later Lord) Morrison.[51] Referring to the American and French system of Committees, he said that Governments tend to become the 'victims or creatures of Committees'; our own Parliament, he continued, would regard the practice as a derogation of its authority. Referring to the Jowett (I.L.P.) proposals, he said they would make the life of the Minister almost intolerable; they might also embarrass the official Opposition, who might find themselves attacking a policy which had been endorsed by their Members on the Committee; and they would, finally, challenge the vital doctrine of the responsibility of Ministers to Parliament as a whole.

The growth of interest in the 1950s in the idea of specialist committees as a remedy for the Commons' shortcomings increased remarkably in the 1960s; Michael Ryle's article in *The Times*,[52] George Wigg's attempts to set up a Select Committee on defence expenditure,[53] the Conservative pamphlet *Change or Decay*[54] and the Labour proposals in *Socialist Commentary*[55] were signs of the new interest. Dr. Crick's thesis that the Commons' duty was not to seek to throw out the Government, but to sustain it with constant advice and scrutiny, influenced the thinking of many commentators and led them, like him, to see salvation in a more effective committee system.[56] Hill and Whichelow showed the difference between the proposed new committees and their foreign counterparts; and argued that the acknowledged faults of the House—its inability to control expenditure, its subservience to party discipline, and its overcrowded programme—would all be remedied by a better use of Committees.[57] The Study of Parliament Group, in its submission to the Procedure Committee of 1964/5, argued the case in great detail; and the adoption by that Committee of the Group's views seemed, at the time, to be the culmination of a hard-fought campaign.[58]

The proponents of the idea did not of course have things all their own way. On the contrary, their arguments were answered with spirit, and it is interesting that the strongest opposition came from some of the most experienced Members of Parliament (see, for instance, an article by George Strauss on the subject[59]). Michael Foot argued passionately against the proliferation of committees which was, he though, not a cure for Parliamentary illness but part of the disease itself. What was needed was to restore the authority of the House of Commons Chamber by bringing spontaneity and flexibility into its 'arthritic' procedures, so enabling debates to be held over a much wider range and at much shorter notice than at present.[60] It was argued that the new committees would provide Members with far more extensive information on government activities; but Sir Edward Boyle could point out that there already existed in the Written Parliamentary Question a means whereby the M.P. could inform himself in these matters.[61] Enoch Powell said roundly that the more information Members had the less effective they would be in debate, and the more likely to approximate to the point of view of the Minister himself.[62]

The General Functions of the Proposed Departmental Committees

We have seen that a wide range of opinion has held that Parliament should set up Committees which would each concern themselves with a particular field of government administration. Not unnaturally, opinions differ as to what would be the precise nature and functions of such Committees, and now we must turn to consider these. However, it should be pointed out that many writers—while they have been keen to stress the virtues of the idea —have not felt it necessary to argue for or against the details of how it would work out. They all envisage a fairly small Committee keeping an eye on each department, and thus being informed— and keeping the House informed—of the reasons on which policy decisions have been taken; but they have not all concerned themselves with the details of the form the Committee should take.

There has been much discussion as to whether the new Committees should concern themselves with administration (as Select Committees are said to have dealt with hitherto) or policy; but the distinction between the two is, as the Procedure Committee ruefully discovered, very difficult to make.[63] Coombes has argued that the experience of the Nationalized Industries Committee shows that Select Committees can and do deal with government departments on questions of policy.[64] He echoes Hanson and Wiseman in saying that the important distinction is not between policy and administration, but between party issues and non-party issues.[65]

The Study of Parliament Group, whose evidence impressed the Procedure Committee,[66] were quite clear about what they were seeking to effect. Parliamentary control, they said, meant 'influence, not direct power, advice, not command, criticism, not obstruction, scrutiny, not initiative, and publicity, not secrecy'.[67]

We now turn to consider the details of the scheme. Some of the general questions to be decided are: Should the Committee have legislative duties? Should it control departmental expenditure? Should it control a department's delegated legislation? What departments are particularly in need of this kind of parliamentary control? A basic factor, which must be clearly defined, concerns the exact relationship between the Committee and the Minister. Finally, we can consider various detailed suggestions about the size, constitution, powers, terms of reference, and staffing of the Committee.

Should the Committee Have Legislative Duties?

A number of those who advocate the setting-up of these departmental Committees contend that they are the appropriate bodies to take the Committee stage of bills affecting their departments. Others go further, and say the Committees should actually initiate legislation.[68]

Among those who favoured the idea of these Committees taking the Committee stage of relevant bills was Jennings. He had elsewhere advocated that Standing Committees, which take the Committee stage of bills, should be composed of specialists; and he thought it would be unnecessary duplication to have two different specialist committees dealing with the same subject-matter.[69] Jowett, speaking for the I.L.P., believed that the one Committee should consider all matters relating to a particular Department, and this would include the Committee stage of bills.[70] The Joint Committee on Indian Affairs (1921–29), which Fellowes suggested as a prototype for future Specialized Committees, included in its duties the examination of bills.[71] Hollis based his views on the procedure of the Parliament in Holland. There, each new bill is presented by the Minister to the relevant departmental Committee, and, together and in private, they go through it in detail. Only after this opportunity for feeling the way and for considering possible modifications is the bill debated publicly.[72]

Others have favoured the idea that these Committees should take more than just the Committee stage of each bill; Stafford Cripps, for instance, said they might themselves suggest legislation.[73] Pollard, who particularized very fully the functions of these Committees, thought they should investigate the need for legislation, and then suggest what form it should take.[74] When the Department produced a bill, it should be examined by the appropriate Committee before being submitted to the House of Commons. The Committee would subsequently take the Committee stage of the bill; they would also consider and report on any private Member's bill specially referred to them by either the Department or the House. He suggested elsewhere that a specialist Committee should look after the Statute Book; that is, supervise the drafting and amending of bills, and prepare consolidation and codification bills.[75]

Point was given to these proposals by Lord Percy, who thought that Parliament's weakness in the field of legislation lay, not in a dearth of time or a waste of time, but in its lack of initiative in formulating bills. Committees should be able to remedy this.[76]

In the sixties the view was being expressed that the new specialist Committees could eventually take the Committee stage of relevant bills[77] or at least form the nucleus of the Committee which did so.[78] Crick thought that Ministers would use the Committees as sounding boards for future legislation;[79] but this belief was attacked by George Strauss, who argued that the Committee, being divided on most political questions, could not give definitive advice.[80] The Parliamentary and Scientific Committee, in its proposal for a Specialist Committee to study the reports of the Research Councils, etc., thought that the new Committee should carry out an *ad hoc* enquiry before legislation was introduced on a particular subject.[81] The Procedure Committee made no recommendation on a legislative role for specialist Committees, but rejected a proposal which considered *inter alia* the desirability of these Committees examining draft Bills before Second Reading.[82]

Should the Committee Control Expenditure?

Several writers have in mind that these Committees should exercise some sort of control over the spending of the Department. Lloyd George said they should be examining expenditure continuously,[83] and Dawkins thought that permanent specialist Committees should consider the Estimates in order to suggest economies (though without questioning the policies behind them).[84] Fellowes suggested more recently that a specialized Defence Committee should consider the Estimates of the relevant Departments and report to the House, by mid-May, what economies (consistent with the Government policy underlying the Estimates) might be effected in them.[85]

Hill and Whichelow thought that a Department's estimates and annual reports would provide the startpoint for the Committee's inquiries, and that the Committee of Supply could debate any suggestions for reduced expenditure which the Specialist Committee might propose.[86] An involvement with expenditure is implicit in the proposals that Specialist Committees could evolve from the Select Committee on Estimates; this was the suggestion of Lidderdale[87] and the Study of Parliament Group,[88] and the basis of the main recommendation of the Procedure Committee.[89]

But some suggestions go further, and say that the Committees should discuss the Department's proposed Estimates of expenditure before these are formally laid before the House. This pre-natal control, which may have been suggested by analogy with local government administration, is suggested, among others, by Pollard.[90] He also believes that the detailed discussion of the Estimates—at present done by the Committee of Supply and the Select Committee on Estimates—should be transferred to the Departmental Committees.[91]

Pollard envisaged a Finance Committee supervising the general arrangements. Laski, however, said that the Estimates were a reflection of Government policy, and that therefore it was wrong for the House to try to exercise 'pre-natal' control over them.[92]

Should the Committee Oversee a Department's Delegated Legislation?

Pollard is again among the several[93] who argue that all the statutory instruments which a Department makes should be subject to the approval of the appropriate Departmental Committee.[94] If the members of the Committee do not agree on the virtues of the proposed instrument, then it should require an affirmative resolution from the House of Commons before coming into force.[95] The Study of Parliament Group advocated a new Select Committee on the merits of Statutory Instruments, and suggested that it should have an overlapping membership with the specialist Committees which they also proposed. The latter Committees were expected to pay particular regard to the way in which instruments were operating in practice.[96]

The Particular Need for Certain Departmental Committees

Some of the demand for specialized Committees stems, not from a general principle, but from a belief that Parliament needs to be better informed of the workings of a particular Department. Thus from 1931—when a witness before a Select Committee averred that the Great War might conceivably have been avoided if there had been an active Foreign Affairs Committee which could have unearthed what was going on[97]—to 1957—when a motion was put down on the House of Commons Order Paper saying that Parliament lacked control over external affairs[98]—there have been proposals that the House should have a committee specializing in foreign affairs.

It has recently been suggested that there is an overwhelming case for more discussion of the affairs of British territories, some of which go unmentioned in the House for years at a time. The remedy proposed was a specialized Committee on Colonial Affairs.[99]

Another subject which suggests itself as suitable for non-party consideration inside a Committee room is Defence. Geoffrey de Freitas and Martin Lindsay have called for a Committee of this kind,[100] and have noted that Members of Parliament know less about the disposition of British forces than do the members of defence committees of foreign legislatures. Grimond included disarmament and the H-bomb as subjects on which Members needed more enlightenment.[101] Fellowes has pointed out that the creation of a Defence Committee would help to spread the debates on the Service Estimates over a longer period than at present.[102] George Wigg had a motion on the Order Paper calling for such a Committee in 1963;[103] it was repeated by Emrys Hughes in 1965.[104]

Laski suggested that there should be a series of Committees specializing in the nationalized industries.[105] He was writing before the creation of the Select Committee on Nationalized Industries, which has been set up sessionally since 1957, and which should, according to John Hall, be divided into two committees, covering the transport and power industries respectively.[106]

Pollard thought that, to make a start, a specialist committee of Members might be set up to concern itself with the Lord Chancellor's Department.[107] The Parliamentary and Scientific Committee proposed to the Procedure Committee that there should be a Committee on Science.[108] Crick lists eighteen possible subjects;[109] Hill and Whichelow suggested, as a start, Committees on science, the social services, agriculture and transport;[110] the Study of Parliament Group asked for Committees on science, crime, the machinery of government (at all levels), housing, and the social services.[111] When the Government was finally convinced of the need for specialist Committees, they chose science and agriculture as the subjects of the first two.

We have noted above that it is sometimes suggested that Departmental Committees should concern themselves with the Estimates presented by those Departments, and that one suggestion was that there should be a supervisory Finance Committee. In step with this is Jennings' proposal that there should be a Committee concerning itself with the work of the Treasury.[112] This Committee would examine not only all the Estimates, but also the Finance Bill and the financial provisions of other bills; its essential functions would be informative, and it should not try to take the place of the Treasury itself. It could, however, act as a kind of court to which the Comptroller and Auditor General could appeal against the Treasury. This notion, apart from its legislative side, has affinities with the idea put by Campion to the Select Committee on Procedure in 1945: a Public Expenditure Committee should be set up, combining the dual roles of the present Estimates and Public Accounts Committee. This proposal was accepted and recommended by the Select Committee,[113] but it has never been put into effect, although it is still occasionally advocated.[114] Basil Chubb, however, after rehearsing the arguments for and against the proposal, concluded that it was not the entire answer.[115]

Relationship Between the Committee and the Minister

The matter of this relationship is clearly central to the whole problem, and most of the writers on the general subject touch on it. Their views, understandably enough, differ.

At one end of the spectrum are those who believe that the Minister should not only belong to the Committee, but be its Chairman. This was how Amery envisaged things,[116] as also did Cottenham,[117] and it what the I.L.P. consistently advocated.[118] Muir thought that, to avoid the Committee over-riding the Minister, he (or someone nominated by him) should be Chairman, with powers to exclude any question from consideration if it was a matter of policy.[119]

Greaves proposed that, if the Minister found that attendance at the Committee took too much time, he should delegate his duties to a junior Minister;[120] Jennings suggested that, normally, it should be the junior Minister's duty to attend.[121] The amendment moved by Leslie Hale to the Report of the Select Committee on

Procedure in 1958/9 envisaged that at least one Minister should be a member of the proposed Colonial Committee, and that any Minister should be entitled to attend and speak, but not to vote.[122]

Others have thought that a meeting between Minister and Committee should only be occasional.[123] Laski (referring to a Foreign Affairs Committee) felt that it should have the power of summoning the Minister or his junior whenever it wanted.[124] Fellowes said it would probably be wiser if the Minister was not a member of the Committee, but senior Ministers could be asked to attend occasionally,[125] and this was the line taken by the Study of Parliament Group.[126] Coombes argued that if the Minister concerned were a regular participant, Members would find it difficult to resist the temptation to make party political advantage out of the proceedings.[127]

These arguments approach the other end of the spectrum, where Minister and Committee do not come together. Percy said that the Committee should agree to recommendations, which would then be passed on to the Minister.[128] The Committee, said Adams, should examine, discuss and advise; in the light of that, the Minister would decide.[129]

The Size and Constitution of 'Departmental' Committees

Most of the writers on the subject specify the need for 'small' or 'workmanlike' Committees; when an actual number is suggested, it is fifteen,[130] fifteen to twenty,[131] twenty-five,[132] or thirty-two to forty.[133] But two Members of Parliament, referring to a proposal to set up a Foreign Affairs Committee, thought that every Member should have a right to attend.[134]

All those who mention the topic agree that the political parties should be represented on these Committees in the same proportion as they are in the House.[135] It has also been suggested that the Committees should consist of Members of both Houses of Parliament.[136]

Incidental Powers, and Terms of Reference, of the Committees

A few writers think that these Committees should be 'unofficial' —that is, presumably, that they would act privately, have no specific warrant from their House, and make no Reports to the

House.[137] As Salter puts it, their talks should have 'no legal effect'.[138]

But the majority have looked forward to official Committees, with specified duties and powers. Of these latter, it seems that all writers imply that the Committees will have the right—as enjoyed by most sessional Select Committees—to send for persons, papers, and records; this would enable them to examine witnesses from the Civil Service, and other appropriate experts. It is also implied that the Committees should have power to report their observations to the House—either annually, as Pollard and Muir suggested,[139] or when it suits them. It is sometimes said that these Reports should be the subject of debates on Supply days, which debates would in consequence be better-informed.[140]

Hale set out the duties of his proposed Colonial Committee with some care. The Committee would meet fortnightly, and could be convened specially if six of its members so desired. It would come to no decisions, except on various procedural points. Any subject could be added to its agenda on the requisition of a quarter of its members.[141]

Fellowes thought that his proposed Defence Committee's terms of reference should be to consider the Estimates of the relevant departments and report what economies, consistent with the policy implied in those Estimates, might be effected therein, and to consider such other matters as might be referred to it by the House or put before it by the Minister of Defence.[142] The Study of Parliament Group, and the Select Committee on Procedure—each of which favoured adapting the Estimates Committee so that it could do the work of specialist Committees—set out proposed new terms of reference for it. The former suggested that the Committee should 'examine the assumptions on which policy decisions have been made, and report on the implementation of policy'; the latter suggested, 'to examine how the Departments of State carry out their responsibilities and consider their estimates of expenditure and reports'.[143]

Some disagreement exists on the question of whether there should be a committee for each Department of State, or whether each Committee should concern itself with a 'subject area', which would take in the activities of several Departments. When explaining his plan for specialized Standing Committees, Dawkins suggested that there were four large subject areas: these were internal affairs and communications; social services; trade and industry; and Scottish affairs.[144] Other writers on the subject seem to prefer the idea of considerably more; nine or ten, suggested Muir;[145] one for each Department, said, for example, Pollard[146] and Greaves.[147] But, as explained above (page 55), when the House began its experiment with specialist Committees, it chose one subject (agriculture in England and Wales) which was the concern of a single department, and another (science) which ranged more widely.

Staffing the Committees

The earlier proposals for specialist Committees did not give much attention to the kind of staff which would be necessary to serve them. Recently, as the idea approached reality, more thought has been given to the subject. The Special Report of the Nationalized Industries Committee in 1958/9 had set out the arguments for and against employing specialized assistance over and above the work that could be done by the Committee's own clerks.[148] Later the Estimates Committee had contended with the same problem;[149] on one occasion they were able to obtain outside assistance as the result of a grant of funds to them from the Acton Society.[150] The Procedure Committee thought that the volume (though not the standard) of the assistance available to the Estimates Committee was lower than a Royal Commission would expect; they recognized the extent to which technical information could already be obtained in evidence; and recommended that the Estimates Committee (in its new role as specialists) should have power to employ and pay for temporary technical and scientific assistance.[151] Coombes argued that expert assistance is unnecessary, and would be the cause of so much suspicion in Whitehall as to hold back the creation of specialist Committees.[152] The Parliamentary and Scientific Committee argued that experience had shown that Committees, with their normal staff of clerks, could make valuable reports on complex matters. Expert staff would in any case not be a match for the Government experts. The Procedure Committee therefore decided against asking for expert staff but would rely instead on expert witnesses. They hoped that an expanded Library staff would also be available to help.[153]

Conclusion

It can be seen that, over the years, there has been a widespread belief in the need for 'specialist' or 'departmental' Committees. Yet the opposition to the idea, allied of course to the formidable forces of inertia, prevailed for a long while. The change, when it came, came with unexpected suddenness. In 1959, as we have seen, the Procedure Committee had dismissed the idea of specialist Committees as a radical constitutional innovation, and the House supported them in a vote along party lines. In October 1965 the House failed to press for the establishment of the modified Estimates Committee structure which the Procedure Committee had recommended. Yet in December 1966 the first specialist Committees were created, and began their deliberations early the following year. Time will tell as to how effective and acceptable—to Parliament and the Executive—these new specialist Committees will prove to be. Their early reports will clearly be awaited and studied with keen interest; and for more than one reason. But the simple fact that they have been set up will be an encouragement to those who have long felt that improved Parliamentary scrutiny of the Executive required a reform along these lines.

(b) FINANCIAL PROCEDURE

The Criticisms

It can be argued that the House of Commons' most important function lies in its control of finance. Yet the working of this control is sometimes criticized, and indeed its very existence is occasionally called in doubt. Lord Samuel said that parliamentary control over finance had fallen into abeyance; that, once presented, every Estimate was approved as a matter of course.[154] Cottenham claimed that it was the Treasury, rather than Parliament, which decided the Estimates; Parliament voted what the Executive demanded: we were governed by officials.[155] These criticisms remain very current; in recent debates in the Commons, it has been said that the House has lost its former role of scrutinizer of the Estimates,[156] and that there is a need for much more control over public expenditure.[157] Lord Butler, when Leader of the House, summed the matter up: 'I think we all feel . . . that there is something not quite right in the manner in which the House of Commons examines Supply.'[158]

The deterioration in the House's control over public expenditure has been a marked feature of post-war years. Lord Hinchingbrooke (now Mr. Victor Montagu) traced back to 1947 the procedure by which the House would agree to a Supply Vote formally—'on the nod'—in order to be able to stage in the time thus left over a general debate on Government policy.[159] But even before then, the 1946 Procedure Committee said that the examination of Estimates by the House had 'almost ceased to serve the purpose of financial scrutiny', and served merely as an excuse for debates on policy.[160] It is a fact, as Lord Butler has pointed out, that the House really prefers a discussion of policy and politics to a detailed examination of Estimates.[161] There nevertheless exists a widespread feeling of discontent at the way huge sums of public money are voted with little or no debate. It is significant that the House's abdication of its duty to scrutinize details of expenditure has taken place in a period which has seen a vast increase in the size of State spending— especially on arms, welfare policies, and the nationalized industries. This has led to the paradoxical situation, noted by Grimond, that nowadays it is Members of Parliament who press for more expenditure, and the Executive which acts as the bulwark against further inflation and heavier taxation.[162]

Another, lesser, criticism is that the financial procedure of the House, in many of its aspects, is too complicated. The existence of two identical Committees of the Whole House—one of Supply, and the other of Ways and Means—was said by Jennings to introduce an element of 'mumbo-jumboism' into procedure.[163] Muir said that the way in which the national accounts were presented made it difficult for a Member to get 'any clear ideas as to the exact financial position of the nation'.[164] Peter Bromhead has described the Supply system as 'mysterious and esoteric'.[165] Hugh Dalton, writing on the Labour Party's proposals for reform in 1934, said that financial procedure took up too much time, and should be abbreviated.[166] Attlee, speaking in the House on the Army Estimates soon after, said it was unsatisfactory that they should have to discuss pages and pages of figures in a debate on the floor of the House.[167] Lidderdale, in his evidence to the Procedure Committee in 1966, said that some of the House's Supply procedures were little short of farcical.[168]

The Suggested Remedies

Attlee's suggested remedy was that Members should meet round a table, and have an official there to explain to them, by question and answer, the purpose behind each Estimate; a later speaker in the same debate answered that that was what the Public Accounts and Estimates Committees already existed to do.[169]

Many of the critics have called for an extension of the Committee system to cover what they feel to be a gap,[170] and there has been discussion of whether the existing Committees could not be made more effective.

The Select Committee of Procedure in 1931 advocated closer liaison between the Estimates and Public Accounts Committees, but this recommendation was later rejected by the Government of the day.[171] It was repeated, however, in 1944 when the National Expenditure Committee (which took the place of both Committees during the war) said that, in the light of their experience, there should be closer bonds between the Committees after the war than there had been before.[172] This in turn led to Campion's proposal to the 1945 Select Committee on Procedure, mentioned above, that both Committees should be coalesced into the one Public Expenditure Committee; the Procedure Committee recommended that this should be done, but the House has never authorized even an experiment along these lines. Chubb traced the arguments for and against this proposal, and himself believed that it was open to criticism.[173] It has, however, been aired again inside the House by Lord Hinchingbrooke,[174] and outside by Paul Einzig, who visualized the new Committee operating through a number of specialist sub-committees.[175]

If part of the fault is in the fact that a Committee of the whole House is an unsuitable instrument for the examination of details, it can be argued that the House should create special Committees to do this kind of work on its behalf. Fellowes suggested to the Procedure Committee in 1958 that the House should refer specific estimates to a Committee, and order the Committee to report on

them by a certain time; the House would thereupon be able to vote the money in the assurance that the need for it had been examined.[176] This proposal was supported by, *inter alia*, Grimond,[177] but the Procedure Committee rejected it on a division.[178]

A new Select Committee on Expenditure has been advocated by Michael Ryle.[179] It was taken up in the proposals for revised financial procedure which the Study of Parliament Group put to the Procedure Committee. These envisaged the Government producing, before Christmas, White Papers on public investment and public expenditure, giving details of the five-year 'forward looks' in respect of expenditure. These papers would be examined by the Select Committee on Expenditure, who would look at the assumptions on which the forecasts had been made, draw attention to variations in the Estimates, and examine their economic implications in terms of availability of physical resources, etc. The White Papers, and the Committee's report, would then form the basis of a two-day debate which would take place before Budget Day. The Group also made a number of detailed suggestions for improving scrutiny of the totals of expenditure on individual services.[180]

Some Conservative Members have argued the need for Standing Economic Committees drawn from back-bench Members with industrial experience. These could include expert advisers called in from outside, and would make preliminary examination of all Government economic bills.[181]

Another proposal by Hinchingbrooke was that every year ten Supply Days should be spent in an examination of the Estimates; a day or half a day should be allotted to a debate on the Estimates of each spending department.[182] Hinchingbrooke also lent his support to another suggestion put by Fellowes to the Procedure Committee. This was that the House—which normally votes a proportion of the Estimates 'on account' in March, and then actually grants the money in July—should, in July, only vote a further sum on account. The formal supply vote would then be made some time towards the end of the calendar year.[183] By interposing this extra step in Supply procedure, the House would ensure that finance was debated in the autumn—the time when, according to Birch (who was supporting the idea), decisions are taken about the Estimates for the following year.[184] But Fellowes' proposal had not been taken up by the Procedure Committee.

Other minds were turning to consider the work at present being done by the Select Committee on Estimates; its terms of reference, said Lord Butler in 1960,[185] left a gap, because it was not entitled to consider administrative policy. This point had been made a long while before, by the 1931 Select Committee on Procedure, which had recommended that the Select Committee on Estimates should no longer be debarred from considering matters of policy on which the Estimates were based. But this had been rejected by the Government, as it would have involved an encroachment on the powers of the Executive; however, it was said, where questions of administration and policy overlapped, with administration as the predominant factor, the Estimates Committee had hitherto considered it within its terms of reference to make recommendations, and the Government saw no objection to such an interpretation.[186] (Point was lent to this by a later Chairman of the Public Accounts Committee, who said that no power on earth could prevent a Committee going beyond its terms of reference, if it so wished.)[187]

It seems to be this bar on the discussion of pure 'policy' which makes some critics prefer the idea of setting up new 'departmental' committees to keep an eye on expenditure, rather than to continue to use the Estimates Committee for this purpose.[188] The Study of Parliament Group, in advocating the adaptation of the Estimates Sub-Committees to perform the functions of departmental Committees, said that their terms of reference ought to be changed so that they could examine the assumptions on which policy decisions were made.[189] The Procedure Committee, in adopting this proposal, preferred that the Estimates Comittee's new terms of reference should be 'to examine how the departments of State carry out their responsibilities and to consider their Estimates of expenditure and reports'.[190] The House, in debating this report,[191] did not however adopt its conclusions.

Another proposal of the 1931 Committee which has failed to be implemented is the suggestion that the Estimates Committee should have the help of a special technical staff. (Samuel suggested elsewhere the appointment of an expert officer, the 'Examiner of Estimates'.)[192] The Government thought this point could be met by having extra Treasury officials available to help the Committee; the National Expenditure Committee in 1941–42, envisaging a new Select Committee to review economies within the machinery of government, said that it would require an Assessor comparable in status with the Comptroller and Auditor General;[193] and a more recent Committee again recommended that the Estimates Committee should have the assistance of an accountant or specially qualified person.[194]

A leader in *The Times*[195] said that the three weaknesses of the Estimates Committee were its preclusion from studying policy matters, its lack of an independent watchdog such as the Comptroller and Auditor General, and the fact that the financial timetable turned each of its inquiries into a post-mortem. It advocated freedom from the restraint on discussing policy, and earlier reports from the Committee. The same newspaper said later that, as the departments now plan their estimates for something like two years ahead, parliamentary control would never mean much until the Estimates Committee could gauge the future financial consequences of policies on which the Government were embarking.[196]

Since the war, the Committee has had to consider whether it could not operate more efficiently if it had more effective powers of travelling to examine the expenditure of British public money abroad.[197] It has had the support of the Procedure Committee in its belief that such powers are necessary.[198]

It would clearly make the Estimates Committee a more formidable instrument if its Reports were, as a matter of course, debated by the House. A proposal that this should be done was made by Samuel in 1931,[199] and has been repeated in more recent times by, amongst others, James MacColl[200] and Einzig[201]; since 1960, three days a Session have been set aside for debating the reports of the Estimates and Public Accounts Committees.[202] The 1946 Procedure Committee, in approving Campion's plans for a National Expenditure Committee, had also recommended that two Supply days should be spent each year in debating its Reports.[203]

Turning again to financial procedure in general, we note that Jennings elaborated his charge that this procedure was too complicated, and made suggestions for improving it. He felt it was unnecessary to have Votes on Account for each department; one single vote should be sufficient for all departments;[204] similarly, the separate Votes which have to be voted when the Supply guillotine falls should be divided on *en bloc*.[205] An annual Appropriation Bill was unnecessary; force of law should be given to the Estimates once they had been passed by the Committee of Supply; or, alternatively, the Appropriation Bill should undergo only one (i.e., a third) reading.[206]

Jo Grimond stressed the need for new machinery that would keep under review the provision of capital for the nationalized industries. His proposal was that an investment board should be set up for that purpose or, failing that, a Select Committee.[207] After a Government announcement that presaged a closer watch by the House over the spending of these industries, a leader in *The Times* pointed out the stagnation of management that might result. The idea that Parliament could itself run the industries was, it said, a delusion.[208]

Muir's suggestion was that the methods of presenting the Estimates and keeping the nation's accounts should be improved, so that they could be better understood.[209] When the Treasury changed the format of the Estimates in 1960, the Estimates Committee complained that the country was thereby to be deprived of useful information.[210]

Various proposals have been voiced for accelerating the passing of the Finance Bill. Thus Ramsay MacDonald suggested, and Baldwin concurred, that it should be divided into two Bills—one dealing with taxation proper, which would be taken on the floor of the House, the other dealing with financial machinery which would be taken 'upstairs'.[211] It has been put forward that the Bills, or parts of the one Bill, could be taken at different times in the Session—administrative parts in the autumn, fiscal parts in the spring.[212] This idea of a divided Finance Bill was echoed by Jennings, who went further; the Taxation Bill would already have been discussed in Committee of Ways and Means, so all it would require would be a formal Third Reading.[213]

The Select Committee on Procedure in 1958/9 recommended that the Finance Bill should be committed, at least in part, to a Standing Committee each year; this, they said, was the greatest single economy that could be made in the time spent on the floor of the House.[214] A possible partition mentioned to them was that between the Bill itself, and the new clauses proposed to it.[215] It was suggested by one witness that the Standing Committee should be an especially large one,[216] and by another that the Committee should split up into two sub-committees, with the Financial Secretary and the Economic Secretary to the Treasury in charge respectively.[217] A Grand Committee has also been suggested.[218] When the Procedure Committee returned to this problem in 1965, they recommended that the Bill should be drafted in such a way that as much as possible of it should be committable to a Standing Committee. The decision as to which parts would be so committed would be recommended by a Select Committee set up for the purpose, and this Committee would also recommend a time-table for the Bill.[219] But the proposal to discuss the Finance Bill in Standing Committee was seen by Einzig as further proof of Parliament's declining control over the nation's finances. The Committee stage, in Committee of the Whole House, is an occasion where the Government comes under the strongest pressure from public opinion. Because, under the Parliament Act, the Bill must be passed by early August, the Government is prepared to make concessions; by sending the Bill to Standing Committee, this inducement would no longer operate.[220]

The criticism, frequently heard in the thirties, about the lack of sufficient Supply days, and the disproportionate amount of time spent on Supplementary Estimates, seem largely to have been silenced by the changes introduced in financial procedure since 1945; though Fellowes, in his proposal to the Procedure Committee in 1958, thought that the House would be able to spend more time on Supply if some of its legislative duties were undertaken by Committees.[221] It was, however, to a more even spread of Supply days throughout the Session that that Procedure Committee turned their eyes.[222]

Grimond has suggested, as a remedy for irresponsible suggestions for increased expenditure, that no member should be allowed to advocate further expenditure without naming the tax which was to be increased to pay for it;[223] the need to stress that every proposed increase in the Estimates would be reflected in a rise in taxation has been mentioned by Birch.[224] Ryle has advocated a Committee to consider the administration of taxation, just as the Estimates Committee examines administration of expenditure.[225]

Financial Resolutions, which authorize the expenditure or taxation contained in Public Bills, are mentioned elsewhere.[226]

The 1966 Reforms

The weight of criticism directed against the House's financial procedure led the Procedure Committee to advocate a number of changes in March 1966,[227] and the House to adopt them in the following December.[228] One of the oldest principles of Commons' procedure was then repealed—the principle that every charge had to be considered in a Committee of the whole House before the House could deal with it. The Committee of Supply was abolished; the business of supply, all Ways and Means resolutions and all money resolutions were henceforward to be taken in the House. The Queen's Recommendation was from then on to be signified in writing, and no longer by the nodding of a Privy Councillor in the House.

These, and a number of other small changes, removed many of the irritations of financial procedure, much of the 'mumbo-jumbo'. But they were largely changes of form, not of content. They did not alter one way or the other the efficacy (or lack of it) of the House's control over the country's finances. Nor were they designed to. Indeed, in commending them to the House, the Leader of the House said that the watchdog control of finance and administration was one of the former functions of the House of Commons which had now been largely lost. To ask for a return of it was, he said, 'crying for the moon'.[229]

(c) LEGISLATION[230]

Although very many proposals have been made for improving Parliament as a legislative machine, very few envisage any radical alteration in the legislative process as such; the proposals, by and large, concern the individual stages of that process. Even Mosley and Cripps, who each looked forward to a much more widespread use of Orders in Council, envisaged that these would be made under General Acts which would have been passed by Parliament in the recognized way.[231] This is in line with what the Clerk of the House told the Procedure Committee in 1958; sooner or later, he said, Parliament would have to lay down general principles, and leave it to the Executive to administer them.[232]

A change in the legislative system was, however, suggested by Sidebotham in 1930. He said that a bill's Committee stage in one House should be followed immediately by the same stage in the other House; on disputed points the Committees could sit jointly. Report stages in both Houses would then follow successively, as would Third Readings.[233] But perhaps the proposal that goes furthest from the House's practice is that a bill which has not completed the legislative process by the end of a Session should be allowed to start the next Session at the point which it had reached before.[234] This had been urged by, for example, Lord Ponsonby in 1933,[235] and was repeated by Pollard in 1944[236] and by some Labour Members in 1964.[237] Lloyd George is among those who have gone on record in opposition to this idea.[238]

Another far-reaching proposal, which was being widely canvassed in the 1930s, was that, as a matter of course, there should be a time-table regulating the progress of all bills. This would have the virtue of obviating tactics of obstruction, and Samuel, for instance, thought that a change along these lines was inevitable.[239] He felt that the Chairmen's Panel would be the right body to allocate what time should be spent on each stage. Sir Austen Chamberlain (repeating an original suggestion of his father) opined that an impartial Committee of Rules might be set up to do this; bills would not automatically be referred to the Committee for an allotment of time, but could be so referred if the member in charge of the bill required; the Committee could, if they thought fit, refuse to allow a time-table.[240] Dalton, writing in 1934, said the Labour Party proposed that a small Committee should be set up at the start of each Session, to allocate time on all Government bills and perhaps on other business.[241] Each Government bill would be given a detailed time-table; as in Samuel's and Chamberlain's proposals, the time-table would not itself be amendable or debatable in the House, but could be divided against. T. C. R. Moore, writing in 1935, said that every bill should proceed according to a time-table,[242] and this idea has been supported by Greaves.[243] A detailed proposal along these lines was put to the Procedure Committee of 1963/4 by the Opposition Chief Whip;

the Committee did not have time to examine it but reported it to the House.[244] A dozen Socialist Members advocated in 1964 the publication, early in the Session, of a sessional time-table for bills,[245] and strong support for the general principle persists today in certain quarters.

Guillotines for bills have, of course, been more frequently used since 1930, and have become almost respectable (though they remain always objectionable to the opponents of each bill). But no general ordinance, imposing guillotines on all or several bills, has been employed; and the time-table itself has always been open to debate and to amendment. There have been cases where the House has agreed to a voluntary time-table on important and contentious bills; 'It would', wrote Lord Campion, 'be a triumph for the spirit of conciliation if this procedure should come in future to be generally adopted.'[246]

Proposals for the automatic guillotining of the Committee stage of bills are mentioned later.

A proposal which could have important repercussions throughout the whole field of legislation was made by the Select Committee on Procedure in 1958/9. This was that an experienced officer or officers of the House should be appointed to assist private Members in drafting bills and amendments to bills.[247] Weight was given to this proposal by a Member who said, in debate, that it had cost him fifty pounds to prepare a bill; [248] but the idea was rejected on a division by the House.[249]

The Study of Parliament Group said that bills were at present too detailed—much more so than in some other countries. As a result, Members spend too much time on legislative processes, and too little on the way in which legislation is working out in practice. They suggested that much of the detail should be left for treatment in statutory instruments. Memoranda (for information only) should be attached to bills indicating the delegated legislation envisaged.[250]

The Bill and its Initial Stages

In 1931, Captain Crookshank told the Select Committee on Procedure that he thought the introduction of all major political bills should be preceded by debates on general resolutions.[251] These general resolutions having been agreed to, a bill would be founded on them (in the same way as the Finance Bill proceeds annually). This might take up more of the House's time, but Second Reading debates could, in consequence, be shorter.

Jennings indeed thought that Second Reading itself might take place on resolutions rather than a bill.[252] After the resolution had been approved, the bill would be drafted.

Lord King-Hall suggested that, prior to legislation, the House should debate the Government's proposals as set out in a White Paper. (A similar proposal was made by twelve Labour Members in July 1964.)[253] This happens not infrequently now, but King-Hall's proposal differs from current practice in advocating that, at the end of the debate, the House should vote on a number of Resolutions (which would be set out in the White Paper, and which would become the basis of the bill).[254]

A number of people have drawn attention to the importance of the Explanatory Memorandum which is sometimes attached to a public bill. Jennings thought there should be one to *every* bill, and hoped that it would give details not only of the proposals in the bill, but also the reasons for putting those particular proposals (instead of the possible alternatives) forward.[255] Pollard agreed that every bill should be accompanied by a memorandum, though this could, he added, be published separately.[256] Sidebotham believed that the reasons for a bill should be set out in the bill's preamble.[257]

It should be noted that the Select Committee on Delegated Legislation in 1953 decided against a proposal that every bill which proposed to delegate legislative powers should be accompanied by a special memorandum drawing attention to the fact. They thought the usual explanatory memorandum could cover this point, but made no special recommendation in the matter.[258]

Jennings drew attention to the blockage that might occur in the legislative machine at the drafting stage. He thought that the Parliamentary Counsel's services should be available to Private Members *after* their bills had been given a second reading (or, in his alternative suggestion, after the House had agreed to some resolutions on the subject—see above); a certificate from the Counsel would indicate whether or not any new principles had had to be introduced in the process of re-drafting.[259]

Muir, drawing attention to the unintelligibility of many statutes, suggested that a draftsman should re-draft every clause after a Committee had amended it.[260]

Hugh Dalton suggested that time could be saved by omitting all financial resolutions to bills: apart of course from the Ways and Means Resolutions on which the Finance Bill is founded.[261] Jennings elaborated the objections to these financial resolutions; debate on them largely repeated the Second Reading debate. He thought they could either be replaced by resolutions of the Standing Committee on Finance (which he elsewhere proposed), or be abandoned altogether.[262] Fellowes has put forward the view that the financial resolution should be considered, not as at present by a Committee of the Whole House, but by the Committee set up to consider the bill concerned,[263] and this suggestion was echoed by the Study of Parliament Group.[264]

In their *Socialist Commentary* article, a number of Labour Members proposed that the Second Reading of uncontentious bills should be taken in a Standing Committee.[265]

Committee Stage

It is towards the Committee stage of a bill that most proposals for legislative reform have been directed. Generally speaking, public bills go after Second Reading either to a Committee of the Whole House, or to a Standing Committee.

Occasional voices have been raised in favour of the principle that all bills should be considered on the floor of the House and not in Standing Committees. Baldwin thought that the right of all Members to take part in the detailed discussion of important measures should be safeguarded in this way;[266] in 1946 Liberal Members of Parliament proposed that bills should be automatically committed to a Committee of the Whole House rather than to a Standing Committee.[267] Ramsay MacDonald urged that there should be an automatic guillotine on the Committee stage of all bills taken on the floor of the House; this stage would thereby be more businesslike, and (presumably) more bills would be taken in that way.[268] This idea has also been aired by Lord Hinchingbrooke, who, however, suggested that bills of constitutional importance should be exempt.[269]

But much louder are the voices of those who believe that the Committee of the Whole House is the wrong instrument altogether for examining the details of bills. Thus Hollis wrote that it was a farce to send bills to a Committee when twenty-five or thirty members debated each proposal and 600 members were then required to vote on it;[270] and Jennings said that the Whole House was 'entirely incapable of dealing with Committee points'.[271]

The remedy they, and others, suggest is that the Committee stage of bills should be taken more often by Standing Committees. Both Wheare[272] and Hollis[273] have drawn attention to the advantages of discussing details in the Committee atmosphere that is so lacking on the floor of the House. Some commentators however stress that certain bills—such as those of constitutional importance, and small uncontentious bills—should continue to go to a Committee of the Whole House;[274] the former because of the need to allow all Members the opportunity of taking part, the latter because they can be disposed of more quickly than in Standing Committee.[275]

The Study of Parliament Group believed that, with a few rare exceptions, all bills should go to Select or Standing Committees. The Standing Committee might have as few as fifteen members; but all Members, whether on the Committee or not, should be allowed to speak (though not vote) on any amendments. A number of substitutes should be named for each Committee to replace members who became sick. Less controversial bills, especially those involving detailed matters, should be committed initially to Select Committees.[276]

Any scheme designed to make more use of Standing Committees must take note of the physical limitations of the House of Commons in this respect. Thus the Procedure Committee in 1958/9 heard of the difficulties of manning more committees, of staffing them, and of accommodating them.[277]

Schemes for the major reformation of the Standing Committee system have been put to Select Committees on Procedure in 1931, 1946, and 1958 by three Clerks of the House, Dawkins, Campion, and Fellowes.

Dawkins proposed that there should be five permanent Standing Committees, four of them responsible for a group of Departments, and one of them dealing solely with private members' bills.[278]

73

The four groups would be Internal Affairs and Communications (which would include the Home Office, Transport, Agriculture, and the Post Office); Social Services (Ministries of Health, Education and Pensions); Trade and Industry (Ministry of Labour and Board of Trade); and Scottish matters. These Committees would consider all bills promoted by their Departments, and would consider their Estimates too.[279] The result would be the creation of Standing Committees of Members who had come to specialize in the subject, and this would result in better-informed debates.

Campion's proposals were more far-reaching, and took in a bill's Report—as well as Committee—stage.[280] He envisaged that, in addition to the Scottish Standing Committee, there should be two large Standing Committees consisting of seventy-five to a hundred members each. For the Committee stage of bills, each Standing Committee should consist of at least three sub-committees of twenty-five each, to whom fifteen should be added in respect of each bill. After the sub-committee had considered the bill, a drafting sub-sub-committee (of not more than seven members) would make drafting and consequential amendments. The bill would then be reported to the parent Standing Committee, which would consider it in the same way as the House does on Report stage. Thereafter, the House would not be able to amend the bill, but could recommit it to the Standing Committee if necessary. The bill, could, however, be debated on the motion for its consideration; once this was agreed to, the bill would stand for Third Reading. Any Member who had given notice of an amendment to a bill committed to a Standing Committee might, although not a member of that Committee, attend and move such amendment and take part in debate upon it, without, however, the right to vote.

Fellowes proposed that, after Second Reading, every public bill should be sent either to the Committee on Unopposed Bills, a Committee on an opposed Public Bill, or the Committee on the Finance Bill. The Unopposed Bills Committee would consist of a Chairman and three Members; a Committee on an Opposed Public Bill would consist of a Chairman and fifteen Members; the Committee on the Finance Bill (which would consider other financial bills, in addition to the Finance Bill itself) would consist of a Chairman and thirty Members. If a bill was reported from a Committee without amendment, it would go at once for Third Reading; if it was amended, it would be recommitted to the former Committee for its Report stage. Fellowes also was in favour of the suggestion that Members should be allowed to speak on amendments before the Committee even though they were not Members of it. But the 1958/9 Procedure Committee rejected this proposal, saying that it might prove inconvenient to the Members concerned, as well as being a potential cause of confusion and of destruction.[281]

Some of the detailed points mentioned in these schemes have been spoken of elsewhere as desirable improvements in themselves. Thus Dawkins' idea of specialized Standing Committees has affinities with the whole scheme of Departmental Committees which is considered at length elsewhere.[282] Jennings took up Dawkins' proposal, but suggested there should be eight Committees.[283] Muir, too, thought Standing Committees should be composed of experts. An article in *Parliamentary Affairs* in 1958 pointed out that 80 per cent of time in Standing Committees was taken up by the 'added Members' (i.e. Members who used to be added to the Committee because of their particular interest in the bill), and suggested that the Committees could usefully be made up entirely of these experts.[284]

Hollis thought there was something to be said for allowing Standing Committees to co-opt experts from outside Parliament, perhaps with the power to speak but not to vote;[285] there was already so much consultation between the Government and outside interests about each bill's proposals, that the machinery should be made constitutional. Jennings believed that, instead of only giving advice to Ministers, the Civil Servants dealing with a bill should be open to questioning by the Committee, as should other experts.[286]

Suggestions are occasionally made that Standing Committees could profit from a change in their times of meeting. Since 1947, the only restriction on the times of sitting has been that the Committee could not meet between 1 p.m. and 3.30 p.m.; but the Committees have continued to meet, generally, on two or possibly three mornings in the week. The multiplication of sittings—combining morning and afternoon meetings—was criticized by Derek Walker-Smith as imposing an intolerable burden on Members.[287]

Morning sittings are, generally, favoured by those who believe in 'full-time' Members of Parliament, such as Jennings,[288] and opposed by those who dislike that concept.

But if it is felt that Standing Committees take up too much of a Member's time, the remedy is at hand. In 1947 the House re-enacted a Standing Order[289] which had previously been repealed in 1933. This would allow the House to adjourn on certain days in order to facilitate the work of its Committees. But the Standing Order has never been used—neither in its new manifestation nor in its old.[290]

A proposal that would, its supporters say, make debates on a bill's details more purposeful, is that a time-limit should be imposed on the Committee stage of all bills; the Standing Committee would be ordered to report the bill by a certain date. This idea, which was suggested in an article in *Parliamentary Affairs* in 1958,[291] was said to give the Committee an incentive to make the best use of the time available; the actual time-table could be agreed either informally through the usual channels, or by some expeditious use of a resolution by the House. The Procedure Committee in 1958/9 favoured this idea, which they set out in some detail.[292]

However, certain opinions tend the other way—to the effect that no guillotines should be allowed to be imposed on a bill until there was definite evidence that obstruction was being met. This point had been made by Lord Winterton in 1931,[293] and was repeated by Captain Crookshank and Sir Charles MacAndrew in a debate in 1946;[294] it ran directly counter to Lloyd George's opinion which was that if a guillotine was to be imposed, it should be imposed from the outset and not after opposition had developed.[295]

For the Committee stage of uncontentious bills, Campion suggested that a Committee much smaller even than a Standing Committee should be employed.[296] Any bill, he said, to the Second Reading of which no Amendment had been moved, might, on a motion by the Member in charge of it, be committed to the 'Uncontentious Bills Committee' of five members. After they had considered it, it would be reported back to the House, who would consider it in the same way as if it had come from a Standing Committee.

Lord Justice MacKinnon suggested that those parts of a bill which amounted to no more than the straightforward consolidation of existing enactments should, after Second Reading, be sent to the Joint Committee on Consolidation, etc., Bills.[297] This would, at the least, remove them from the field of controversy, and, at the most, diminish the opportunities for obstruction.

Later Stages

The proposals of Campion and Fellowes each, as we have seen, visualized that the Report stage of bills should be taken by a Committee rather than, as at present, on the floor of the House, and this idea won the distinguished support of Hugh Gaitskell.[298] The Procedure Committee, however, rejected this idea in 1959, saying that it was improper to depart from the principle that the Whole House should assume responsibility for the details of legislation.[299] The proposal was renewed afresh in 1965 by the Study of Parliament Group.[300]

Several other writers, such as Greaves, have put forward the view that the Report stage, although taken on the floor, should be more restricted in time.[301] Similarly, Pollard thought that both the Report stage and Third Reading of a bill could always be dealt with in a single sitting in the House,[302] and Jennings felt that a rule to this effect should be incorporated in Standing Orders.[303] His view, which was attendant upon the change he had proposed for the Committee stage of bills, was that the Report stage would be considerably less important if the Committee had made a more thorough job of the amendments required. He suggested that amendments still necessary on Report should be moved to the Motion 'That the Bill as Reported be read a third time'; after they had been disposed of, the Motion, 'That the Bill as Reported (and amended) be read a third time' would be debated. This device would, he claimed, abolish the possibility of having a general debate on the operative clauses on Report, which would be repeated on the bill as a whole on Third Reading.[304]

Dawkins suggested that time could be saved if all drafting amendments at Report stage should be sent to a special committee of Members and legal experts;[305] Michael Stewart echoed this idea.[306]

Percy was more forthright in his proposals. Apart from certain major bills, which would be debated in Committee and on Report on the floor of the House, all other bills, having passed through Standing Committee, should go straight to Third Reading.[307]

Jowett aimed to remove Report stage from the floor of the House; amendments put down for Report stage would be referred back to the Standing Committee to whom the bill itself would be recommitted, with instructions as to how to deal with them.[308] A point of detail recommended by the Select Committee on Procedure in 1958/9 was that all amendments imposing or varying a charge which would be in order on Committee stage should in future be held to be in order on Report stage. This would obviate the need to recommit the bill in order to consider such amendments.[309] But the House subsequently negatived this proposal.[310]

The Study of Parliament Group suggested that all Lords Amendments should be referred to the Committee which, they had urged, should take Report stage; the reference would be undebatable except on an amendment to agree to all the Lords Amendments. The report of the Committee could be agreed to on a debatable motion in the House. If necessary, instructions could be moved to require the Committee to reconsider any particular Lords Amendment.[311]

Private Bills

Private Bills are bills for the particular interest or benefit of some person or persons; as such they can be sharply distinguished from measures of public policy, and are treated by Parliament in an entirely different way. Unlike Public Bills they are initiated, not by Members, but by parties outside the House; they are founded on Petitions made by those parties to Parliament, and opposed largely by other Petitions from other outside parties. In the Committee stage of the bill—which is its most important parliamentary hurdle—a small Committee of Members assess the arguments for and against the bill, and either reject it, or allow it to proceed (with any amendments they may think desirable). Other stages of the bill are generally formal, but it is always competent for either House to defeat a bill by direct action after a debate on the floor of the House.

Private Bill legislation has had a long and important history, but it is, says Campion, 'definitely on the downgrade'.[312]

Writing in 1930, Muir urged that the time taken by Private Bill legislative procedure in Parliament should be reduced by throwing more of the burden on to Government Departments.[313] This contention, like many of the other suggestions about Private Bill procedure made in the thirties, has been overtaken by events. The Provisional Order system which had, since the nineteenth century, been replacing the Private Bill system, was itself largely replaced in 1945 by the introduction of Special Procedure Orders.[314]

But if Private Bill legislation is on the downgrade, its vestigial rites have been attended by some hard words. It was in answer to powerful criticism of its procedure that a Joint Committee was set up in 1954. It reported in 1955,[315] and many of its proposals have duly been put into effect; since then, the critics have been quieter.

The above Committee, however, considered three proposals for the amelioration of Private Bill procedure which they did not recommend. These were: first, the adoption of a system of joint committees on Private Bills in substitution for the present procedure; secondly, the institution of a permanent Commission to authorize the extension to certain local authorities, or to local authorities generally, of powers granted to other 'pioneer' authorities; thirdly, the application to England and Wales of Scottish private legislation procedure.[316]

(d) GENERAL PROCEDURAL REFORMS

Length of Sessions and Hours of Sitting

There has been a considerable change in the attitude of Members to these subjects. In 1931, Ramsay MacDonald said that the length of Sessions was 'absolutely intolerable'; Baldwin thought longer recesses were necessary to avoid the danger of government by tired men; and Winston Churchill said that a shorter session, of five to six months, would encourage the House to stick to the more important topics.[317] Gaitskell has said that the summer recess is too long, but that the Easter, and possibly the Christmas recess could reasonably be made longer.[318] Philip Goodhart, on the other hand, wanted to see the Christmas recess shortened.[319] But in all, nowadays, it is more usual for voices to be raised in simple protest against the length of the recesses (which are, in any case, shorter than in 1931);[320] an article in *Socialist Commentary*, for instance, thought that the working year should be expanded from one hundred and sixty to two hundred days.[321] The Procedure Committee of 1966/7 thought, however, that the most that could be added to the Session was 'a week here and there'.[322]

A suggestion with more life in it was that the House should revise its hours of sitting. Motions on the Order Paper from 1952 to 1966 have been calling for morning sittings of the House,[323] and several Members have referred to it in debates on Procedure[324] and in correspondence to *The Times*.[325] Typical of the proposals are those of Sir Gerald Nabarro, suggesting an 11.30 a.m. to 9 p.m. parliamentary day, and of the Labour Members in *Socialist Commentary*, one from 10 a.m. to 7 p.m.[326]

Fellowes' scheme for procedural reform envisaged morning sittings on Mondays and Wednesdays; junior Ministers would be present to put the Government's point of view. Business to be taken would include debates to affirm or negate statutory instruments; opposed private business; Private Members' adjournment motions. There would be a time-limit on speeches, no divisions, and no counting out. The 1958 Committee which considered this scheme set out the case for and against morning sittings; on a division they rejected the idea,[327] and the House later confirmed this rejection.[328]

When, however, a Government defeat in the division lobbies in 1965 led to the Committee stage of the Murder (Abolition of Death Penalty) Bill being taken on the floor of the House, instead of in Standing Committee, the Government instituted morning sittings for the purpose. The 1966 Procedure Committee presumably adjudged these sittings a success, as they recommended that sittings should be regularly held on Wednesday and Thursday mornings.[329] The Government accepted the idea in principle, but preferred the detail of Fellowes' proposals, noted above (although they did not advocate a time limit on speeches). The House agreed on a division to have these twice-weekly morning sittings (on Mondays and Wednesdays), and they began on 1st February, 1967.

The idea of having a fixed hour for the rising of the House every day has its supporters;[330] late sittings are frequently named as one of the principal causes of dissatisfaction with Parliament.[331] Fellowes has suggested that, if the House wishes to be able to sit late, the motion to enable it to do so should be debatable (at present, it must be decided without amendment and without debate).[332]

Another proposal has been that the parliamentary week should be shorter; this is sometimes allied with the suggestion (see under *Committee Stage*) that on one day a week the House should not sit, in order that its Committees could dispatch more business.

But all talk on the hours that the House should sit must really be reviewed in a broader context; for it is an aspect of two other wider problems. Should Parliament require full-time professional politicians? What ought to be the relationship between Parliament and the Executive? (For, even if Members gave up all other jobs in order to attend Parliament, Ministers would still have their Departments to attend.) These problems are discussed in Chapters IV and V of this book.

Speeches

The tool of the politician's trade is the speech. It is hardly surprising, then, that the writings considered in the present study are spattered with suggestions for improving the effectiveness of the speech as a weapon, or, at the least, of making sure that all Members have fair opportunities of employing it. Members constantly complain of the length of others' speeches; since 1930 there have been very many instances of this criticism and it is perhaps the aspect of procedure that gets more mention in the House than any other.

It is essentially a domestic problem and on the whole has had little attention from commentators outside the House; though Muir (who had, of course, himself been a Member for a short while in 1923–4) saw a point of principle involved. All Members should, he said, have the opportunity of expressing an opinion on each Government Bill; in those debates, then, some control of the length of speeches was essential.[333] But, by and large, it is within the House that the matter is generally raised. Frequently a major debate, in which few back-benchers have been able to speak, sparks off a new series of complaints. As a result, there has been a constant succession of demands for some sort of time-limit on speeches.

If Members err, they do so in the face of constant exhortations from the Chair. Mr. Speaker Morrison pointed out that the one attribute of a good speech within the reach of all is brevity.[334] Mr. Speaker Fitzroy said his experience was that short speeches were the most effective. Yet he had to admit that his previous advice on the subject had fallen on 'deaf ears or on unruly tongues'; Members, who promised to speak for ten minutes, went on for half an hour.[335]

Members have specified different time-limits as the desirable maximum. Thus a Whip suggested twenty minutes to the Select Committee on Procedure in 1931;[336] a self-denying ordinance by back-benchers, limiting themselves to fifteen minutes, was said in 1947 to have a good deal of support from both sides of the House.[337] Another suggestion has been that, during the dinner hour from seven o'clock to eight o'clock, there should be a ten-minute time-limit.[338] R. T. Paget has proposed the same limit should be in force between five o'clock and seven o'clock;[339] his suggestion led to a unanimous recommendation of the Select Committee on Procedure in 1958/9 that an hour should be set aside, at the discretion of the Chair, for five-minute speeches. They agreed, however, that this could not be governed by Standing Order, but should be left to the good sense of Members.[340]

It has also been said that there is special need for a time-limit during debates under a guillotine. Campion (although he was on the whole opposed to a time-limit) thought that, if introduced, it could best begin in certain Supply debates.[341] As noted above, Fellowes' scheme for morning sittings envisaged that speeches then would be limited in time.[342]

If a time-limit were introduced, allowance would need to be made for the time first taken up by interruptions, and then spent in answering them. Speakers have pointed out that many speeches were prolonged for this reason;[343] and a Procedure Committee, in recommending short speeches, suggested that by convention Members should not be interrupted in them.[344] A later Committee, however, suggested that the Chair should allow an extension of time to make up for interruptions.[345] A practical suggestion from Alfred Morris was that there should be a stop-clock visible in the Chamber, so that Members could see for how long they had been talking.[346]

Supporters of an imposed time-limit generally agree that front-bench speakers require special consideration, since they frequently have to make lengthy expositions of, for example, a bill.[347] On the other hand, it is precisely these lengthy speeches that some back-benchers object to and think should be curtailed.[348]

Various references have been made in the House to a voluntary time-limit which operated in some Scottish debates. Thus in a 1936 debate on the Scottish Estimates, speeches were limited to fifteen minutes.[349] Other references, in 1941, 1948 and 1953 indicated that some degree of restraint continued to be shown by Scottish Members.[350]

It is rare that a case is made out in favour of the *status quo*; when it is, it is based on the sanctity of preserving minorities' rights, and on the dissatisfaction which a formal time-limit would cause.[351] Thus, one Member described a debate of short speeches as a parliamentary Children's Hour.[352] It has also been said that the thing Ministers fear most is the long, well-informed speech of criticism.[353] The Government, when questioned for their views on the subject, have always said that it is a matter that must be left to the good sense of individual Members;[354] a voluntary time-limit might be worth trying.[355] When appeal is made to the Speaker, his invariable reply is that he has no powers in the matter —the remedy must lie with the House.[356]

Until the 1958/9 Procedure Committee, the nearest the House had got to considering it had been in the deliberations of the Select Committee on Procedure in 1946. They heard no evidence in favour of the idea, and they did not recommend it.[357] It may be that their final opinion mirrored that of the Member who claimed in 1948 that the main trouble was not excessive oratory, but an overloaded parliamentary programme.[358] It could be that they were aware of the paradox pointed out elsewhere—that some speeches, which were very short in time, seemed very long to the House.[359]

Herbert Morrison has drawn attention to the deleterious effect of Members making speeches which do not try to follow what has been said before; as a result, there is no cut and thrust.[360] 'What kills debate', said Grimond, is 'the old rule that it is Buggins's turn now, and if Buggins wants to talk about something different from what went before, he gets up and does so.'[361] Speeches such as these, said Charles Pannell, should be ruled out of order.[362]

As a means by which more Members can have their opinions made public, Kennedy suggested in 1936 that Members should be allowed to circulate in the Official Report those speeches which they had not been able to make orally in the Chamber.[363] This suggestion was subsequently taken up by Anthony Wedgwood Benn,[364] but the Procedure Committee of 1958/9 found the practice undesirable.[365]

If some Members have favoured written speeches, there has been no encouragement for speeches which are read out in the House. Opinions on this point are frequently expressed; specific objection was taken in 1947 to the delivery of prepared winding-up speeches, which made no answer to the detailed points raised during the debate.[366] But, as the Speaker pointed out in 1952, although the conventions of the House still stood out against the reading of speeches, it had 'become the practice in recent years for Ministers to be allowed greater latitude in this respect'.[367]

In view of Members' sensitivity on the matter of their speeches, it is not surprising that the Speaker has often found his duty of choosing Members to speak an invidious one. Thus it is sometimes objected that, in his zeal to see that all points of view are heard, he is too indulgent towards minority parties, and the Government back-benchers got less than their fair share of the House's time.[368] (This latter argument, incidentally, is also sometimes employed in support of a set time-table for bills.) It has also been suggested that the Speaker's eye should rest less frequently on the more garrulous of Members,[369] though this was a proposal that he had already scouted.[370]

A Member suggested that there should be a rationing of time among Members, to make up for the uncertainty of the favours of the Speaker's eye: he could have got little comfort from the then Father of the House, whose experience was that the people who didn't get called often were, in general, the people no one wanted to hear.[371]

Other suggestions have been that speakers should be chosen by ballot; that those who write to the Speaker, asking to be called, should automatically be disqualified; and that those who wish to speak, but on whom the Speaker's eye is not going to alight during a particular debate, should be informed, so that they no longer need wait in hopeless expectation. It has been said that a list should be circulated beforehand of those Members who are likely to be called on to speak in a debate, as happens in the House of Lords.[372] Criticism was also made of the conversations which took place behind the Speaker's chair and which appeared to influence the choice of who should speak in the debate.[373]

The Speaker's answer to these criticisms has been that he had to see that every expression of opinion had a fair chance, and that he tried to call all minorities; he chose speakers from amongst those who continually rose just as much as from those who wrote to him.[374] On another occasion, a Speaker had said that it had always been the practice for minorities to get more than a generous share of time, and that to call on speakers according to the numerical strengths of parties would not improve the character of debates.[375]

It is a fact that a Member, anxious to be able to put his point of view, and the Speaker, charged with the duty of preserving the House's traditions, must sometimes be at odds. This is most clearly seen in the objection that Members take to the 'right' of Privy Councillors to be heard whenever they offer themselves to speak, and it has been in the post-war period that this right has been most heavily attacked. Constant objection has been taken to it; a number of Motions on the Order Paper have called for its rescission.[376] But when the subject is raised in the House, the Speaker can do no other than point out that the traditions and practice of the House have always allowed Privy Councillors a greater right to be called.[377]

However, when the Select Committee on Procedure came to consider the matter in 1958/9, they reported that the rule no longer operated in the best interests of the House; they suggested that Privy Councillors should have only the same rights as other Members in asking supplementary questions, and, in debate, the Speaker should not be bound to call them in preference to other Members. This virtual abolition of the rule was, they thought, better than the modifications of it which had been suggested to them—namely, that Privy Councillors should only have priority when the debate was on a subject for which they had previously been departmentally responsible, or that two (or more) Privy Councillors should not be called in succession.[378] The House, however, negatived the recommendation of the Select Committee.[379]

Question Hour

The right to ask a Minister for a public reply to a particular Question is amongst the most prized of a private Member's privileges.[380] The popularity of the Question has grown, and in 1931 the Procedure Committee was told by the Clerk of the House that it might become necessary to reduce the number that a Member is allowed to ask orally, from three to two per day.[381] This idea, though supported by MacDonald and Sinclair,[382] did not commend itself to the Committee; but another Select Committee (which had been set up to consider the relationship between Parliament and the nationalized industries) recommended the change twenty years later,[383] and it has since been adopted. Kennedy, in 1931, was more drastic; he suggested that Members should only be allowed to ask one oral Question per day.[384] Sir C. Osborne, in 1959, suggested that a Member should only be allowed to put down one Question to a particular Minister on a particular day.[385]

An alternative that Dawkins put to the 1931 Committee was that the Speaker should be allowed (possibly with the Member's consent) to direct that a Question should be 'unstarred'. This proposal was supported by Sir Austen Chamberlain,[386] but the Committee did not recommend it. (When Clement Davies made a similar proposal to the Clerk of the House, he was told it would destroy the confidence between Members and Clerks.[387])

But the Committee did propose that a new class of Questions—'daggered' Questions—should be introduced;[388] these should be for accelerated written answer. The House did not give effect to this proposal, which was, however, more recently resuscitated by Wedgwood Benn.[389]

A different suggestion, put forward by de Freitas, was that the total number of Questions which a Minister should be required to answer on a particular day should be limited.[390] (At present, the whole of Question Hour can be taken up by Questions to one Minister.) The 1958/9 Procedure Committee turned down a suggestion along these lines.[391]

The idea is sometimes voiced that more time should be allowed for Questions. It has been suggested that there should be a Question Hour on Fridays; but the then Leader of the House thought this was not a day that saw the House at its brightest.[392] With the House's decision in 1958 that Members' letters to Ministers were not privileged, a number of Members thought that Question Hour should be extended to ninety minutes in order to give more time for the (privileged) laying of grievances before Ministers by means of Questions.[393] A 'modest proposal' by Tom Driberg has been that Question Hour should at least last a full hour.[394] In the standard work on the subject, however, Chester and Bowring consider why there is not more enthusiasm in the House for increasing Question Time. They conclude that this is partly due to the domination over the House of the two front benches, especially the Treasury bench; partly to the fact that questioning is a minority activity; and partly to the fact that no increase would be possible without detracting from time available for debates.[395]

The 1931 Procedure Committee did not accept the Clerk's suggestion[396] that they could usefully review the rules which have accreted on the subject of Questions (a proposal that was repeated by the Study of Parliament Group in 1965).[397] They considered, but did not concur in, the proposal that the right to ask a supplementary Question should be limited to the asker of the substantive Question.[398]

Wedgwood Benn has suggested that no Minister should be allowed to refuse an answer to an oral Question, except with the consent of the Speaker.[399] Emrys Hughes thought, in 1949, that Members should be allowed to put parliamentary Questions to the Leader of the Opposition, in addition to Ministers.[400]

In Fellowes' scheme for procedural reform, he suggested that Questions should be taken, not in the House, but in three Grand Committees, which would sit, twice a week, at an hour when the House was not sitting.[401] The Study of Parliament Group thought that at least Scottish and Welsh questions might be taken in their respective Grand Committees.[402]

The most radical change that has been suggested, however, is that by Lord Percy. Question Hour should, he thought, be abolished, and its time taken up by short debates on topical matters.[403] Sidebotham was thinking along the same lines; better five or ten Questions exhaustively treated, than one hundred answered perfunctorily. These five or ten should be chosen by a small committee of members, and the rest should be answered in writing.[404]

Summing up their opinions on Question Hour, the 1945 Procedure Committee said it was 'perhaps the readiest and most effective method of parliamentary control over the action of the executive'. Therefore the very powerfulness of the right imposed a proportionate responsibility on Members in its use; Questions should only be put down when other and less formal methods had failed to produce a satisfactory result, or when some information or action was urgently desired.[405]

The 1958/9 Procedure Committee said that the root of the problem of Question Hour lay in the fact that supplementary questions were more frequent and longer, and the answers longer, than they used to be. They urged the House to support the Speaker when he tried to curtail questions.[406] This view has been echoed by *The Times*, which expressed the hope—'a naïve hope'—that members would exercise more discrimination in their questioning.[407]

Throughout the fifties and early sixties, the vitality of Question Hour seemed to be in doubt. 'Both questions and answers are grossly abused,' said the Speaker in evidence to the Procedure Committee, whose report on the subject in 1965 is the most thorough parliamentary enquiry to date into the subject. The evidence of the Second Clerk Assistant, in particular, shows the ingenuity practised by Members in this parliamentary game; mysterious devices, such as 'pre-emption', 'tacking', and 'farming out', are exposed. The 1965 Committee thought a brisker approach by Members was desirable; an average of fifty Questions a day should be readily attainable. Besides a three-week limit on notice allowable of new questions (since adopted by the House) it recommended that Members should be limited to eight oral questions a month, and that the House should agree to a resolution which would arm the Speaker in his demands for shorter questions and answers. It considered, but did not recommend, a longer

Question Time, the taking of questions in Grand Committees and at morning sittings, and a proposal of Michael English that a Member's first question on a particular day should have priority over other Members' second questions.[408]

Divisions

Among the more bizarre discoveries of this research has been the fact that H. G. Wells, while spanning *The Work, Wealth and Happiness of Mankind,* [409] should have paused to observe that the method of voting in the House of Commons—in contrast to that used in Texas—was 'processional' and inefficient. Voting procedure in the Commons is certainly a matter that frequently engages the mind of those who think about Parliament. Ross lists it first among the causes of dissatisfaction with Parliament today;[410] and it was repeatedly adverted to in 1957 in a correspondence in *The Times.*[411] Moreover, every Procedure debate in the House of Commons brings out complaints on the system employed.

The usual epithet used—'time-wasting'—is hard to gainsay; in 1946, the average time taken for a Division was 10·8 minutes, and it sometimes requires two or more Divisions to conclude the debate on a question.[412] Yet experienced parliamentarians do not always agree that the system is bad. Baldwin thought it was useful to relieve tension: 'In the heat generated by the gag . . . a walk through the lobbies restored the House to a sense of perspective.'[413] Herbert Morrison said that, 'Anyway, moving through the Division Lobbies is a useful and pleasant social occasion.'[414] An Opposition Chief Whip found in the system 'something rather wonderful'.[415]

The critics of the present system have suggested a number of palliatives. First, that a mechanical, press-button system of voting could be introduced. Secondly, that various improvements could be made in the present arrangements. Thirdly, that Members should be allowed to vote, *in absentia*, by proxy. Fourthly, that all Divisions should take place at a convenient, pre-arranged, time. Fifthly, that there should be fewer Divisions.

(i) Mechanical Voting: This is frequently put forward by commentators inside and outside Parliament; both Pollard and Greaves suggest it. It is rare, however, that the scheme is set out in detail, so that the practical difficulties are hard to assess. One critic of the idea, thinking it required specified seats in the Chamber for each Member, believed that a larger House would have to be built before the scheme could be introduced.

One practical scheme was put before the Select Committee on Procedure in 1946.[416] By it, Division time could be cut down, but it would still require seven and a quarter minutes; for the great proportion of the time taken is the six minutes which must be allowed for Members to get to the Chamber from wherever they are. There were various shortcomings in the device, and the Committee felt it was 'neither so convenient nor so accurate a means of counting votes and recording names as the present method'.

Another scheme was considered by the Select Committee on Procedure in 1958/9; this was calculated to cut the time of a division down to six minutes. In dismissing the scheme, the Committee could only cite the congestion which they deemed to be inevitable in the lobbies as a result, and the loss of the present amenities in the lobbies.[417]

The Procedure Committee considered the problem again in 1966. They found that a push-button system of voting would cost £80,000; but that, even then, a Division would still take seven to eight minutes. There were other drawbacks to the system, and the Committee could not recommend its adoption. They did, however, suggest that tellers should be appointed as soon as their names were handed in, so that they could begin counting straight away.[418]

(ii) It has been suggested that the Division would take less time if there were six division clerks, or eight tellers; or if the present division lobbies could be duplicated somewhere else in the House.[419]

(iii) Proxy voting has occasionally been advocated as a minor reform that would help.[420] Hollis has drawn attention to the Norwegian example, where each Member has a substitute who can perform the Member's duties when he is away;[421] and Acland has also stressed the desirability of substitutes.[422]

The 1958/9 Procedure Committee turned down the idea of proxies. They did not take up two other ideas—that Members should be allowed a proxy vote once a month,[423] or that they should be allowed a registered pair twice a month.[424] Though they deplored the fact that seriously ill Members had had to be brought to the House to vote, they did not recommend any ameliorative. Their successors in 1964/5, however, thought there was no alternative to proxy voting for sick Members 'unless the usual channels could agree on some other way';[425] this later prompted the parties to make suitable arrangements which removed the necessity for sick Members to vote.

(iv) If it was known at what time Divisions were going to take place, Members could arrange other engagements without the fear that in so doing they might miss an important vote; thus they sometimes suggest that the procedure be changed in this regard.[426] Also, they suggest that the vote on 'prayers', which may not end till late at night, should be held over until the next day.[427]

The idea is never fully worked out. Sir Herbert Williams cited the absurdity of holding the Divisions that would follow a Committee stage, all together, at a time when people have forgotten the detailed points that were at issue.[428] It was, however, one of the features of the morning sittings introduced in 1967 that Divisions should be held over until the conclusion of the day's business.

(v) When Members suggest that there should be fewer Divisions,[429] they appear to do so out of pious hope rather than practical expectation; Parliament works by means of debates leading up to Divisions, and it is hard to say how its right to divide can be restricted. Ramsay MacDonald, however, suggested in 1931 that it was unnecessary to hold Divisions on the Closure, since these were a foregone conclusion;[430] and the 1945/6 Procedure Committee was reminded that the Speaker already had power to require a vote to be taken by counting Members, for and against, in the House, after only two minutes, if he thought the Division had been unnecessarily claimed. The Committee did not however, as urged, recommend a more frequent use of this Standing Order.[431]

Procedural Miscellanea

There are, of course, innumerable proposals made from time to time for improving the minutiae of parliamentary procedure. Many of the old traditional processes arouse the ire of some of today's Members of Parliament. Emrys Hughes wrote a book about them, called *Parliament and Mumbo-Jumbo*, in which he inveighed against such things as adjusting the mace when the House goes into Committee, the enacting formula used in all Bills, the need for a Queen's Speech at the start of the Session, the circumlocutions ('the honourable and gallant gentleman') by which Members talk of each other, etc. Minor changes like these hardly rate attention in a project of this kind but, taken together, they might conceivably amount to a 'reform of procedure'; some of the more interesting suggestions are accordingly listed here.

Adjournment Motions. The half-hour debates at the end of each day's sitting, in which some private Members can raise matters on their own initiative, should be moved to an earlier part of the sitting.[432]

Philip Goodhart has also expressed the wish that these debates should be longer and more frequent.[433]

As noted above, Fellowes suggested that these debates should take place in the morning, and they were a feature of the morning sittings introduced in 1967. MacAndrew put forward the idea that no adjournment motion should be allowed after 11.30 p.m. Other suggestions have been that incidental references to legislation should be allowed in them, and that any change of subject should be announced beforehand.[434] (See also *Standing Order No. 9*, below).

Black Rod, who summons the Commons to attend in the Lords to witness the Royal Assent to bills, should not do so in the middle of a debate.[435] There has been increasing resentment at his interruptions which led, on one occasion, to a disorderly debate being carried on by Members in the Chamber after the Speaker had led the House in procession to the Lords.[436] It is argued that his entry should be at fixed, pre-ordained times.[437]

The Business of the House should be known longer in advance.[438]

Casting Vote. Sir Kenneth Pickthorn has questioned the propriety of the Chair's casting vote being exercised in favour of a taxing proposal in a Finance Bill. The Procedure Committee of 1965/6 were, however, not prepared to recommend anything that would limit the discretion reposed in the Chair.[439]

The Closure, which at present requires a hundred assenting votes, should only require a simple majority of the House in its favour.[440] The Procedure Committee in 1958/9 saw no reason for lowering the number required for the closure (and for the quorum), as had been suggested to them by the Government Chief Whip.[441]

Debates on large general topics should be split up into more manageable compartments.[442] Furthermore, it is said that the House could not lead public opinion on contemporary problems if it went on fixing its debates ten days ahead.[443]

A *'Judge'* for the House of Commons should be appointed. He would be a non-party officer of the House, who would assess impartially the cases put by each side during a debate.[444]

Ministerial Statements are at present made after Question Hour. Since they are made, as it were, *in vacuo*, and not on a formal motion, debate on them is irregular; the disorderly kind of debate that follows them was described by Sir Kenneth Pickthorn as one of the worst abuses of procedure.[445] It has been suggested that Ministers should move the adjournment if they wish to make a statement.[446]

The Order Paper should be made more readily intelligible.[447]

Pairs, it is said, should be easier for Members to arrange.[448] The Procedure Committee in 1958/9 declared themselves satisfied with the present arrangements, and did not take up the idea of the pre-war 'pairing book' that was favourably mentioned to them.[449] The whole system of pairing, however, has never been officially recognized by the House. It remains a strictly private enterprise.

Public Petitions were once a powerful means of bringing pressure to bear on the House. The procedure on them should be changed, to make them more effective today.[450] An article in *The Times* suggested that the House's Committee on Public Petitions could be revitalized by giving it the power to investigate the allegations and merits of petitions received.[451]

Points of Order are made promiscuously, and should be penalized.[452] One Member counted forty-two false points of order in a month.[453]

Standing Orders should be more amenable to change; at present, they were narrowed down from precedent to precedent. There should be a sessional Select Committee which would consider the working of an Order whenever a hundred Members asked for it to be amended.[454]

Standing Order No. 9 (Adjournment on a definite matter of

urgent public importance) was falling into desuetude and should be more liberally interpreted.[455] Fellowes, who thought these debates could best take place at the end of the day's sitting, urged that the onus of defining 'urgency' and 'public importance' should be placed on the House; the Procedure Committee went some of the way with him, and recommended a rather wider interpretation of the Order.[456] The House, however, did not lay down any changes in the procedure, on the understanding that discussions would take place to see if any relaxation could be afforded.[457]

In the 1960s, nevertheless, while many people were arguing that what the Commons needed was a new committee system which could expose the shortcomings of Government and provide fuller information for Members, others argued that it was in the Chamber of the House that improvements were most needed. What was wanted, they said, was not more Committees, but more opportunities for the House to debate the urgent topical matters that most concerned the country as a whole. Perhaps both were right— the 1965 Procedure Committee, at least, seemed to think so, for soon after advocating changes in the Committee system it produced a scheme for providing more debates on matters of current concern. S.O. No. 9 lays down the conditions under which the House could set aside its arranged programme in order to turn to matters of urgent public importance; but the precedents which guided the Speaker in allowing an application for an urgent debate had so agglomerated over the years as to make it very difficult for the application to succeed. The Procedure Committee sought to get away from this difficulty by drafting a new Standing Order; under this the Speaker would be able to grant the application if he was satisfied that the matter was proper to be discussed. Such a debate would take place on the following day at 3.30 p.m. unless extremely urgent, in which case it would take place at 7 p.m. on the same day. The Committee thought that about five debates of this kind should be allowed per session. They also favoured the idea that the Opposition should be allowed to earmark for short-notice debates four half-Supply Days out of the twenty-nine available to them; not more than one such debate should take place per month. Other recommendations were that Private Members who won the ballot for notices of motion should not need to nominate the subject for debate until a week before it took place; that the ballot for daily adjournment motions should take place weekly instead of fortnightly as hitherto; and that one of these adjournment motions per week could, at the Speaker's discretion, be debated for up to two hours.[458]

The Swearing-in of Members at the start of a new Parliament took an inordinate time, and should be curtailed.[459] (Jennings suggested this might be done before a justice of the peace, or before the Speaker privately.[460])

Conclusion

We have seen that, amongst the suggestions for reform of Procedure, it is the proposed system of Departmental (or Specialist) Committees that offers change on the broadest front—spanning as it does Parliament's three functions, financial, legislative and deliberative. Furthermore, in the piecemeal criticisms of today's Procedure, it is the Committee stage of bills, and the Commons' control of finance by means of its Committees, which come in for the most comment. It becomes clear that the core of any large-scale procedural reform lies in the use the House of Commons makes of its Committees.

There is visible, too, a trend towards smaller Committees— from a Committee of the Whole House to a Standing Committee, from a Standing Committee to a Committee of the size of today's Select Committees. Underlying all this, perhaps, is the shining way in which Select Committees have in the past been able to deal with controversial matters in a non-party way.

But, before any proposal is advocated to increase greatly the work done by Commons' Committees, four notes of warning should be sounded. In the first place, the House has always insisted on the *subordinate* character of its Committees; they are never allowed executive powers; and the House reserves its right to reject, or even ignore, any suggestions they make. So any change which will increase the effectiveness of Committees should allow for the House's traditional concern to remain the master of all that happens in its subordinate bodies.

Secondly, if too many important decisions are to be taken by small groups of members, one may be getting away from the principle that each elected representative ought to have an equal opportunity of influencing events.

Thirdly, the success of Select Committees in the past may have been due in part to a careful selection of matters which have been referred to them. If they had to deal with too many subjects of party-political controversy, it could be that they would not prove so successful. There is the danger that, if you move too many subjects from the floor of the House to the Committee rooms, the party-political guns will be moved with them.

Finally, it is important that changes and improvements in the Committee system (however far-reaching, however urgently required) should be viewed in the overall context of the House of Commons as a practical and integrated working system. A 'curate's egg' solution, making Commons' procedure good in parts, is unlikely to prove wholly satisfactory. Thus, the introduction of specialist Committees may well pose new problems of hours of sitting, the admissibility of certain types of Questions, payment of Members, research and information facilities, and so on. If it were not outside the scope of this study, one could point to the desirability of relating changes in the Commons' Committee system to the functioning of Parliament as a *bicameral* legislature. The use which the House of Commons makes of its Committees, in other words, is a means to an end and not an end in itself; as the Study of Parliament Group said in 1965, 'Nothing can or should be changed unless M.P.s are quite clear what it is they have and what it is they want to have.'[461]

Nevertheless, the experimental introduction of specialist Committees and the other procedural changes made or proposed in 1966 are likely to add considerably to the vitality of the House. The abolition of the Committee of Supply and of the old principle that a charge must originate in committee, have removed, at a stroke, much of the 'mumbo-jumbo'.

It seems unlikely that the reforms will stop there. The historian of the future may look back and note that the introduction of a permanent Procedure Committee in the 1960s was the start of an era of greater change than anything seen this century.

NOTES AND REFERENCES*

[1] H.C. Deb. 617, c. 70.

[2] *ibid.* c. 38.

[3] See articles by A. H. Hanson in *Parliamentary Affairs*, Vol. X, No. 4, and Vol. XI, No. 1.

[4] This important aspect of the relationship between Parliament and the Executive is considered in the present chapter because of its essentially 'procedural' nature. Other problems and proposals for reform are discussed in Chapter V.

[5] H.L. Deb. 86, cs. 791ff.

[6] H.C. 161 of 1931, Q. 656.

[7] Greaves: *The British Constitution*, 1948, p. 50.

[8] *English Review*, Vol. LIX, 1934, pp. 29–39, 163–74.

[9] *Public Administration*, Vol. XXIV, 1946, pp. 75–85.

[10] Lord Campion and others, p. 281.

[11] H.C. 161 of 1930/1, Q. 408.

[12] Greaves, pp. 49–51.

[13] Amery, pp. 53–4.

[14] Lord Campion and others, p. 34.

[15] *ibid.* p. 84.

[16] Spectator, 10th November 1933, pp. 653–4.

[17] *English Review*, Vol. LIX, 1934.

[18] H.C. 161 of 1930/1, Q. 481.

[19] Lord Campion and others, p. 34.

[20] *Manchester Guardian*, 22nd July 1957, p. 6.

[21] H.C. 92 of 1958/9, pp. xlix–l.

[22] Lord Campion and others, p. 34.

[23] Grimond: *Manchester Guardian, loc. cit.*

[24] Fitzroy: H.C. 161 of 1930/1, p. 406.

[25] Lord Campion and others, p. 83.

[26] Lord Cottenham: *English Review*, Vol. LIX, 1934; and John Hall: H.C. Deb. 617, c. 113.

[27] Adams: *Listener*, Vol. VII, 17th February 1932, pp. 236–7.

[28] Grimond: *Manchester Guardian, loc. cit.*

[29] Lord Campion and others, p. 119.

[30] Jennings, p. 141.

[31] Lord Campion and others, p. 83.

[32] *ibid.* p. 33.

[33] See *Speed up Law Reform*, Fabian Research Series, No. 194, 1958, p. 25.

[34] A better and more recent example might be the Select Committee on Nationalized Industries.

[35] *Listener, loc. cit.*

[36] H.C. 92 of 1958/9, Q. 276.

[37] *ibid.* p. 18.

[38] *ibid.* para. 47.

[39] *Manchester Guardian*, 13th November 1952.

[40] H.C. 161 of 1930/1, p. 154. Jowett's views were mostly expressed before the period covered by this research, but his name should be remembered as one of the chief begetters of the specialized committee system.

* All references to Jennings in this chapter are to his *Parliamentary Reform*

[41] Jennings, pp. 126–9.
[42] H.C. 161 of 1930/1, p. 259.
[43] Laski, pp. 87–8.
[44] Lord Campion, and others pp. 33–4.
[45] H.C. 92 of 1958/9, p. xxv; also p. xlix.
[46] Writing on behalf of Mosley's New Party: *Political Quarterly*, Vol. II, 1931.
[47] H.C. 92 of 1958/9, Q. 1161.
[48] H.C. 161 of 1930/1, p. 406.
[49] *Political Quarterly*, Vol. II, 1931.
[50] *Manchester Guardian*, 25th May 1934.
[51] Morrison, pp. 155–9.
[52] 17th April 1963.
[53] See the Order Paper of 17th July 1963.
[54] Published by C.P.C., January 1963.
[55] July 1964.
[56] Crick, *The Reform of Parliament, passim.*
[57] *What's Wrong with Parliament?, passim.*
[58] H.C. 303 of 1964/5.
[59] *The Times*, 9th June 1966.
[60] H.C. 303 of 1964/5, p. xiv.
[61] *ibid.* Q. 352.
[62] *ibid.* Q. 346.
[63] *ibid.* para. 9.
[64] *The Member of Parliament and the Administration*, pp. 211–12.
[65] *Public Law*, 1959, p.286.
[66] H.C. 303 of 1964/5, para. 4.
[67] *ibid.* p. 139. The Group were quoting from Professor Crick's book, *The Reform of Parliament*, p. 77.
[68] At present, bills are sent after Second Reading to a committee—either a Committee of the Whole House, or a Standing Committee (which consists of from twenty to fifty members). These Committees do not specialize in a particular class of bill, although the Scottish Standing Committee deals with bills of all kinds that pertain to Scotland. The Scottish Grand Committee—consisting of all Scottish members, plus ten others—holds general debates on Scottish matters, some of them being virtually Second Reading debates on Scottish bills, and considers the Scottish Estimates; the Welsh Grand Committee, consisting of all Members for Welsh constituencies, and twenty-five others, holds general debates on Welsh matters. None of these Committees, of course, initiates legislation.
[69] Jennings, p. 145.
[70] H.C. 161 of 1930/1, p. 154.
[71] H.C. 92 of 1958/9, p. 18.
[72] *Manchester Guardian*, 13th November 1952.
[73] *Political Quarterly*, Vol. IV, 1933.
[74] *Speed up Law Reform*, pp. 24ff.
[75] *How to Reform Parliament*, 1944, p. 43.
[76] *Spectator*, 10th November 1933.
[77] Hill and Whichelow, p. 72.
[78] H.C. 303 of 1964/5, p. 138.
[79] *The Reform of Parliament*, p. 199.
[80] *The Times*, 9th June 1966.

[81] H.C. 303 of 1964/5, p. 143.
[82] *ibid.* p. xvii.
[83] H.C. 161 of 1930/1, pp. 41–60, *passim.*
[84] *ibid.* Appendix 6.
[85] H.C. 92 of 1958/9, p. 18.
[86] Hill and Whichelow, pp. 72, 75.
[87] H.C. 303 of 1964/5, pp. 8–11.
[88] *ibid.* pp. 137–8.
[89] *ibid.* p. viii.
[90] *Speed up Law Reform*, pp. 24–5.
[91] *How to Reform Parliament*, pp. 43–4.
[92] Laski, p. 37.
[93] Others include Cripps, Muir, Wise, Lord Eustace Percy, and Crick.
[94] *How to Reform Parliament*, p. 43.
[95] *Speed up Law Reform*, pp. 24–5.
[96] H.C. 303 of 1964/5, p.133.
[97] H.C. 161 of 1930/1, Q. 3111.
[98] Motion, 22nd January 1957.
[99] H.C. 92 of 1958/9, p. 1; *Hill and Whichelow*, chap. 3; and see *Parliamentary Affairs*, Vol. XIX, pp. 191–207.
[100] H.C. Deb. 581, c. 697; and the *Observer*, 14th December 1958.
[101] *Manchester Guardian*, 22nd July 1957.
[102] H.C. 92 of 1958/9, p. 18.
[103] See, e.g., Order Paper of 17th July 1963.
[104] Early Day Motion 47 of 1965/6.
[105] Laski, p. 91.
[106] H.C. Deb. 617, c. 113. Since then, the Committee has been given power to set up sub-committees.
[107] *Speed up Law Reform*, p. 25.
[108] H.C. 303 of 1964/5, p. 143.
[109] Crick, *The Reform of Parliament*, pp. 200–1.
[110] Hill and Whichelow, p. 78.
[111] H.C. 303 of 1964/5, p. 138.
[112] Jennings, pp. 127–9.
[113] H.C. 189 of 1945/6.
[114] e.g. H.C. Deb. 557, c. 1322.
[115] Chubb: *The Control of Public Expenditure*, 1952, p. 239.
[116] Amery, p. 53.
[117] *English Review*, Vol. LIX, 1934.
[118] H.C. 161 of 1930/1, Q. 1775; and Memo (unpublished) to Select Committee on Procedure in 1945.
[119] H.C. 161 of 1930/1, p. 259.
[120] Greaves, pp. 42–4.
[121] Jennings, p. 144.
[122] H.C. 92 of 1958/9, p. 6.
[123] Thus Molson (unpublished memo to Select Committee, 1945); and H.C. Deb. 400, c. 1093.
[124] Laski, pp. 87–8.
[125] H.C. 92 of 1958/9, Q. 274–7.
[126] H.C. 303 of 1964/5, p. 138.
[127] *The Member of Parliament and the Administration*, p. 212.
[128] *Spectator*, 10th November 1933.

[129] *Listener*, 17th February 1932, pp. 236–7.
[130] Lloyd George, Pollard.
[131] Fellowes (Defence Committee).
[132] Greaves.
[133] Hale (Colonial Committee).
[134] Amendment to Motion, 22nd January 1957.
[135] Jennings, Pollard, Greaves, Brogan, etc.
[136] e.g. by Amery, p.53.
[137] e.g. Young, Salter and Wheare.
[138] Lord Campion and others, pp. 118–9.
[139] *Speed up Law Reform*, pp. 24–5; and H.C. 161 of 1930/1, p. 259.
[140] e.g. Lloyd George, H.C. 161 of 1930/1, Q. 391.
[141] H.C. 92 of 1958/9, p. 16.
[142] *ibid.* p. 18.
[143] H.C. 303 of 1964/5, pp. ix, 138.
[144] H.C. 161 of 1930/1, Appendix 6.
[145] H.C. 161 of 1930/1, p. 259.
[146] *How to Reform Parliament*, p. 43.
[147] Greaves, pp. 49–51.
[148] H.C. 276 of 1958/9.
[149] H.C. 161 of 1964/5.
[150] H.C. 308 of 1964/5.
[151] H.C. 303 of 1964/5, p. ix.
[152] *The Member of Parliament and the Administration*, pp. 204–11.
[153] H.C. 303 of 1964/5, pp. 143–4.
[154] *Political Quarterly*, Vol. II, 1931.
[155] *English Review*, Vol. LIX, 1934.
[156] e.g. Ellis Smith, H.C. Deb. 557, c. 1313.
[157] Lord Boothby, H.C. Deb. 581, c. 688; see also H.C. Deb. 619, cs. 1315–75 *passim*.
[158] H.C. Deb. c. 1368. 16th March 1960.
[159] H.C. Deb. 16th March 1960, c. 1317.
[160] 3rd Report of Select Committee on Procedure, 1946, para. 36.
[161] H.C. Deb. 16th March 1960, c. 1373.
[162] *Manchester Guardian*, 22nd July 1957.
[163] Jennings, p. 119.
[164] Muir, p. 224.
[165] *Parliamentary Affairs*, Vol. XII, Nos. 3 & 4, pp. 337–48.
[166] *Political Quarterly*, Vol. V, pp. 469–79.
[167] H.C. Deb. 262, c. 1668–9.
[168] H.C. 122 of 1965/6, p. 46, Q. 63.
[169] H.C. Deb. 262, c. 1764.
[170] The proposals to set up 'Departmental' Committees, which might concern themselves, *inter alia*, with a department's expenditure, are considered above.
[171] H.C. Deb. 277, c. 669–70.
[172] H.C. 122 of 1943/4.
[173] Chubb, *The Control of Public Expenditure*, 1952, p. 239.
[174] H.C. Deb. 619, c. 1321–2.
[175] Einzig: *The Control of the Purse*, 1959, p. 330.
[176] H.C. 92 of 1958/9, Q. 191, 184, 284.
[177] *ibid.* p. 122.

[178] *ibid.* p. 48.
[179] *Political Quarterly*, Vol. 36, p. 302.
[180] H.C. 303 of 1964/5, pp. 136–7.
[181] *Change or Decay*, p. 11–12.
[182] H.C. Deb. 619, c. 1323.
[183] H.C. 92 of 1958/9, p. 13.
[184] H.C. Deb. cs. 1341–2, 16th March 1960.
[185] H.C. Deb. cs.1371–3, 16th March 1960.
[186] H.C. Deb. 277, cs. 669–70.
[187] H.C. 189 of 1945–6, Q. 4091.
[188] e.g. H.C. Deb. c. 1345, 16th March 1960.
[189] H.C. 303 of 1964/5, p. 138.
[190] *ibid.* p. viii.
[191] On 27th October 1965. See *Parliamentary Affairs*, Vol. XIX, No. 1, pp. 113–17 for an article on the report and the debate.
[192] *Political Quarterly*, Vol. II, 1931.
[193] H.C. 120 of 1941/2, p. 38.
[194] H.C. 184 of 1953/4, para. 39.
[195] *The Times*, 18th March 1960.
[196] *ibid.* 27th July 1960.
[197] See, for example, H.C. 149 of 1953/4; H.C. 290 of 1953/4; H.C. 162 of 1964/5.
[198] H.C. 303 of 1964/5, para. 13.
[199] H.C. 161 of 1930/1, Q. 2537.
[200] H.C. Deb. 510, c. 615–6.
[201] Einzig, p. 330.
[202] H.C. 303 of 1964/5, Q. 387.
[203] H.C. 189 of 1945/6, para. 44.
[204] Jennings, p. 122.
[205] Jennings, pp. 124–5.
[206] Jennings, pp. 131–2.
[207] H.C. Deb. c. 1330, 16th March 1960.
[208] *The Times*, 2nd June 1960.
[209] Muir, p. 224.
[210] H.C. 184 of 1960/1.
[211] H.C. 161 of 1930/1, Q. 133, 323.
[212] H.C. 92 of 1958/59, p. 174n.
[213] Jennings, *op. cit.* p. 133.
[214] H.C. 92 of 1958/59, para. 9.
[215] *ibid.* Q. 678; p. 208.
[216] *ibid.* p. 4.
[217] *ibid.* p. 196.
[218] *ibid.* Q. 1085.
[219] H.C. 276 of 1964/5.
[220] Einzig, pp. 12, 326–7.
[221] H.C. 92 of 1958/59, pp. 15–16.
[222] *ibid.* para. 43.
[223] *Manchester Guardian*, 22nd July 1957.
[224] H.C. Deb, 619, c. 1342.
[225] *Political Quarterly*, Vol. XXXVI, pp. 295–303.
[226] Under 'Legislation', section (*c*) below.
[227] H.C. 122 of 1965/6.

228 H.C. Deb. 738, cs. 471–4.

229 *ibid.* c. 479.

230 Proposals which affect the procedure for Private Members' Bills are considered later, in Chapter IV.

231 H.C. 161 of 1930/1, pp. 311–2; and *Political Quarterly*, Vol. IV, 1933, pp. 467–81.

232 H.C. 92 of 1958/9, p. 2.

233 *Political Quarterly*, Vol. I, 1930.

234 Parliament sometimes allows this to occur in the case of Private Bills, but never with Public Bills.

235 *Contemporary Review*, Vol. CXLIII, February 1933.

236 Pollard: *How to Reform Parliament*, 1944.

237 *Socialist Commentary*, July 1964, p. vi.

238 H.C. 161 of 1930/31, Q. 1065.

239 *Political Quarterly*, Vol. II, 1931, pp. 305ff.

240 H.C. 161 of 1930/31, Q. 2514.

241 *Political Quarterly*, Vol. V, 1934.

242 *English Review*, Vol. LXI, pp. 657–64.

243 Greaves, pp. 42–4.

244 H.C. 306 of 1963/4, p. 3.

245 *Socialist Commentary*, July 1964, p. iv.

246 *An Introduction to the Procedure of the House of Commons*, 3rd ed. 1958, p. 131.

247 H.C. 92 of 1958/9, para. 20.

248 H.C. Deb. 617, c. 121.

249 H.C. Deb. 617, cs. 158–62. It was repeated in *Socialist Commentary*, July 1964, p. vii.

250 H.C. 303 of 1964/5, p. 133.

251 H.C. 161 of 1930/1, p. 284.

252 Jennings, p. 73.

253 *Socialist Commentary*, July 1964, p. v.

254 H.C. Deb. 400, cs. 1089–90.

255 Jennings, pp. 69–70.

256 Pollard: *op. cit.* p. 43.

257 *Political Quarterly*, Vol. I, 1930.

258 H.C. 310 of 1952/3, p. xxiv.

259 Jennings, pp. 61–3.

260 Muir, p. 210.

261 *Political Quarterly*, Vol. V, pp. 469–79.

262 Jennings, pp. 73–7. Some of the objections which Jennings raised have been obviated by subsequent changes in Standing Orders. His Standing Committee on Finance is mentioned in section (*a*) of this chapter.

263 H.C. 92 of 1958/9, p. 16.

264 H.C. 303 of 1964/5, p. 134.

265 July 1964, p. v.

266 H.C. 161 of 1930/1, Q. 258.

267 Motion, 18th December 1946.

268 H.C. 161 of 1930/1, Q. 35.

269 H.C. Deb. 557, c. 1322.

270 *Parliamentary Affairs*, Vol. VI, 1952–3, pp. 165–72.

271 Jennings, p. 79

272 *The Machinery of Government*, O.U.P. 1945.

273 *Parliamentary Affairs*, Vol. VI, 1952–3, pp. 165–72.
274 H.C. 161 of 1930/1, p. 174.
275 *ibid.* p. 443.
276 H.C. 303 of 1964/5, pp. 133–4.
277 H.C. 92 of 1958/9, para. 6, Q. 1089, 1122.
278 H.C. 161 of 1930/1, p. 442.
279 The use of Committees to consider a Department's Estimates is considered in section (*a*) of this chapter.
280 H.C. 189 of 1945/6, pp. 39–42.
281 H.C. 92 of 1958/9, para. 13; and pp. 3–4.
282 See pp. 43–55 above.
283 Jennings, p. 85.
284 *Parliamentary Affairs*, Vol. XI, No. 3. A change along these lines was later made.
285 *ibid.* Vol. VI, pp. 165–72.
286 Jennings, pp. 86–90.
287 *The Fortnightly*, Vol. CLXI, pp. 425–32.
288 Jennings, p. 93.
289 Now S.O. No. 10.
290 *Parliamentary Affairs*, Vol. XI, No. 3.
291 *Parliamentary Affairs*, Vol. XI, No. 3.
292 H.C. 92 of 1958/9, para. 7.
293 H.C. 161 of 1930/1, p. 330.
294 H.C. Deb. 430, cs. 1102–30.
295 H.C. 161 of 1930/1, Q. 949.
296 H.C. 189 of 1945/6, p. 43
297 In a memorandum (unpublished) to the Select Committee on Procedure in 1945.
298 H.C. 92 of 1958/9, Q. 1045.
299 *ibid.* para. 10.
300 H.C. 303 of 1964/5, p. 134.
301 *op. cit.* pp. 42–4.
302 Pollard, p. 43.
303 Jennings, pp. 107–8.
304 It seems probable that Jennings was thinking of Recommittal (when some Clauses might be debated), rather than Report (when there is no opportunity for debating individual Clauses).
305 H.C. 161 of 1930/1, p. 443.
306 Stewart: *The British Approach to Politics*, 3rd rev. ed., 1955, p. 117.
307 H.C. 161 of 1930/1, p. 174. This reverses the emphasis which the House at present places on the relative effectiveness of a Committee stage in Standing Committee and on the floor of the House. For if a bill is unamended in Committee of the Whole House, it can go for Third Reading without a Report stage; but a bill unamended in a Standing Committee *must* still go for a Report stage on the floor of the House.
308 *ibid.* p. 155.
309 H.C. 92 of 1958/9, para. 11.
310 H.C. Deb. 617, cs. 157, 181–2.
311 H.C. 303 of 1964/5, p. 134.
312 *Introduction to the Procedure of the House of Commons*, 3rd ed., 1958, p. 296.
313 Muir, p. 213.

[314] Lord Campion, p. 296.

[315] H.C. 139 of 1954/5.

[316] *ibid.* paras. 60–5, 73, 74.

[317] H.C. 161 of 1930/1, Qs. 175, 333, 1527.

[318] H.C. 92 of 1958/9, Q. 1045.

[319] *Crossbow*, Vol. 4, No. 10, p. 12.

[320] e.g. H.C. Deb. 574, cs. 1525ff.

[321] July, 1964.

[322] H.C. 153 of 1966/7, p. ix.

[323] e.g. Motions, 18th November 1952, 19th June 1956, and Early Day Motion 13 of 1966/7.

[324] H.C. Deb. 581, c. 669–771 *passim*; 557, c. 1293–352 *passim*; 510, c. 529 *et seq.*

[325] M. Lindsay: *The Times*, 28th December 1957.

[326] Early Day Motion 13 of 1966/7; *Socialist Commentary*, July 1964.

[327] H.C. 92 of 1958/9, pp. 6–7; and para. 24, pp. 39–42.

[328] H.C. Deb. 617, c. 165.

[329] H.C. 153 of 1966/7.

[330] H.C. Deb. 510, cs. 529ff, and H.C. 92 of 1958/9, p. 3 and Q. 667.

[331] e.g. H.C. Deb. 510, c. 533.

[332] H.C. 92 of 1958/9, pp. 8–9.

[333] Muir pp. 206–7.

[334] H.C. Deb. 577, c. 782.

[335] H.C. Deb. 347, c. 2500–4.

[336] H.C. 161 of 1930/1, Q. 574–6.

[337] H.C. Deb. 434, c. 1500–6.

[338] H.C. Deb. 459, c. 1621.

[339] See H.C. Deb. 510, c. 547 (mentioned in a speech by A. Greenwood).

[340] H.C. 92 of 1958/9, para. 27. The proposal was repeated in an Early Day Motion (No. 27) in 1966/7 supported by 115 Members.

[341] H.C. 189 of 1945/6, p. 45.

[342] H.C. 92 of 1958/9, p. 6.

[343] e.g., H.C. Deb. 577, c. 781–2.

[344] H.C. 92 of 1958/9, para. 27.

[345] H.C. 153 of 1966/7, p. vii.

[346] Amdt. to Early Day Motion 70 of 1963/4.

[347] e.g., H.C. 161 of 1930/1, Q. 573; Early Day Motion 46 of 1959/60, Early Day Motion 70 of 1963/4.

[348] H.C. Deb. 581, c. 694.

[349] See H. C. Deb. 315, c. 25.

[350] H.C. Deb. 369, c. 1148; 459, c. 1616–28; 510, c. 541.

[351] e.g. H.C. Deb. 459, cs. 1616–28.

[352] H.C. Deb. 617, c. 41.

[353] H.C. Deb. 510, c. 573–4.

[354] e.g. H.C. Deb, 310, c. 1625–6.

[355] H.C. Deb. 510, c. 602.

[356] e.g. H.C. Deb. 266, c. 1339; 347, c. 2500–4.

[357] H.C. 189 of 1945/6, para 59. For a full description of the difficulties, see para. 31 of the Appendix to that Report.

[358] H.C. Deb. 459, 1624.

[359] H.C. Deb. 266, c. 1340.

[360] H.C. 92 of 1958/9, Q. 535.

[361] H.C. Deb. 617, c. 110.
[362] H.C. Deb. 617, c. 138.
[363] H.C. Deb. 310, c. 1625–6.
[364] e.g. H.C. Deb. 557, c. 1334.
[365] H.C. 92 of 1958/9, para. 55.
[366] Motion, 1st May 1947.
[367] H.C. Deb. 504, c. 397.
[368] H.C. Deb. 307, c. 300–2; 459, c. 1618.
[369] H.C. Deb. 272, c. 61–2.
[370] H.C. Deb. 266, c. 1339.
[371] H.C. Deb. 443, c. 1584–6.
[372] H.C. Deb. 617, c.111
[373] H.C. Deb. 434, cs. 1500–6 (raised by Ellis Smith and others.)
[374] *ibid.*
[375] H.C. Deb. 307, cs. 300–2.
[376] e.g. Motion, 24th November 1956.
[377] e.g. H.C. Deb. 347, cs. 2500–4.
[378] H.C. 92 of 1958/9, para. 29.
[379] H.C. Deb. 617, col. 164–5. It was repeated in *Socialist Commentary*, July 1964, p. viii.
[380] For a full exposition of the subject see P. Howarth: *Questions in the House*, Bodley Head, 1956.
[381] H.C. 161 of 1930/1, p. 443.
[382] *ibid.* Q. 159, 1250.
[383] H.C. 332 of 1951/2.
[384] H.C. 161 of 1930/1, p. 64, p. 443. A Member may now put down two starred Questions (i.e., Questions for oral answer) for a particular day within the next three weeks, but any number of unstarred Questions (i.e., Questions for written answer) which must be answered within about a week.
[385] H.C. Deb. 615, c. 1463.
[386] H.C. 161 of 1930/1, Q. 2500.
[387] H.C. 92 of 1958/9, Q. 86.
[388] H.C. 129 of 1931/2, p. 14.
[389] H.C. 92 of 1958/9, Q. 1067.
[390] H.C. Deb. 510, c. 567.
[391] H.C. 92 of 1958/9, para. 41.
[392] H.C. Deb. 418, c. 1713.
[393] Motion, 10th July 1958; and H.C. Deb. 612, cs. 67–8.
[394] H.C. Deb. 615, cs. 175–8.
[395] Chester and Bowring, pp. 273–7.
[396] H.C. 161 of 1930/1, p. 444.
[397] H.C. 303 of 1964/5, p. 138.
[398] H.C. 161 of 1930/1, p. 443, Q. 159, 605.
[399] H.C. Deb. 557, c. 1332.
[400] Motion, 14th March 1949.
[401] *ibid.* pp. 9–10.
[402] H.C. 303 of 1964/5, p. 138.
[403] H.C. 161 of 1930/1, p. 172.
[404] *Political Quarterly*, Vol. 1, 1930, pp. 351–67.
[405] H.C. 58 of 1945/6, para. 3.
[406] H.C. 92 of 1958/9, para. 38.

[407] *The Times*, 25th April 1960.

[408] H.C. 188 of 1964/5.

[409] Heinemann, Ltd. 1932, p. 573.

[410] Ross, *Parliamentary Representation*, p. 9.

[411] e.g. cf. *The Times*, 28th December 1957.

[412] H.C. 58 of 1945/6, p. 50. It should be pointed out that this was at the start of a new Parliament which included a high proportion of new members; as the Division Clerks familiarized themselves with the new faces, the time was likely to drop to nine minutes (Q. 1687). In 1966, the time taken was between eight and eleven minutes—H.C. 283 of 1966/7.

[413] H.C. 161 of 1930/1, Q. 339; and echoed by C. Davies, H.C. Deb, 510, c. 581.

[414] Morrison, p. 215.

[415] H.C. 92 of 1958/9, Q. 1046.

[416] H.C. 58 of 1945/6, pp. 50–2.

[417] H.C. 92 of 1958/9, para. 32; pp. 218–223.

[418] H.C. 283 of 1966/7.

[419] *ibid.* p. 223; Q. 784.

[420] e.g., *Manchester Guardian*, 1st December 1952; Hinchingbrooke, H.C. Deb. 557, c. 1322.

[421] H.C. Deb. 510, c. 561.

[422] Acland, p. 170.

[423] H.C. 92 of 1958/9, para. 37; and Q. 815.

[424] H.C. Deb. 617, cs. 104–5.

[425] H.C. 361 of 1964/5.

[426] e.g. Hollis, *Parliamentary Affairs*, Vol. VI, pp. 165–72.

[427] H. Hynd, H.C. Deb. 510, c. 541.

[428] H.C. Deb. 510, c. 552.

[429] e.g., H.C. Deb. 581, c. 752; *Observer*, 14th December 1958; *Socialist Commentary*, July 1964, p. v.

[430] H.C. 161 of 1930/1, p. 115.

[431] S.O. No. 34; see H.C. 58 of 1945/6, p. 51.

[432] H. Hynd, H.C. Deb. 510, c. 541.

[433] *Crossbow*, Vol. 4, No. 10, pp. 11–13.

[434] H.C. 92 of 1958/59, p. 6; and Q. 653–4, paras. 31, 34.

[435] Delargy; H.C. Deb. 581, c. 747; and Bevan, H.C. Deb. 400, c. 1108.

[436] The debate is reported in *The Times* of 6th August 1965. Since that date changes have been made as a result of which Black Rod's visitations are now infrequent: see H.C. Deb. 738, cs. 481–2.

[437] H.C. 92 of 1958/9, Q. 143–7.

[438] H.C. Deb. 617, c. 108.

[439] H.C. 122 of 1965/6, p. xii.

[440] Hinchingbrooke, H.C. Deb. 557, c. 1322.

[441] H.C. 92 of 1958/9, para. 16; and Q. 1162.

[442] de Freitas; H.C. Deb. 510, c. 568.

[443] C. Davies; H.C. Deb. 510, c. 579.

[444] Acland, p. 171.

[445] H.C. Deb. 617, cs. 70–2.

[446] Wedgwood Benn, H.C. Deb. 557, c. 1333; and 581, cs. 681–2.

[447] de Freitas, H.C. Deb. 581, c. 696; and H.C. 92 of 1958/9, para. 53. There have been a number of improvements designed to this end since 1959.

[448] *Manchester Guardian*, 1st December 1952.

449 H.C. 92 of 1958/9, para. 37, p. xlvi.
450 Wedgwood Benn, H.C. Deb. 557, c. 1335; and 581, c. 683.
451 *The Times*, 12th December 1960.
452 Boyle, H.C. Deb. 510, c.588.
453 Keeling, H.C. Deb. 508, c. 628.
454 Lord Winterton, H.C. Deb. 400, c. 1074–6.
455 Bevan, H. C. Deb. 400, c. 1096; and 443, c. 1569; see also Jennings, p. 138 and an article by H. V. Wiseman in *Parliamentary Affairs*, Vol. XII, Nos. 3 and 4, pp. 377–91.
456 H.C. 92 of 1958/9, p. 12, para. 34.
457 H.C. Deb. 617, c. 161–4.
458 H.C. 282 of 1965/6.
459 Hynd: H.C. Deb. 510, c. 542.
460 Jennings, p. 165.
461 *Reforming the Commons*, pp. 271–2.

IV

The Party System in Parliament

(a) THE NEED FOR POLITICAL PARTIES

It is possible to distinguish between two ways of viewing the whole question of parliamentary reform.[1] There is, on the one hand, the comparatively restricted field of parliamentary procedure proper, such as that covered by the previous chapter. Reforms in this field are designed to make the House of Commons, *as it is*, function more effectively. The alternative approach is to consider every factor, large and small, which affects the working of Parliament as the central point of the country's governmental system. Electoral reform, for example, demands these broader terms of reference if it is to be properly discussed. Similarly, any detailed examination of the supposed merits and defects of the party system must fall into this second, wider category.

However true it may be that political parties, as we know them today in their parliamentary context, just grew while nobody was looking, their importance is now as great as it is incontestable.[2] A galaxy of illustrious parliamentarians, from Burke by way of Disraeli to Winston Churchill, have at some juncture testified not only to the importance but also to the desirability of party politics. 'I know of no equal force', declared Winston Churchill in the House of Commons over fifty years ago, 'which assures the stability of democratic institutions.'[3] Government exists for the benefit of the governed, but democracy in Lincoln's sense of 'Government by the People' is an impossible ideal. Twentieth-century Britain accepts political parties—bodies of individuals and affiliated organizations having similar views on leading issues and uniting in order to gain the power to apply their beliefs—as the

For Notes and References see pages 127–131

best way of combining effective government with a reasonably democratic expression of the electorate's wishes.[4] Distinguished former Independent Members, such as Sir Alan Herbert, themselves subscribe to the above belief.[5] Michael Foot, who has in his time had much to say against certain aspects of party discipline, concedes unreservedly that the disappearance of party politics would mean the death of democracy. A robust repudiation is needed, he continues, of those sneers which have aimed at making 'Party' a dirty word in the political dictionary.[6] Because of these practical advantages, none of the suggested reforms discussed below aims at the total abolition of parties, even supposing such a carnage to be possible. The answer to the question: 'Why have parties?' is quite simple: 'For convenience'.[7]

Contradictory though it may seem, this widespread acquiescence in the existence of such highly organized political bodies has been accompanied over the years by criticisms which, in volume and intensity, surpass those attacks levelled against all other aspects of parliamentary government. The explanation of this apparent paradox is not hard to find. The party system influences almost every ingredient of present-day British democracy. Hence, its real or imagined defects assume enhanced, far-flung significance because of their potential consequences. Since the system is held to be practically indispensable, its workings have been minutely examined and its supposed weaknesses pitilessly exposed.

(b) GOVERNMENT AND OPPOSITION

In British national government today, the political scene is almost always dominated by two great parties. The two-party system, remarked Sir Harold Nicolson at the Caxton Hall on 14th March 1946, is illogical and indefensible—but it is the best means of running representative institutions.[8] In like vein, Sir Ernest Barker speaks of the struggle for power between two parties as the salt of British democracy.[9] The two-party system, in short, has its protagonists. But others have not been slow to emphasize its dangers. Maurice Duverger claims that, although this country *officially* maintains a parliamentary system (that is, a system with modified separation of powers, Cabinet and Parliament each specializing in a particular function), *in practice* Parliament and Government are like two machines driven by the same motor—

the party in power. The Opposition provides the alternative (party) motor.[10] Muir points out that an elector is frequently confronted with a choice between two parties; he appreciates that no other party can possibly form a Government,[11] yet he may not agree with the fundamental policies of either alternative.[12] It remains for him to vote for the lesser of two evils, to 'waste' his vote on another candidate whose hopes of success are negligible, or to abstain. This sort of drawback appears even more pernicious to those who believe that the differences between the two main contesting parties are less great than would appear at first sight. Not many are as bitter as Belloc and Cecil Chesterton, who spoke of 'collusion' between the two front benches, from which the Speaker himself was not exempt.[13] Yet a leading article in *The Times* commented harshly on a House of Commons containing 'far too many little men' and engaging in 'desperate fighting over things that do not matter'.[14] Fulford, putting the Liberal case, refers to 'two monstrous, inhuman party political machines' existing only to smash each other.[15] Much snapping and snarling goes on, he asserts, over comparative trifles.[16] R. T. McKenzie, at the close of his lengthy survey, pictures 'two great monolithic structures' facing each other in the Commons, debating furiously the comparatively minor issues which divide them.[17] The condition of Parliament's impotence, writes Hollis, is the two-party system.[18] If one accepts that these grave indictments are not wholly false, then the complaint that Cabinet government is a polite title for alternating party oligarchy cannot be lightly dismissed.[19]

The proposals for remedying such serious charges (assuming for the moment they are not groundless) vary considerably in type and magnitude. The most far-reaching suggestion, perhaps, is that party government should be replaced by Coalition government—the parties would not disappear, but the best men from all parties would take office under an accepted leader. The experience of the war years is plainly discernible here. Laski says that the Asquith and Lloyd George Coalitions of 1915 and 1916 respectively were essential contributions towards ultimate victory in 1918, and he refers to the inspiring change in the spirit of the whole nation when the Labour Party agreed to serve under Churchill in May 1940.[20] But the same author goes on to illustrate at some length that such Coalitions are highly unsatisfactory in time of peace;[21] the Coalition of 1931 he condemns as a dangerous threat to parliamentary institutions.[22] An administration of this sort blurs responsibility, prevents issues being clearly defined, and hampers their realistic discussion.[23] Many others argue cogently against peace-time Coalitions on the grounds that the quintessential virtue of parliamentary democracy depends upon the full freedom of articulate constitutional opposition.[24] 'Mr. Ramsay MacDonald's conception of the ideal Parliament as a Council of State in which the Opposition co-operate with the Government for the common good', concludes Laski, 'seems to me to come near to opening the door to the one-party state'. And, as Sir Ernest Barker has pointed out, 'party uses its giant's strength most like a giant when it stands solitary'.[25] Broadly speaking, then, Disraeli was an accurate prophet when he said in 1852 that 'England does not love Coalitions'.

Following his critical survey of the two-party system, R. Muir[26] advocates Minority Government as desirable, since it compels the party forming the Government to follow policies which are not totally unacceptable to all the other major parties represented in the Commons. Undeniably, the task which faces a party not disposing of an overall majority, yet setting out to legislate as a Minority Government, is difficult. But Muir does not consider the task impossible, providing the following conditions obtain:

(a) A Minority Ministry must accept that it cannot hope to carry out measures for which it has no support outside its own party. In other words, it is powerless to effect policies for which there is not a majority of support in the country as a whole.

(b) Parties outside the Government must not devote themselves primarily and exclusively to opposing the Government. Free criticism would not be barred, but the current Ministry would be afforded 'reasonable facilities' to pursue its policies, provided these were not generally unacceptable.

(c) In return for this concession, the Minority Government must allow greater freedom of debate in the Commons, and accept a greater amount of amendments to its Bills.

(d) Nothing less than a vital issue of principle should prompt the Government to threaten resignation.

(e) The most important of all conditions, if effective administration is to take place under a balance of parties, is that a Minority Government should have *no* right to claim a dissolution. If the Ministry's resignation is felt to be imperative, then Parliament should embody its majority decision in an Humble Address to the Crown.[27]

Given the establishment of these very considerable understandings or conventions, Muir postulates that parliamentary government 'can work very well in a condition of balanced parties: not only so, but an opportunity will be opened for the House of Commons to perform its true, but long abdicated, functions of criticism and control'.[28] Ross also has something to say in favour of Minority Government—the 'bloated majorities' of the two great parties are not conducive to healthy government.[29] This whole question is, of course, intimately associated with the campaign for the introduction in this country of Proportional Representation—under this latter electoral system, it might easily happen that no party would obtain an absolute majority in the House. Muir goes further, postulating such electoral reform as essential to the long-term success of Minority Government.[30] But critics of this form of administration heavily outnumber those who favour it. Barker points out that such a system might easily lead to the secret 'backstairs' tyranny of a cabal which would unite the leaders of several parties in an interested coalition—a cabal which would control both the nominal Government and the legislative body. Perhaps, too, the opportunity of pressing a Minority Government for concessions might tempt the parties not in power to demand their own pound of flesh, to the detriment of both Executive and Parliament.[31] Bulmer-Thomas similarly emphasizes the potential menace of secret inter-party negotiations under such a system: not only is this inherently vicious, but the election promises of the various parties would become meaningless.[32] Elections leading to Minority Government, in fact, would play virtually no part in deciding the eventual policy of the administration. Responsible, effective rule on behalf of the people would be considerably weakened.[33] Above all, Minority Government could well lead to some sort of Coalition; the arguments against this last possibility have been mentioned.

Many of those who prefer the two-party system to the alternatives discussed above, nevertheless believe that the debates staged on the floor of the House between the two main opposing factions have lost a great deal of their former significance. It is sometimes alleged that the now firmly established practice of holding private party meetings at Westminster, when affairs of national import are discussed behind closed doors, is a major cause of this decline. Michael Foot claimed in 1959 that 'the higher the party meeting rises on the see-saw, the lower sinks the Commons'.[34] The fact that decisions reached behind closed doors are often regarded by the parties as critical and binding, leads Mr. Foot to a melancholy pen-portrait of a House of Commons where two well-whipped forces confront each other in formal, pre-arranged combat. Speeches of Gladstonian power or Disraelite piquancy are unlikely to shift a single vote.[35] Hollis inveighs with comparable vigour against 'the very disgraceful truth' that the private Member, though relatively impotent in the Chamber, can influence the policy of his party (and often of the Government) at some secret meeting.[36] Foot's proposed remedy is simple: if votes have to be taken at private gatherings, then the results should not be binding on a Member's conduct in the House. An M.P. would, as a result, be fully answerable to the country and his constituents for his public speeches and/or votes.[37] The controversial nature of such a suggestion scarcely requires emphasizing. Beyond doubt, the potential consequences of diminishing in this way the status of the private party meeting could strike at the very heart of the party system, so dependent on unity for its continuing success. Internal feuds, once exposed to open view, could be exploited by political opponents. Peter Richards writes that 'the repeated inability of Liberal Members since 1916 to vote together in the same division lobby has done much to accelerate the decline of their Party'.[38] Granted the existing pattern of our political life, observes the same author, it is 'idealistic' to suppose that the claims of party loyalty will be much diminished.[39]

The movement for the compulsory publication of political parties' accounts has attracted considerable attention for many years. The matter was raised during a debate on Procedure on 26th May 1944, when King-Hall suggested that the funds of political parties should be opened to public inspection. On 15th December 1949, Geoffrey Bing moved 'that . . . political parties, and all other organizations having political action as one of their aims, should publish annually full and adequate statements of their accounts'.[40] The principal point of this proposal, as regards parliamentary reform, is that the vital financing of those political organizations competing for the electors' support should be open to proper public investigation, criticism and control. The whole question of political expenditure was again debated in the Commons on 21st July 1960, when the Labour Party called for an Inquiry into the matter. P. Gordon Walker, moving the amendment, quoted from *The Times* of 9th June 1960:

> In so far as the law regulating election expenses is supposed to set a reasonable limit to the electioneering budgets of political parties so as to cancel the undue advantage of wealth, the law is obviously defective.

When the Labour Party was subsequently returned to power, they promised legislation on this subject; and the point was duly included in the Companies Bill of 1966.

Butler and Rose have pointed out that, since people now tend to vote for a party rather than for a candidate, there is nothing in the law to prevent parties or interested organizations from intervening on a national scale during and before the electoral campaign.[41] They concluded that if the necessity for legislation regarding control of political expenditure had still to be proved, the case for an investigation into the situation nevertheless appeared overwhelming.

Protagonists of the two-party system emphasize consistently the importance of an articulate, effective Opposition. Parliamentary democracy would falter without it: the Heaven of the Right is the Hell of the Left, observes Jennings, and it is only in totalitarian states that the populace can be made to exclaim 'Excelsior!' whether the Government moves forwards or backwards (or in both directions at the same time).[42] It is also now an accepted fact that the Opposition's function is constructive as well as destructive. But the argument is sometimes advanced that the two-party system would work better if the official Opposition were informed earlier, and more fully, of all major Government policies. Acland contends that the principal party not in power should be allowed representatives *within* the State Departments. 'Shadow Ministers' privileged in this way would not be permitted to monopolize the precious time of senior officials, but their inevitably improved knowledge of Government matters would transform democratic criticism into an effective reality. The Civil Service, concludes Acland, belongs to the nation, not to the Government.[43] The principle underlying such a suggestion is not new, but the question seems to have come to a head in recent years. According to Laski, speaking in 1950, 'it is not easy to believe that the House of Commons has been honestly informed of the facts which have led to its approval of policies which have concerned grave issues like those of Abyssinia, Spain, Italy, Greece, Germany and Russia; and not without skill, it has been manœuvred into something like an organized silence over the atomic bomb and the present state of our military commitments'.[44] The gravity of the accusation is clear. The charge is not infrequently levelled against the party in power, as it was, for example, during debates on the Suez crisis. Hollis, in his pamphlet *Has Parliament a Future?* deplores the frequency with which Government and Opposition agree *not* to debate a matter under discussion elsewhere. This detracted from Parliament's efficiency. As distinct from Acland's and Hollis's suggestions, many informed critics would like to see all-party Committees of the House of Commons set up to investigate various aspects of national affairs; such Committees would always contain Opposition Members, who would thus be able to investigate, intimately and in detail, the particular aspect of Government policy allotted to their Committee.[45] These different suggestions underline the generally accepted idea that Parliamentary democracy needs an active, informed Opposition if it is to continue to flourish under the aegis of the party system. It has been said that no Government can be long secure without a formidable Opposition; the fact that the Government pays an official salary to the Leader and the Chief Whip of the Opposition testifies to the unanimous acceptance of the latter body's importance.[46]

(c) THE PRIVATE MEMBER AND HIS PARTY

The influence of political parties in Parliament is by no means confined to the Government and Opposition, conceived of as two organized bodies facing each other in the House of Commons. Indeed, the most substantial volume of post-1945 criticism has been directed at the pressure and discipline exerted on the individual Member by his or her own party. The comparative decline in the Private Member's independence and initiative is regarded by many as a serious, deplorable feature of modern politics. Describing the individual as the obedient servant of the party machine, Hollis has suggested that it would be simpler (and certainly more economical) if a flock of tame sheep, kept conveniently at hand, were guided through Westminster's division lobbies in appropriate numbers at agreed times.[47] Hollis's pessimistic view of the situation is echoed less spectacularly by other informed observers. R. T. McKenzie feels that genuine political dissent is unduly discouraged by the parties' inflexibility;[48] Bulmer-Thomas warns that fewer men of ability will enter Parliament if the present restrictions on free speech continue.[49] Criticism of this kind is not restricted to the post-war years, but it has certainly come to the forefront following the abolition of university constituencies by the 1948 Representation of the People Act.[50] Since then, the one Independent candidate to be *elected* to Parliament (other than successive Speakers) has been Sir David Robertson—and he, himself a former Conservative, was not opposed by a Conservative candidate.[51] Generally speaking, therefore, the contention that mass electorates are fatal to the politically unorthodox is justified.[52] Voters are swayed by national issues rather than by personalities. A candidate, in short, depends on his party affiliations. Given this post-war state of affairs, the independence or otherwise of an M.P. *within* his party is a matter of extreme importance—for honest, informed political dissent is accepted without question as the life-blood of Parliamentary democracy.[53] As Crossman emphasizes, if the Member is responsible primarily to his party, not to his electors, then a Government cannot be wholly responsible to the House of Commons.[54] How, then, can 'honest political dissent' be best encouraged?

Acland has suggested that all Members of the Commons should

be guaranteed a reasonable income for life, even when no longer serving at Westminster.[55] The consequence of such comparative security would be that men and women of modest means would be more willing to speak out against their party's policy, since an enforced or voluntary farewell to Westminster would no longer incur extreme financial hardship. Ross advocates that a Member, on giving up or losing his seat, should receive for a 'limited time' that part of his remuneration ranking as salary. This 'limited time' would not exceed his previous active service in the Commons, and would in no case be longer than three years. A person's private income would also have to be considered before an award of this type was made.[56] An inquiry into the operation of the House of Commons Members' Fund was undertaken by the Select Committee on Members' Expenses which reported in 1953–4, and which put forward a suggestion for a non-contributory pensions scheme.[57] The Committee argued in favour of its proposal (which would of necessity impose upon the taxpayer) that M.P.s were servants of the public—a capricious employer with the right to dismiss them without ceremony.[58] The scheme as such was not implemented, although on 22nd February 1957 it was announced that an annual Government contribution of ten thousand pounds would be made to the Members' Fund; and in October 1964 a new contributory Pensions Scheme was introduced by which, in return for an annual payment of £150, a Member on ceasing membership after ten years' service, will, at the age of sixty-five, receive a pension calculated at the rate of £60 per annum for each year's service up to fifteen, and £24 per annum for each subsequent year.[59]

The plea for some financial security for former M.P.s has had its opponents. An article in *The Times*, for instance, declared categorically that a Member of Parliament who asks for security in his career is seeking a prize to which freely elected representatives were not entitled.[60] Lady Tweedsmuir has observed: 'Whatever any of us may feel about the necessity for pensions, for example, for past Members of this House . . . all of us who sit in the House now knew exactly the terms and conditions of service and the risks to our dependents when we decided to stand for Parliament.'[61] Fears that improved financial security might attract more 'professional politicians' to Parliament have also been voiced on a number of occasions. But there seems now to be general recognition of the need for a fairly wide sprinkling of 'full-time' M.P.s—however artificial or invidious that term may sound.[62] As Peter Richards pointed out, the introduction of payment to Members as far back as 1911 had led inevitably to the presence in Parliament of men without private means.[63] Such Members, moreover, often make sacrifices to serve in the Commons. Whilst any discussions of the country's moral obligations in the matter would be out of place here, the popularity of the argument that some financial security as regards his future might well lead to a Member's greater independence within his party is undeniable. For example, following criticism in *The Times* of the proposal for non-contributory pensions,[64] both Attlee and Acland wrote letters in defence of some such scheme.[65]

The recommendations of the Select Committee regarding a non-contributory scheme for Members' pensions, mentioned in the preceding page, were the subject of a free vote in the Commons on 24th May 1954. This leads us to another proposal aimed at increasing Private Members' independence: there should be more free votes. Grimond has said that Parliament ought to be 'less dragooned on every issue by the Whips';[66] Hollis has also campaigned assiduously for relaxed discipline of this sort. Foot claims that dignity, spontaneity, suspense, surprise and significance will return to Commons debates if more free votes are permitted: the division lobby will no longer be a 'corridor of humiliation' where the M.P. must wear the badge of his tribe.[67] It is true that more free votes would entail extra work, sharper headaches and, possibly, confusion of the issues as far as the Government is concerned. In particular, Ministers can expect trouble if they decline to follow a clear-cut verdict reached by the House without the assistance of the Whips.[68] Some would simply say that such a price was well worth paying. Others, more mindful of the Government's problems, suggest that more free votes would be possible if the result were not necessarily regarded as a vote of confidence. Cripps said in 1933 that unless the Cabinet threatened to resign less regularly the 'take it or leave it' atmosphere engendered in the Chamber would render discussion abortive.[69] In like vein, Captain Cunningham-Reid wanted to see a Government resign only if defeated on a vote of censure, which would *follow* a Government defeat in the lobbies.[70] Whether this latter proposal is accepted or not, keen advocates of increased free-voting argue that their proposals would not render a Government's task impossible. 'Honest political dissent' need not be incompatible with basic loyalty to one's party, and few Members would abuse their freedom since they must face their electors at regular intervals. The Government back-bencher with hopes of office would have added reasons for treating such liberty with respect and restraint. It is probably true that convinced supporters of a stable Executive would still claim that free votes should remain an occasional luxury, whilst no Government is itself likely to encourage such a policy.[71] Nevertheless, the charges levelled against excessive 'dragooning' in the division lobbies, whether justified or not, have been sufficiently frequent and outspoken to merit serious attention being paid to the question inside and outside Parliament.

Bulmer-Thomas, supporting the plea for more free votes and fewer questions of confidence, adds that tolerance of personal dissent within the party should be accompanied by similar tolerance on the part of an M.P.'s constituency organization: 'An executive committee which is always brooding over the Member's speeches, passing resolutions of censure on his votes, and threatening him with the withdrawal of support at the next election is doing a great disservice to representative government.'[72] The important issue as to whether a Member is a representative or a delegate is involved here. Without debating the merits or defects of Burke's classic answer to the question, we may fairly say that the Suez crisis— which provoked definitive ruptures between several M.P.s and their constituency organizations—revealed substantial support for the eighteenth-century statesman's words to his electors at Bristol. 'Your *representative*', Burke had said, 'owes you, not his industry only, but his judgement, and he betrays, instead of serving you, if he sacrifices it to your opinion.'[73] King-Hall, in the debate on Procedure of 26th May 1944, detected a tendency that the electorate, more and more, wanted to feel that their *representatives* had minds of their own, and were not 'perambulating rubber stamps'. In a speech to his constituency association, Nigel Nicolson declined in public an invitation to resign his seat because he had opposed his Party's policy in the Suez affair.[74] Shortly afterwards, Nicolson published in *People and Parliament* his own account of the quarrel between his constituency organization and himself; in support of his views, he quoted Bagehot's axiom that constituency government is the precise opposite of parliamentary government,[75] and noted Amery's preference for 'democracy by consent and not by delegation; government of the people, for the people, with but not by the people'.[76] The impression derived from this book is that party discipline can on occasions be wielded more firmly by the constituency associations than by the Whips at Westminster.[77] This was but one of several similar clashes between Members and their constituencies during 1956/7, and there have been others since then. In *Pathways to Parliament* (1965), Ranney identifies in the Conservative Party alone twelve instances since 1945 in which local constituency organizations have declined to re-adopt their sitting Member.

How are the perils of excessive 'constituency government' to be avoided? First, a number of practical suggestions have been made concerning the selection of candidates by local associations: these proposals have been considered in an earlier chapter.[78] The second safeguard put forward is of a more general, abstract kind. If accepted, it would involve the acceptance locally of the principle that a Member of Parliament is not his electors' 'delegate', but their 'representative' in Burke's sense of the word. The Member would thus have the acknowledged right to speak against his party *in exceptional circumstances*. This last proviso is important—for few would deny that electors rightly attach significance to a party's being sufficiently united in order to form an effective Government or Opposition.[79] There is one more reason why a Member should not lightly go against his constituents' known wishes: local Party workers, mostly unpaid, toil hard and selflessly to support his candidature, and quite naturally expect loyalty from their elected representative as their just recompense.

(d) PRIVATE MEMBERS' TIME

Proposals to increase the independence and effectiveness of the Private Member fall into two broad categories. One of these categories—the right of an individual to express his personal views, even if they clash with his Party's official policy—has now been considered. The other broad type of proposed reform relates to the actual opportunities of back-benchers to make their presence felt in Parliament. That such opportunities have been seriously curtailed over the past hundred years is a well-known fact,[80] and suggestions to prevent the 'threatened eclipse'[81] of the individual Member's initiative have acquired a definite sense of urgency. The proper place for the consideration of the majority of these proposals is in the chapter devoted to 'Procedure' (Chapter III). Those concerning Private Members' time, however, may perhaps be most usefully discussed here, if only because the subject is so typical of the constant struggle for time, opportunity and recognition waged today by the average back-bencher on both sides of the House. Of Private Members, Sir Alan Herbert said (to his prospective electors at East Harrow in December 1958): 'This is a fine and precious institution which must never be surrendered or belittled—especially the time set aside for Private Members' Bills.'

Although public interest fixes almost entirely on to Private Members' bills, it is as well to note that the House has lately allotted more time to Private Members' motions than to bills (the equivalent of twelve full days for motions, as against ten days for bills, each session); the Study of Parliament Group wished to reverse these figures.[82]

The threat to Private Members' time comes from three directions. There is, first, possible direct action by the Government, who can commandeer all or some of the available time for their own purposes when they feel that events justify it; this happened for example, in 1929–30, 1934–5, the war years, and the sessions from 1945–6 to 1947–8. In 1948–9 there were no motions, and in 1950 no bills.

A second and perhaps more sinister threat is the use Private Members can make of this time in order to bring forward official Opposition or Government business in disguise: Campion notes that Members often ballot in effect for the privilege of introducing a bill or moving a motion on behalf of their party.[83] A recent motion in the House showed resentment at the practice of party whips being applied to Private Members' business.[84] And there can be said to be something cynical in the way in which a Government spokesman in the Lords, referring to a particular piece of future legislation, could say: 'All the necessary preparatory work . . . is

being done to ensure that everything will be ready for the introduction of a Private Member's bill early next session.'[85]

Thirdly, there is the gravest threat of all; it is the apathy of
Private Members themselves. On the motion to restore some
Private Members' time after the war, the then Father of the House
said: 'The House . . . has ceased to take any real practical interest
in this matter.'[86] Nearly four years later, a former Leader of the
House said that if Divisions on a Friday showed as small attendance as in the previous session, 'Private Members' business might
very well fall into some contempt amongst the public outside.'[87]
There now seems, however, less need for alarm on this score; the
private Member has been acting robustly in defence of his legislative
rights. When, after the 1966 Election, the Government sought to
deny to Private Members any legislative time before the Summer
recess, they were persuaded to give way. Nor were they able to continue the practice, introduced as an experiment during the previous
Session, of moving the introduction of bills under the 'Ten Minute
Rule', from the commencement of public business (a time of peak
parliamentary interest) to the end of the day.[88]

Precedence on Private Members' days is allotted by ballot. There
is one ballot for bills early in the session, and Members successful
may choose on which of several allotted days they will move the
Second Reading of their bills; a suggestion that this ballot should
take place in the Session before (which proposal was supported
by a draft Standing Order on the subject) was not taken up by
the Procedure Committee in 1959.[89] Ballots for motions are held
at various dates throughout the session; the successful Members
are able to move motions of their choice on the appropriate day.
The Select Committee on Procedure in 1946 recommended that
one ballot should be held for both motions and bills;[90] winning
Members could then choose to initiate whichever they preferred.
The House, however, never gave effect to this proposal.

Private Members' motions, suggested Campion, could be given
precedence according to the weight of support accorded to them
by Members. Alternatively, the ballot could decide between the
motions proffered, rather than between the Members who put
their names down.[91] Neither of these views commended itself to
the Committee. Nor did they accept the late Clerk's point that 20
half-day debates would prove more satisfactory than 10 full days.

They did not advocate reverting to the pre-war practice, where a Motion Day was divided into two, so that two short debates would invariably be held, instead of (possibly) one longer debate only; this was, however, the view of the Study of Parliament Group and, provided the hours of a Friday Sitting were slightly extended, of a later Procedure Committee.[92] Other suggestions have been that the motions should be selected by a Committee, rather than by ballot; and that the ballot should be held, not as a choice between Members, but as a choice between known motions (possibly those motions placed on the Order Paper for debate on 'an early day').[93]

As to Private Members' bills, one point should be made clear from the outset; it has been emphasized by two Procedure Committees, in 1958/9 and 1963/4 respectively.[94] The procedure by which they pass into law is identical with that of all other public bills, their only peculiarity being the way in which the best opportunities are ballotted for. It is to this peculiarity that most writers on the subject apply their minds; it is objected that the persistence of the eccentric is rewarded too often, so that too many Private Members' bills have a touch of the 'crank' about them.[95]

Campion suggested that Private Members' bills should be given precedence according to the amount of support they carried in the House; once a bill had been given precedence, no Member who had supported it could put his name to another bill for the remainder of the session.[96] This method (or its corollary, by which Members sign their name as objectors to a bill, and the bill with least objectors gets precedence) was considered by Pollard; his conclusion was that the best bills would still not necessarily get precedence in this way.[97]

The 1931 Procedure Committee recommended that, as the Session proceeds, the Committee of Selection might give precedence on Standing Committees to such bills as seemed likely to command general assent.[98] The House never gave effect to this, but Muir[99] and Michael Stewart[100] suggested that an all-party Committee should sit to select which of the Private Members' bills offered should have precedence. Bromhead also thought the idea worth considering.[101] But Pollard said it would be placing an invidious task upon the Committee.[102]

Laski suggested something which had a touch of both proposals:

a bill with certain specified support (for example, twenty-five Members) could, if it involved law reform, be referred to a special Committee. This Committee would take evidence in public, and report to the House. If the report was favourable, the Government would be bound to allow time for the bill's further progress.[103]

Pollard's own view[104] was that the Speaker should, under certain stipulated conditions, certify bills as non-contentious. Such bills would then be given special facilities, perhaps on the lines of the Consolidation of Enactments (Procedure) Act, 1949.[105]

With this idea, we are getting away from the principle that the legislative process for a Private Members' bill should be the same as for any other public bill. Pollard goes even further from this principle when he postulates a lower quorum (twenty instead of forty) for the House when it is considering Private Members' business;[106] the Procedure Committee of 1958/9 rejected both this idea, and a proposal that it should be easier to carry the closure on a Private Members' day.[107]

From time to time Members with bills of their own have shown resentment at the ease with which these can be blocked by their colleagues. Following some instances of this in 1964, a Procedure Committee recommended that objectors to bills at a time of unopposed business should at least have to stand up to signify objection. However, they rejected proposals that objectors' names should be recorded, and that a bill that had been blocked on a certain number of occasions should then be allowed to proceed.[108]

Finally, mention should be made of a suggestion by Ernest Davies that the Government might grant time for all Private Members' bills which had got Second Reading to make further progress even though all the allotted Fridays were used up.[109] Pollard believed that, after some general resolutions had been agreed to by the House, an Advisory Committee should consider the bill. If they reported favourably the Government should be bound to provide time for the bill.[110]

Bills and motions in Private Members' time do not, of course, exhaust the potentialities of the Private Member for taking part in the parliamentary game; the other resources are still there— questions, adjournment debates, the introduction of bills under other procedures, speeches on other people's proposals, etc. But the former present the only opportunity by which Members are actually encouraged to take action on matters in which they feel that a great issue is at stake; that is why, for instance, S. Gordon has described Private Members' time as 'the precious initiative'.[111]

(e) PARTY COMMITTEES

In all that has been written about political parties, surprisingly little attention has been paid to the role of party Committees. Lord Morrison has explained how he advocated the formation of these groups in order to give employment to the landslide of Labour backbenchers who had entered the House after the General Election of 1945.[112] The Committees prospered and today have considerable influence on events; in a series of radio talks on Power and Parliament, Norman Hunt said, 'Insofar as the Commons does have any influence on affairs, it is exerted privately in party Committees rather than publicly on the floor of the House.'[113] Hill and Whichelow believe that the provision of these Committees is one of the most useful services rendered by the party to its Members; but this does not stop them from arguing that it would have been better for Parliament had the Commons in 1945 set up a number of *official*, all-party, specialist Committees instead of these *unofficial* party Committees.[114]

Conclusions

The volume and complexity of the work to be done at Westminster, combined with the existence of universal suffrage, make the party system an important and indispensable aspect of the Commons' present-day activities. The most zealous advocates of reform acknowledge the fact. A substantial amount of support for the two-party system is also evident, though such support is naturally by no means unanimous. Moreover, the criticisms and suggestions discussed in the preceding pages have of necessity focused attention on the real or supposed shortcomings of the system, and it is only right and proper that brief mention should be made, in concluding, of some of the arguments in the contrary sense. In the first place it has been pointed out that beneath the surface of parliamentary life, there are a number of tides opposing the pull of party discipline; a Member's reliance on his 'pair' from the other side, and his tendency in committees to make non-party points, are only two of the factors that moderate his party's control over him.[115] 'People tend to exaggerate the effect of party control on back-bench Members of Parliament,' says Robert Rhodes James, 'the House of Commons has a very strong collective spirit, and is as proud as the devil.'[116] Apart from its eminent practicality,[117] the party machine, even as it exists today, does not completely stifle the initiative and independence of the Private Member. Chief Whips from the two main parties are united in declaring that government back-benchers working behind the scenes make a bigger impact on government policy than is often apparent.[118] A Private Member may not possess 'power'—that belongs to the Cabinet of the day—but he still has 'influence'[119] for it is of the essence of democracy that minority and even individual opinions must be heard and respected. Further, in times of crisis the Whips can lose their force. To the charge that it demands 'almost heroism' to defy one's Whips when voting,[120] many would retort that this is a quality not unknown to the British. Roy Jenkins has pointed out that freedom from the Whips, even if it could be granted, would not mean freedom from other 'pressures'[121]—the writer refers, no doubt, to Pressure Groups, the influence of which on Members of Parliament has been given some prominence in post-war years.[122]

These are but some of the strong arguments advanced in support of the part played by political parties in the Commons today. Nevertheless, it is still true that a vast body of current informed opinion does not regard their present influence as an unmixed blessing. The details of such criticisms and indictments, together with proposed remedies, have been discussed; it remains to speak of the general fear which underlies the bulk of those criticisms. Often this 'general fear' is implied rather than expressly stated. It is that the strong party system may eventually deprive Parliament of its vital role as the nation's safeguard against possible Executive dictatorship. One impartial observer who pointed *explicitly* to this threat was the late Lord Campion, sometime Clerk of the Commons: 'To their authority as servants of the King, wielding the powers of the prerogative, Ministers have added a second power, the power of Parliament itself. Through their command of a devoted party majority they have to a large extent in practice reversed the constitutional relationship of the Executive to the House of Commons—as party leaders, they are in a position to control the controllers.'[123] Jo Grimond, mentioning the relentless pressure on the Private Member of Government business, emphasizes the 'erosion of the defences once erected against the Executive'.[124] That the influence of the latter is too considerable, in the eyes of many, will emerge from the following chapter. It is already clear, however, that the preservation of some independence and personal initiative by the Private Member in the face of potential 'alternating Party oligarchy', 'constituency government' and other similar perils is regarded by many as quintessential if Parliament is to hold fast as the nation's watchdog. Speaking in support of increased opportunities for *Private* Members, one back-bencher recently declared: 'After all, Parliament was not intended simply as a machine to ratify measures proposed by the Executive. . . . We (i.e. Private Members) have constitutional rights in this place which are important, rights for which men have died in the past and which we should not lightly sacrifice to the Executive. Much of the early history of this House, as all hon. Members know, is the struggle for the preservation of those rights against the eroding domination of the Executive. In stressing that, we are really only stressing *the rights and freedom of the nation as a whole.*'[125]

NOTES AND REFERENCES

[1] H. V. Wiseman: 'Parliamentary Reform' in *Parliamentary Affairs* Vol. XII, No. 2 (Spring 1959), p. 240.

[2] W. Harrison: *The Government of Britain*, 1948, p. 50. This in no way invalidates the fact that political parties today are highly organized bodies.

[3] 31st March 1910.

[4] Curtis, pp. 18–20. R. T. McKenzie likewise emphasizes that policy cannot be initiated by the electorate as a whole.

[5] *Independent Member*, 1950, p. 337.

[6] M. Foot: *Parliament in Danger*, 1959, pp. 7–8.

[7] S. Gordon: *Our Parliament*, 5th ed., 1958, p. 80. The author, who points out that there is 'nothing sacred' about parties, goes on to say that they appear to suit the taste of the people, and that over a long term the party system seems to be indispensable to the success of parliamentary government.

[8] Hansard Society Pamphlet, No. 2.

[9] Bailey (ed.): *The British Party System*, 1952, p. 198.

[10] M. Duverger: *Political Parties: Their Organization and Activity in the Modern State*, 2nd revised ed., 1959, p. 394. Lord Morrison of Lambeth has noted that one Labour Party publication referred to an Opposition Front-bencher as '*Minister* of — in the Shadow Cabinet'. (Morrison, pp. 349–50.)

[11] The Liberal Party manifesto at the 1959 General Election conceded to the elector; 'You will get a Tory or Socialist Government after this election . . . .'

[12] Muir, p. 145.

[13] In *The Party System*, 1911.

[14] 23rd December 1957, p. 7.

[15] *The Liberal Case*, 1960, pp. 18–19.

[16] *ibid.* pp. 25–6.

[17] McKenzie: *British Political Parties*, 1955, p. 586.

[18] H. Thomas (ed.): *The Establishment: A Symposium*, 1959, p. 186.

[19] *New Statesman*, 2nd April 1955, pp. 460–1.

[20] Laski, p. 57.

[21] *ibid.* pp. 58ff.

[22] *ibid.* p. 65.

[23] *ibid.* p. 71.

[24] e.g. (i) Jennings: *Parliament Must be Reformed*, 1941, pp. 15ff. (ii) Lord Samuel: 'The Party System and National Interest' (address to the Hansard Society at Denison House, 10th October 1945). (iii) Gaitskell: 'In Defence of Politics' (oration at Birkbeck College, December 1954).

[25] Barker: *Reflections on Government*, 1953, p. 212.

[26] Muir, Chap. IV, 'Political Parties and the Party System'.

[27] *ibid.* pp. 190–3.

[28] *ibid.* p. 193.

[29] *Parliamentary Representation*, pp. 225–9.

[30] Muir, pp. 193–4.

[31] In *The British Party System*, p. 196.

[32] Bulmer-Thomas, pp. 102–3.

[33] Butler: *The Electoral System in Great Britain 1918–1951*, 1953, pp. 188–9. This real or supposed defect of Minority Government is constantly emphasized by opponents of Proportional Representation—the electoral system most likely to lead to such a form of administration.

[34] Foot, p. 14.

[35] *ibid.*

[36] In *The Establishment: A Symposium*, p. 174.

[37] Foot, p. 27. Hollis has said, in similar vein: 'If the floor of the House should become the place of decision, then we shall have no need to worry about its prestige.' *Daily Telegraph*, 14th March 1959.

[38] Richards, p. 143.

[39] *ibid.* p. 254.

[40] H.C. Deb. 470, cs. 2972–3040. The Motion was carried by 213 votes to 104. Bing's case was based partly on his claim that, whereas the Liberal, Labour and Communist Parties published their accounts, the Conservative Party did not. c. 2972.

[41] Butler and Rose, Appendix 5.

[42] Jennings: *Parliament*, 2nd ed., 1957, p. 167.

[43] Acland, p. 171.

[44] Laski, p. 84.

[45] The proposals regarding such all-party Committees are considered more fully in Chapter III.

[46] 'The right honourable gentleman, the Member for South Leeds [Hugh Gaitskell], is in his place on the Front Opposition Bench to exercise a function which is almost as important as the function of the right honourable gentleman (i.e. the Prime Minister) opposite.' Jennings: *op. cit.* p. 532.

[47] *Can Parliament Survive?*, pp. 64–5.

[48] McKenzie, pp. 585–6.

[49] Bulmer-Thomas, p. 271.

[50] See, for example, an article by Sir Bryan Fell written in August 1935: 'Nineteenth Century and After', Vol. CXVIII, pp. 129–41.

[51] Sir David resigned the Conservative Whip in January 1959. At the General Election of October 1959, he defeated a Labour opponent by 5,725 votes.

[52] Richards, p. 13.

[53] 'Honest political dissent' does not mean the right of 630 individual M.P.s to voice their differing opinions on all subjects. This 'fallacy of self-defeating individualism' (Crick: *Reform of the Commons*, 1959, p. 3.) would destroy Parliament's effectiveness. Lord Attlee has pointed out that the conception of Parliament as an assembly of individuals all using their individual judgement on every particular subject is 'hopelessly impractical' (*Fabian Journal*, November 1958, p. 8). Nigel Nicolson similarly concedes that party organization is needed to make vague aspirations 'articulate and effective'. (Nicolson, p. 17.) The general recognition of the necessity of some party organization and discipline has been mentioned above.

[54] Crossman, *Socialism and the New Despotism*, Fabian Tract 298, p. 18.

[55] Acland, p. 171.

[56] Ross: *Parliamentary Representation*, p. 209. The author does not conceive of this type of extended remuneration as a 'pension', but as a means of allowing the former Member to re-establish himself, outside Westminster, without suffering financial hardship.

[57] H.C. 72 of 1953/4.

[58] H.C. 72 of 1953/4, para 36.

[59] Ministerial Salaries and Members' Pensions Act 1965.

[60] *The Times*, 8th March 1954, p. 9. The article agreed that an extended Members' Fund might be considered, but no general statutory right should exist.

[61] H.C. Deb. 613, c. 1183. Lady Tweedsmuir was speaking during the Second Reading of Mr. Speaker Morrison's Retirement Bill, on 18th November 1959.

[62] The question is discussed more fully in Chapter VI.

[63] Richards, p. 242. A summary of the then position regarding Members' pensions is given in the following pages of Richards' book, pp. 242–7.

[64] *The Times*, 17th February 1954, p. 9.

[65] *ibid*. 18th February 1954, p. 9. The related question of Members' pay is discussed in Chapter VII.

[66] In *The New Liberal Democracy*, Part II, p. 7.

[67] *op. cit.* 23–5. Foot adds, however, that more free votes will not be possible until the status of private Party meetings is diminished.

[68] Lord Morrison, who was not a keen advocate of too many free votes, nevertheless declared that a Government should abide by the result when such a liberty has been granted (Morrison, p. 355).

[69] 'Democracy and Dictatorship' in *Political Quarterly*, Vol. IV, 1933, pp. 467–81.

[70] H.C. Deb. 399, cs. 1866–67.

[71] The relations between Parliament and the Executive are discussed in the following chapter.

[72] Bulmer-Thomas, p. 272.

[73] *Speeches and Letters on American Affairs*, Everyman edition, pp. 72–3. For an excellent summary of opinions in this matter, see Richards, pp. 157–72.

74 At the Selwyn Hall, Boscombe, 5th December 1956.

75 Nicolson, p. 166.

76 *ibid.* p. 167.

77 Morrison said of Nicolson's *People and Parliament*: 'In general I agree with the views he expressed in it.' (Morrison, p.353.) A leading article in *The Times* of 3rd October 1958 similarly approved of the author's general principles, (p. 11). Following a postal ballot in February 1959 among members of his constituency association, Nigel Nicolson was defeated (by 91 votes) and did not stand at the 1959 General Election.

78 Chapter I: 'Elections and Representation'.

79 See also note 55, above.

80 cf. a diagram in *Our Parliament*, 6th ed., 1964, p. 165—The Precious Initiative of the Private Member.'

81 *ibid.* p. 165.

82 H.C. Deb. 615, cs. 1456ff., SO. No. 5, and H.C. 303 of 1964/5, p. 135.

83 *An Introduction to the Procedure of the House of Commons*, 3rd ed., 1958, p. 114.

84 Early Day Motion 120 of 1966/7.

85 H.L. Deb. 183, c. 951. (The subject under discussion was the Protection of Wild Birds, 28th July 1953.)

86 Lord Winterton: H.C. Deb. 460, c. 80.

87 Ede: H.C. Deb. 507, c. 149.

88 H.C. Deb. 727, cs. 846–907, 2007–9.

89 H.C. 92 of 1958/9, Qs. 119, 995–6, p. 194. It was repeated by the Study of Parliament Group—H.C. 303 of 1964/5, p. 135.

90 H.C. 189 of 1945/6, para. 51.

91 *ibid.* para. 29.

92 H.C. 303 of 1964/5, p. 138; and H.C. 153 of 1966/7.

93 H.C. 92 of 1958/9, p. 11; and Qs. 802, 969.

94 See H.C. 306 of 1963/4, p. 4.

95 H.C. 189 of 1945/6.

96 *ibid.*

97 *Speed up Law Reform*, pp. 27–8.

98 H.C. 129 of 1931/2, p. xvii.

99 Muir, p. 205.

100 Stewart, p. 118.

101 Bromhead: *Private Members' Bills*, pp. 42–3.

102 *Speed up Law Reform*, pp. 27–8.

103 Cited by Pollard, *op. cit.* p. 29.

104 *ibid.* p. 28.

105 Under this procedure, Acts can be consolidated, and have minor improvements made in them, by a Joint Committee; subsequent progress of the Consolidated Bill in both Houses is largely formal.

106 *Speed up Law Reform*, p. 27.

107 H.C. 92 of 1958/9, paras. 15–16.

108 H.C. 306 of 1963/4, p. 4.

109 *Political Quarterly*, Vol. XXVIII, 1957, pp. 32–9.

110 *Speed up Law Reform*, p. 29.

111 Gordon, 6th ed., 1964, p. 165.

112 Morrison, *An Autobiography*, p. 253.

113 *Listener*, Vol. LXX, No. 1791, 25th July 1963.

114 Hill and Whichelow, Chap. 4.

[115] *ibid.*
[116] James, p. 19.
[117] See section (*a*) above.
[118] *Listener*, Vol. LXX, No. 1791, 25th July 1963.
[119] This very sensible distinction between *power* and *influence* is made by Richards in *op. cit.* p. 260.
[120] Hollis in *The Establishment: A Symposium*, p. 175.
[121] *Listener*, 26th January 1956, pp. 127-8.
[122] King-Hall, H.C. Deb. 400, 26th May 1944, cs. 1087-8. H. Eckstein: *Pressure Group Politics: The Case of the British Medical Association*, 1960; S. E. Finer: *Anonymous Empire*, 1958; J. D. Stewart: *British Pressure Groups: Their Role in Relation to the House of Commons*, 1958. There have also been numerous articles on the subject.
[123] Lord Campion and others, p. 26.
[124] In *The Unservile State*, Book I, Chap. 2, pp. 27ff.
[125] H.C. Deb. 612, c. 217. (Business of the House: Private Members' Time; 28th October 1959. The speaker was Nigel Fisher.)

V

Parliament and the Executive

(*a*) CABINET AND PARLIAMENT

An outstanding constitutional development of the first sixty years of this century has been the substantial increase of the Cabinet's authority and activities. To a large extent this development was prompted by the advent of two world wars within a relatively short space; but the enhanced powers of the Cabinet (and, consequently, of the Executive as a whole) survived into the post-war years, and the relationship between Parliament and the Executive soon became a major peace-time issue. Our modern system of democracy has been termed 'Parliamentary bureaucracy',[1] 'Cabinet Government',[2] and 'Cabinet bureaucracy';[3] whether such definitions emphasize the superiority of the Executive or of the House of Commons, it is clear that no account of proposed reforms for the latter would be complete without considering the mutual interdependence of these two great bodies.

Apart from extremist views such as those of Mosley and his present or former supporters,[4] recent opinion has accepted unanimously the need for both these aspects of the constitution. The difficulty is the preservation (some would say, 'the discovery') of a fair, effective balance between the Parliamentary and bureaucratic elements—for an unhappy marriage between the two could develop into a most dangerous situation for the nation. And from the briefest survey of relevant criticisms, it is beyond doubt that most writers regard the unprecedented authority of Cabinet and Executive as the true source of existing dissatisfaction. The Cabinet is too omnipotent, declared Muir in 1930; by subjecting Parliament to its power, it has 'atrophied' control on behalf of the nation by the latter's elected representatives.[5] In the House of

For Notes and References see pages 157–161

Lords on 17th May 1950, Lord Cecil of Chelwood moved to resolve 'that the growing power of the Cabinet is a danger to the democratic constitution of the country', and countless others have found it difficult to reconcile such 'growing power' with democracy. In his *Reform of the Commons*, Bernard Crick claims that 'the Executive has reached a point where the divorce in attitude between Minister and M.P. is such that both front-benches have grown more and more prone to think that Parliamentary criticism is nuisance enough at the moment, without contemplating radical reforms of Parliamentary procedure.'[6] Edward F. Iwi, recalling how Parliament has in the past defended its powers successfully against the Monarch, adds that it is now delegating its authority, almost recklessly, to the Executive, which is now the strongest component in our Constitution.[7] Because of his professionally unbiased position, one can do no better than quote again as representative the view of the late Lord Campion, who regretted the increasing subordination of the Commons to the Executive, through the influence of Ministers.[8]

Here we find the main theme of the present chapter. How can we arrive at the best possible compromise between liberty and authority—between Parliament and Government—which Lord Salisbury described as 'the basis of ordered freedom'?[9] The problem is difficult and delicate, but not insuperable: there is, as Crick points out, no necessary contradiction between desiring both a strong Executive and a strong, efficient Commons.[10] The question is too complex, however, to be dealt with in a single, tidy chapter; related matters such as the influence of the Party system, the question of Private Members' time in the House, and proposals for an extended system of Committees are discussed more fully elsewhere. Moreover, the internal workings of the Civil Service proper are not considered here, unless directly involved in some specific suggestion for parliamentary reform. The present chapter is thus concerned primarily with the structure and responsibilities of the Cabinet, regarded as the link between Parliament and the Executive; with the Cabinet's influence on the duties and effectiveness of the ordinary Member of Parliament; and with the questions of Parliament's control over delegated legislation and nationalized industries.

(b) THE OFFICE OF PRIME MINISTER[11]

The whole *modus operandi* of the Cabinet depends very largely on the ability and personality of the Prime Minister, whose position, once elected, is one of great authority. Considerable attention has been paid in recent times to the way in which the power of the Prime Minister has increased at the expense of that of the Cabinet. Richard Crossman, who dates the change from the wartime premiership of Winston Churchill, argues that the Prime Minister has now replaced the Cabinet as—in Bagehot's phrase—'the hyphen which joins, the buckle which fastens, the legislative part of the State to the executive part'.[12] In this he follows J. P. Mackintosh whose book stresses the primacy of today's Prime Minister.[13] Crick, too, takes issue with Morley's classical description of the Prime Minister as 'the keystone of the Cabinet arch'; he is, he says, 'not merely the arch, but the foundation stone and the cement for all the other stones as well. . . . As long as the Prime Minister carries with him the conviction of his party that he will get them victory again, his power remains almost absolute.'[14] Crick also draws attention to the strength of a modern Prime Minister's powers of patronage—'beyond the wildest dreams . . . of a Walpole or a Newcastle', he says.[15]

Suggesting (in 1960) that the best name for our constitution is 'elective monarchy', R. W. K. Hinton has explained: 'Government by a single person is monarchy, and it is because the Prime Minister is the real ruler that I think our constitution ought to be called a monarchy. We recognise this practice when we vote.'[16] As Laski remarked, little short of carefully organized revolt can shake his position within or without the Cabinet, and the Professor goes on to point out that a problem of real constitutional significance is involved in this growth of the Prime Minister's powers: 'Great authority may . . . accrue to one, the greatness of whose leadership may fairly be regarded as doubtful'.[17] That Laski is thinking in particular of Neville Chamberlain is quite clear from what follows: his fears are that the mistakes of an authoritative Premier may leave Parliament, and even the Cabinet, with nothing better than a chance of *ex post facto* control which (as in the Munich crisis) could come too late.[18]

The seriousness of the whole question of the power of the Prime

Minister in Parliament is heightened, in the view of many, by the method of his appointment: 'It is still the Monarch who selects the individual who is likely to make the most effective Prime Minister, and that individual who acts on his own responsible judgement of the situation.'[19] Thus the two institutions of Government (the Prime Minister and the Cabinet he selects) and of Parliament are to some extent at least separate, independent entities —each starting from separate historical origins and each perpetuating itself by its own methods.[20] Since the Cabinet remains in essence a 'Committee of the party in power', one may fairly say that this question of the Prime Minister's appointment attracts serious criticism only when that same party has no obvious leader to assume the mantle of supreme authority. An example occurred on the resignation of Sir Anthony Eden. Would his successor be Mr. Harold Macmillan or Mr. R. A. Butler? Speculation was widespread, but the responsibility of making the final choice rested not with the people or Parliament, or even with the Conservative Party, but with the Queen. The exercise of the royal prerogative at this juncture aroused much comment—was it asking too much of Her Majesty, at a comparatively young age, to select a Prime Minister who would then choose his own Cabinet?[21] There was the added risk that on such occasions the Sovereign might become involved in party politics.[22]

The problem, as summarized above, is twofold: is it desirable to limit the Prime Minister's authority, and is his method of appointment sufficiently democratic? To begin with the latter question, one may say that there have been more criticisms than constructive proposals for reform.[23] Referring to the Australian system of choice by the party caucus, Laski observes that such a method does not always make for that mutual confidence between a Premier and his back-benchers which the British system does.[24] Laski means that the Sovereign normally chooses the man which the party in power has itself singled out as its leader. But since this leader is not always an obvious choice (as has been seen above), the Professor's defence of the British method of appointment is not totally waterproof. He also mentioned 'the French system (in and before 1950) of continuous, though short-lived, coalitions in which each group insists to the Prime Minister both upon his choice of certain men, and, hardly less, of the places they must occupy . . .'[25]; and concluded 'that that profoundly highly influences the tendency of a French Cabinet to move towards dissolution upon the day the Chamber has given to it its first vote of confidence'.[26] In 1957, the Labour Party outlined the procedure it wished to see adopted if a Labour Premier were to be appointed under similar conditions. It declared that the Monarch should not make the appointment until a new leader had been elected by the Parliamentary Labour Party.[27] This and the recent changes made by the Conservative Party mean that there is now no question of leaving the real choice in the hands of the Monarch.[27]

No wholly acceptable alternative to the present method of nominating the Prime Minister has been discovered to date, however. Those who point out its dangers, yet favour its retention, rely on the ultimate safeguards of public opinion and the need for party unity as means of ousting a man whose appointment proves to be a mistake. In their recent factual survey of the contemporary powers of a British Prime Minister, Menhennet and Palmer (*Parliament in Perspective*, pp. 62–5) point out that 'party' can not only bring about a Premier's downfall, it also circumscribes the exercise of his unique powers: 'No Premier is entirely free in forming an administration: while a primary consideration will be the ability of his colleagues, the Prime Minister will also be careful to balance the different elements in the party.' The same authors also point out that examples sometimes cited in support of the thesis that Britain today has 'Prime Ministerial' government—the decision to develop British nuclear weapons and the 1956 Anglo-French attack on Port Said, for instance—could be regarded as 'aberrations from the path of parliamentary government' but not 'the heralds of the new norm'.

As to other possible limitations on a Prime Minister's powers, once elected, Laski had two suggestions for reform, and both underlined the need for *collective* Cabinet responsibility. First, no Prime Minister should submit to the Sovereign a request for dissolution until he had obtained full Cabinet assent. In a deeply divided Cabinet, the personal power of one man to seek a dissolution might stifle honest dissent, force the resignations of able Ministers or promote intrigue and confusion in the whole Government.[28] This personal power of asking for a dissolution is also emphasized by Carter, who points out that the American President has no comparable power of dissolution over Congress.[29] Laski also disapproved of the limits a Prime Minister might set to the circulation of Cabinet papers; if the Cabinet is to remain a 'unit' then no Minister should be held responsible for an action of which he has not been fully and opportunely informed.[30]

Such reforms are not the whole answer to the problem; Laski himself, who saw (in 1950) the increasing authority of the Prime Minister as one aspect of the process of centralization taking place in all spheres of government, admitted that.[31] He added that the most effective reform to limit such powers is likely to occur in the area of the Premier's relations with his party, both inside and outside the House of Commons, and that a national crisis might well precipitate a consitutional change of this sort.[32]

There remains, however, one indirect means of limiting or modifying the Prime Minister's position—reform of the Cabinet structure as a whole.

(c) THE CABINET

As has been seen, there is no inherent contradiction between a desire for a vigilant, efficient House of Commons on the one hand, and a desire for a strong, policy-making team of Ministers on the other. Hence, suggested reforms deal not only with Parliament's control over the Executive, but also with the welfare and effectiveness of the Government's representatives. L. S. Amery, amongst many others, has asserted that the present Cabinet machinery is totally inadequate for the immensely wide, complex responsibilities now facing Ministers.[33] His principal contention is that a group of overworked departmental chiefs, absorbed in the details of their respective routines, is not a fit body to plan vital long-term policy and see that it is properly carried out. When each Minister attempts to 'father' the wishes of his own Department, the Cabinet is inevitably subject to internal friction and delay, and is unable to make collective decisions on important, supra-departmental matters.[34] Amery's suggested remedy, illustrated in the diagram overleaf, is that a definite division should be made, within the Government, between policy and administration.[35]

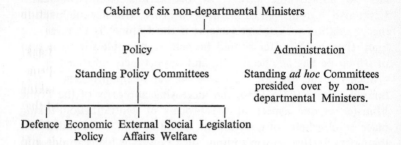

Cabinet of six non-departmental Ministers

A smaller Cabinet, as above, with its subordinate committee-system, would then be able to perform the vital work of supervision and co-ordination. A similar suggestion for a small inner Cabinet of non-departmental Ministers engaged essentially in the formation of policy was made in an unsigned article in *The Economist* on 27th October 1934,[36] and since Amery published his views, they have received considerable support.[37]

Others have pointed out the potential defects of such proposals. First, the creation of a small, formal ministerial hierarchy could easily promote jealousies and frustration within and without the Cabinet.[38] Laski, whilst agreeing that the traditional Cabinet is too large,[39] could not believe that the separation between policy and administration would be as easy as Amery suggests.[40] The latter, Laski adds, was probably influenced by an unduly roseate view of Lloyd George's Cabinet in 1916–19: what is best in times of war is not always most suitable for peace.[41] A more serious objection to Amery's proposals is that a 'Policy Minister' might not be able to control a 'subordinate' Minister having all the status and executive power of his Department behind him.[42] Moreover, to conceive of 'policy meetings' in the absence of departmental chiefs is unrealistic; discussion of general principles must involve consideration of detail, and Amery's Cabinet would not have such details at its finger-tips.[43] Finally, would a select group of backroom boys brooding over future policy be able to afford effective, informed political leadership to the Party in power, to the House of Commons, and to the country as a whole? Lord Morrison does not believe it could.[44] He observes that Amery, in his enthusiasm, has carried his idea too far, and adds that it is possible both to avoid the very large Cabinet[45] and to use non-departmental Ministers to secure a measure of co-ordination and policy planning without restricting the Cabinet to six super-Ministers.

In the Romanes Lecture of 1946, Sir John Anderson (later Lord Waverley) also brought forward the criticism that supervising Ministers without portfolio were not a practical proposition, since their existence would clash with the accepted parliamentary responsibilities of departmental chiefs.[46] Instead, Sir John suggested a careful development of the system of Cabinet Committees; there would be groups to consider Defence, Economic Policy, Foreign Relations, Social Welfare, Establishment Affairs and Legislation, special attention being given to general policy. Joint meetings between two or more of these groups would contribute to co-ordination of policy. A similar suggestion was made by a committee of Conservatives in the same year, in a publication called 'Some Proposals for Constitutional Reform'. For Economic Policy, for instance, the Chancellor of the Exchequer should preside over a Standing Committee of Ministers, which would supervise economic research, report regularly to the Cabinet on trade, agriculture, etc., and also to Parliament. Sub-Committees would exist for particular economic problems, and Civil Servants, as well as outside representatives of industry, would participate in these.[47] These suggestions aim at extending and elaborating, rather than at innovating: since, to a certain extent, the system of Cabinet Committees has been realized already. Lord Morrison has given a first-hand account of their functioning under the Labour Government of 1945–50.[48] He concludes that they saved the Cabinet a great amount of work, without impairing the doctrine of ultimate collective Cabinet responsibility. With a few exceptions,[49] the existence of these Committees was kept secret during the Labour Government's period of office—a policy which Anderson himself had advocated.

Agreeing with Anderson's contention that supervising Ministers are not a practical proposition, Lord Morrison has elaborated his objections with particular reference to Winston Churchill's so-called 'Overlord' system. In October 1951, the appointment was announced of Lord Leathers as Secretary of State for the Co-ordination of Transport, Fuel and Power; simultaneously, Lord

Woolton was given supervisory authority over the Ministers of Agriculture and Food. Attlee criticized these appointments on several grounds. Above all, he raised the important constitutional issue of answerability to the House of Commons: 'Here it seems that the power of decision is left with Ministers in another place, and we here are to be faced only with departmental Ministers responsible merely for administration. I want to know this: when questions of major policy arise concerning food and agriculture and transport and fuel and power, who will answer in this House?'[50] Morrison added his objections to those of Attlee. The House faced a position, he declared, in which Ministers not in the Commons had been given public and specific responsibilities which could not but move certain responsibilities away from the departmental Ministers concerned. There could be no fair comparison between these 'Overlords' and the system of Cabinet Committees used by the Labour Government—these latter (secret) Committees were the domestic concern of the party in power, and there was no question of the Chairman of such Committees being answerable to the Commons.[51] The 'Overlord' system eventually came to an end in September 1953, with the resignation of Lord Leathers. There had been sharp disagreement between supporters and opponents of the idea, and it must be admitted that neither side was able to convince the other as to its notion of the precise responsibilities of the 'Overlords'.

Morrison has drawn the important distinction between a 'supervising' and a 'co-ordinating' Minister. Whereas his feeling is that the former imperils an essential of the constitution—namely, a departmental Minister's accountability to Parliament—he does concede that the volume and complexity of Cabinet business make out a strong case for a sprinkling of senior 'co-ordinating' Ministers. The latter normally work as Chairmen of Cabinet Committees; they can advise, consult, urge and persuade; they can view the policy of a single Department against the broader background of the several other Departments which they seek to co-ordinate. But a co-ordinator 'is a helpful colleague and not a master'—there is no question of his impairing the responsibility to Parliament of the individual political heads of Departments.[52] The idea of co-ordination within the Cabinet is not new. In 1937, Attlee had argued in favour of non-departmental appointments which would facilitate both Cabinet cohesion and policy-planning.[53] When he became Prime Minister, he sought to secure 'supervision without blurring the responsibility of departmental Ministers',[54] and two senior Ministers—Morrison and Arthur Greenwood—became Cabinet co-ordinators.[55]

A full exposition of the way in which the Cabinet operates has recently been made by Dr. Mackintosh. He believes it is misleading to describe British Government today as Cabinet Government. Today the country is governed by a Prime Minister who leads, co-ordinates and maintains a series of ministers all of whom are advised and backed by the Civil Service. The Cabinet holds the central position because most decisions pass through it or are reported to it. The use made of the Cabinet, and the power it possesses, depend on the Prime Minister. The Government may be pictured as a cone with the Prime Minister at its apex, and widening rings of senior ministers, Cabinet, Cabinet Committees, non-Cabinet ministers, and departments below. Governments, he avers, are restrained not so much by Parliament or by the Opposition as by their own desire to keep in step with public opinion and to increase their strength. This has come about because of the widespread desire in the country for strong leadership; it has come about, in other words, because the country wants it.[56] Yet, as Richard Crossman points out, the British people retains the right to throw off its deferential attitude and reshape the political system. It could, if it so wished, rapidly reinstate the House of Commons as a popular check on the executive.[57]

A miscellany of other proposed Cabinet reforms may be mentioned briefly here. Advancing the familiar thesis that a Minister can attend either to his Cabinet papers or to his Department, but not to both, Desmond Donnelly has suggested that day-to-day control of the Departments should be vested in the Parliamentary Secretaries, who would also answer most Questions in the House. Ministers would deal with major departmental policies, but their principal concern would be the Cabinet.[58] Apart from relieving an overworked Minister, this scheme would clearly add to the status of the Parliamentary Secretary—which Ellen Wilkinson, in a profoundly melancholy moment, described as 'less than the dust'. Lord Mansfield proposed in July 1938 that Ministers should be able to address the House to which they did not belong. They could thus answer attacks made on them in 'another place'; good Ministers would never have to resign on receiving a peerage; it would be easier for the Premier himself to be a peer. Lord Crewe, however, felt that such an innovation would increase a Minister's burdens and reduce still further the status of Parliamentary Secretaries. An added complication would stem from the differences in practice and procedure between the two Houses. Lord Londonderry also listed practical obstacles in the way of this reform, whilst Lord Onslow felt that peers might not attend in the Lords if their hopes of office were diminished in this fashion.[59] The idea nevertheless came to the fore again following the appointment in July 1960 of a peer (Lord Home) to the office of Foreign Secretary.

Then there is the suggestion that there should be a special Ministry of Research, the work of which would be divorced from the responsibilities of actual administrative routine. The Haldane Committee[60] favoured such a Ministry. But both Amery and Laski rejected this proposal, the latter in particular maintaining that research which is to affect policy must be controlled by those who are directing policy. Research undertaken in an academic fashion would not have that sense of reality vital to its success.[61] Laski similarly points out that proper contact between research and the realities of everyday political administration is absent from the idea of an Economic General Staff, of which Lord Beveridge was an enthusiastic advocate. As a practical illustration of this potential defect, Laski claims that much of the value of the 'Beveridge' Report on Social Insurance and Allied Services came from its principal author's previous practical experience as an official at the Ministry of Labour.[62] Finally, we have Philip Goodhart's antidote for front-bench fatigue: the ministerial sabbatical year. A number of Ministers and/or Parliamentary Secretaries should be 'rested' every year, and have the opportunity of refreshing mind and body —for further front-bench exertions on their return—in the Caribbean, Paris or elsewhere. An innovation of this sort would also make it possible for the Premier to 'spread the chance of promotion and so reduce feelings of frustration below the gangway'.[63]

To sum up, it is clear that supporters of the scheme for a very small supervisory peace-time Cabinet of 'Policy Ministers' are outnumbered by their critics. The latter point out in particular that policy and departmental administration are in practice inseparable, and that the answerability to Parliament of heads of Departments might well be confused if there were 'super-Ministers' above them. But there is almost general agreement that present-day Cabinets tend to be too large. The authors of the 1918 'Machinery of Government' Report advocated a Cabinet membership of from ten to twelve.[64] Muir thought ten an ideal number for general efficiency and collective responsibility.[65] Laski set the limit at fifteen, the Secretary of State for Scotland and the Lord Chancellor being excluded under his scheme.[66] A Cabinet of 'moderate size, say sixteen to eighteen' seemed to Morrison to be the best solution.[67] (In January 1967 Mr. Harold Wilson reduced the size of his Cabinet from twenty-three to twenty-one.)

There is also substantial support for a good measure of general policy-planning and 'co-ordination', to be effected by senior Ministers within the Cabinet and by the use of Cabinet Committees, rather than by 'Overlords'. It could be argued that recent developments within the Labour Cabinet—in the fields of Economic Affairs, Commonwealth Affairs and Defence—are a move in this direction.

One suspects that three major requirements, or aims, motivate the bulk of these proposals. The first is to enhance the collective responsibility of the Cabinet on all important questions of policy, in order that such great decisions should not be made wholly on the initiative of the Prime Minister, or of a small caucus within the Cabinet itself. As Sir David Lindsay Keir puts it, genuine Cabinet solidarity ensures that the administrative business of the nation is co-ordinated by a unanimous collective will.[68] The second aim is intimately related to the first. Since the Cabinet is the link between a permanent Executive and Parliament, it is vital that Members should themselves know that the Cabinet is genuinely 'collectively responsible' for major items of policy. Only if this is so can effective control on behalf of the people become a reality. It is particularly important that the Cabinet should be regarded as a unit when a vote of confidence is taken—since each Cabinet Minister is staking his position, in theory at least, on the result.[69] The third, and most obvious, point of proposed Cabinet reorganization is the increased efficiency of the Cabinet itself. This last objective is not incompatible with the other two: as has been said already, there is no automatic contradiction between desiring both a strong, efficient Executive and a keen, effectively critical Parliament.

Up to now, the question of the relationship between Parliament and the Executive has been considered from the viewpoint of the Cabinet and its head, the Prime Minister. In addition, of course, there have been proposals aimed at effecting a better balance between Parliament and the Executive by increasing the powers of the ordinary M.P. over the Cabinet. The majority of these suggestions concern the opportunities afforded the private Member of raising grievances and of initiating legislation in the House: these are discussed in the chapters devoted to Procedure and to the Party System respectively. There remain to be considered here three outstanding problems. To what extent has the growth of delegated legislation impaired the prestige and effectiveness of Parliament? Should Parliament's control over nationalized undertakings be extended and/or tightened? And finally, what is the place in our constitutional set-up for a British 'Ombudsman'?

(d) DELEGATED LEGISLATION

A subject on which Parliament and the Executive can cross swords is Delegated Legislation—the granting by Parliament of some of its legislative powers, with safeguards, to Ministers. The principle of delegated legislation is one that is attacked on two fronts; first, that Parliament's sovereignty over the legislative machine is gainsaid; secondly, that the setting-up of administrative tribunals can prove to be a derogation of the Rule of Law. This second principle carries us rather far from our subject of Parliamentary (as opposed to Law) Reform; but the first principle is in the heart of the subject. Lord Hewart's *The New Despotism* (1928) struck out at the abuses that had grown up; the Donoughmore Committee on Ministers' Powers was set up to consider them, and to report what safeguards were necessary to secure the principles of the sovereignty of Parliament and the supremacy of the law.[70] Their report, says Sir Cecil Carr, was comforting.[71] 'The country was told that delegated legislation was valuable and indeed inevitable. The Committee suggested that, with reasonable vigilance and proper precautions, we had nothing to fear. . . .'

The Committee made a number of detailed recommendations, but two years later complaint was being made in the House that effect had not been given to them.[72] In 1937, although one Member could say: 'The particular clauses against which [*The New Despotism*] was written ... are finding their way less and less into modern statutes'[73], another said: 'I believe that almost every week in this House the Executive is usurping the function of Parliament.'[74] In 1944, it was still being said that it was time to enforce the Donoughmore proposals.[75]

Meanwhile, the problem had increased in size; in 1950, about three times as many Instruments of general—as opposed to local—applicability were made as in pre-1931 (during the war, the number had reached nearly five times as many).[76]

Needless to say, this increased use of delegated powers has not lacked supporters. Ponsonby[77] and Dalton[78] in the thirties, Stewart in the fifties, Fellowes and the Study of Parliament Group in the sixties,[79] for example, have all gone on record as thinking that more, and not less, legislation should be delegated. Acts of Parliament should, they say, state broad general principles; the details should be left to the Minister to work out.

As an answer to its critics, in 1943 the House of Commons set up—in accordance with one of the Donoughmore Committee's recommendations—a Select Committee which scrutinizes every Instrument laid before the House on which the House may or must move a resolution. The Committee draws the attention of the House to any Instrument that appears to make unusual or unexpected use of the power conferred by the parent statute. Carr says of this Committee that '... it acts with independence and without partisanship; it can do so because it is debarred from reporting on matters of policy or merits; it is entirely uninfluenced by the Executive, and it has established the interesting convention that its chairman must be a member of the Opposition'. Its work, however, he says, is imperfectly geared to the machinery of parliamentary control; Members table their motions for annulling Instruments long before the Committee has reported on them, and the reasons for their challenge will probably be reasons which the Committee was debarred from considering.[80] The most important result of setting up this Committee, said H. W. R. Wade, was that it gave government departments a lively consciousness that critical eyes were kept upon them. He thought it the one successful enterprise which had resulted from the tireless efforts of reformers to impose discipline on 'this unruly activity'.[81]

The setting-up of this Committee might have been a modest step forward, but various powerful indictments of the whole system continued to appear. The works of Sir Carleton Allen,[82] W. A. Robson,[83] G. W. Keeton (who was able to cite the case of Crichel Down),[84] and Carr,[85] among others, have framed the case. Curtis cites the following among their main criticisms:[86]

> (i) Delegated legislation is sometimes made on matters of principle, and may therefore result in an evasion of parliamentary statute.
> (ii) Taxing power is occasionally delegated.
> (iii) There has been some retrospective legislation.
> (iv) Sub-delegation is always dangerous.
> (v) The courts of law are by-passed.
> (vi) The legislation is not always well-publicized, so that it is possible to offend against it in ignorance.
> (vii) Parliamentary control is unsatisfactory.

As far as this last complaint is concerned, various amelioratives have been put forward. Thus, Campion suggested to the Select Committee on Procedure in 1946 that the Statutory Instruments Committee should be empowered to report on the *merits* of Instruments, and to inquire into grievances out of those Instruments actually in operation.[87] The Committee agreed that this scheme 'would go some way to supplement the inadequate and unsatisfactory opportunities which the House . . . possesses for exercising . . . control', but considered it was beyond the scope of their investigation, and urged that a later Committee should be set up to consider the specific matter.[88] The Study of Parliament Group later suggested a Select Committee to look at the merits of all instruments requiring an affirmative resolution of the House, and such of those requiring a negative resolution as might be referred to it by the House.[89]

Those who support the idea of 'departmental' Committees— Committees, that is, which will specialize in the work of a particular Ministry, and can act as a link between the House and the Department—sometimes urge that these Committees will be able to supervise the delegated legislation which emanates from that department.[90] Pollard, for instance, suggested that, if the departmental Committees do not agree on the need for a particular Instrument, then it should be left to the House to affirm or reject it.[91] It is interesting in this context to note that the Select Committee on Procedure in 1957 recommended that, provided certain safeguards were allowed, debates on affirmative resolutions relating exclusively to Scotland should take place in the Scottish Standing Committee.[92]

A Select Committee was set up by the House of Commons in 1952 to cover all this field of delegated legislation; in so doing they resurrected and reconsidered those of the Donoughmore proposals which had not yet been brought into force. Principal among these was the suggestion that each House of Parliament should set up a sessional Committee to examine every bill for the purpose of drawing attention to any unusual or novel proposal in it to delegate legislative authority.[93] Such a Committee, was, said Carr, 'potentially more valuable' than the other Scrutiny Committee which had been set up;[94] but the 1952 Committee disagreed with the idea, preferring to rely on the vigilance of private members.

Among the more important of the other questions which members of this Select Committee asked themselves, in seeking to improve the House's control over delegated legislation, were:

    (i) Should the Government issue with each bill a memorandum explaining what sort of powers are to be delegated by it?

  (ii) Should there be a Committee of the House to consider all Statutory Instruments, and separate the important ones from the less important?

 (iii) Should Statutory Instruments be amendable?

 (iv) Could the resolutions relating to Statutory Instruments be taken in a Committee, rather than in the House?

  (v) Should a Minister have to explain his proposals to a Committee before laying his Instruments?

 (vi) Should the House meet at special times—say, in the morning—to debate prayers for annulling Statutory Instruments?

147

These questions span most of the proposals still current for the better controlling by Parliament of delegated legislation; the Committee, with great consistency, answered each one in the negative.[95]

One proposal they did make, and which the House adopted, was that debates on prayers to annul Instruments should be concluded at a definite hour. This prevented such debates from continuing indefinitely into the night, and made sure they would be conducted on the merits of the motion, rather than as a weapon of obstruction. But this was a change more of convenience than of principle.

The main charge remains. Committees of inquiry may continue to find that the sovereignty of Parliament over delegated legislation is secure; but if Parliament is content to divest itself of its powers, and give to the Executive the right to make Orders in Council under unlimited statutory powers, is not the trouble that Parliament is all too sovereign? This was the question that Carr, with his vast experience of the matter, posed.[96] He gave his own answer thus:

> With the intensification of party politics, parliamentary control has ... in effect disappeared; when ... the Government side has secured the enactment of the parent statute, the Opposition side has little hope of success in moving a motion for the annulment of the resultant Statutory Instrument. These are issues of political partisanship, not of political theory. Only the Opposition will be challenging the Executive, and the Executive has the means and the will to crush the challenge.[97]

(e) PARLIAMENTARY CONTROL OVER NATIONALIZED INDUSTRIES

In the earliest of the nationalized undertakings—such as the Post Office, the Royal Ordnance factories, and the state management of public houses in Carlisle—responsibility and powers were vested wholly in the Minister for the Department involved. Accordingly he was answerable in Parliament for everything to do with those undertakings, and parliamentary control could be said to be total.

In the inter-war years, however, a new type of nationalized

148

undertaking came into being—the public corporation; early examples were the B.B.C., the London Passenger Transport Board and the Central Electricity Board. In these cases, governmental control was indirect.

Much of the political argument on the subject in the thirties was directed to the point of whether subsequent undertakings should be controlled by a Minister or a Board; with the nationalization of the transport and power industries after 1945—and the acceptance of the public corporation as the type to be employed[98] —much of this argument becomes only of academic interest. Today's problem is a post-war one.

The post-war nationalization Acts place a number of duties upon the Minister—and on these points, of course, the Minister is answerable to Parliament; these duties are noticeably more extensive than those of Ministers in respect of the pre-war Corporations.[99] The pattern of these Acts is to give the Minister the responsibility for nominating members of the Board; the power of issuing general directions to the Board on matters affecting the national interest; and certain wide controls over the Board's finances.[100] To this extent, parliamentary control could be openly exercised; but beyond it, as one of the chief architects of nationalization pointed out, '. . . the precise character of the public accountability of these Boards [had] to be worked out in the light of experience'.[101]

This 'working out' has occasioned much thinking, both inside and outside Parliament. In 1950, Morrison listed six ways in which the House of Commons could exercise control over the Boards;[102] but his list was, said Goodhart, 'more formidable in length than in content',[103] and the House appeared to believe that, as things were, it was not able to exercise effective control.

The first battle that the House had to fight was over its right to ask Parliamentary Questions. If the Minister has no direct responsibility for a matter, he cannot be questioned on the point: and thus many Questions on nationalized industries had to be refused by the Table. The Speaker, however, allowed a relaxation of the rules to be made. Questions on nationalized industries which he deemed to be of sufficient public importance would in future be allowed. The Minister could still, theoretically, refuse to answer the Question, but the right of asking it was formally admitted.[104]

While this might have been a palliative, it was hardly a cure for the House's complaint. The next step was to set up a Select Committee to enquire into the relationship between the House and the industries, and this occurred in 1951. Its first report dealt with Questions and it concurred in the view that 'Questions on matters of detail in the Nationalized Industries are inappropriate'.[105] This point is of particular significance for, as a paper published by the Acton Society Trust has pointed out, Members, both in Questions they attempt to ask and the speeches they make, are preoccupied with local problems of management as opposed to overall efficiency.[106]

It should be added, on the subject of Questions, that the Boards make special provision for the answering of the letters sent to them by individual members. The Chairman of one Board told the Select Committee that his average correspondence with Members was about 1,700 letters a year;[107] Morrison suggested that these letters gave 'fuller and perhaps more satisfactory information than could be condensed into a parliamentary answer'.[108] In his view (writing in 1954), the controversy about the eligibility of Parliamentary Questions had tended to diminish.[109] But with the decision of the House in 1958 that letters from M.P.s, forwarded to the Boards by the Minister, had only a qualified privilege, there were renewed demands for wider facilities for asking parliamentary questions.[110] In 1960, the Leader of the House promised that Ministers would in general view more broadly their responsibility for answering Questions on the nationalized industries; *The Times* thought this indicated that some sensible progress was being made.[111] A further easement, of perhaps greater significance, was made in July 1963; under this, Questions seeking statistical information about the nationalized industries were in future to be allowed.[112]

In 1950 it was still being suggested that the Minister's control over the industries should become closer, thereby allowing Parliament the right of asking a greater area of Questions. Thus, Austen Albu said he thought the Minister himself should actually be Chairman of the Boards which he appoints.[113] But argument tended then to move on to different ground. If these Boards were not to be departmentally controlled, what other form of parliamentary control should be tried? Curtis suggests there were two possibilities open.[114] First, a Committee of Inquiry could be set up—perhaps on the lines of a Royal Commission—periodically; or secondly, the House could set up a Select Committee to act as some sort of link. The former idea was urged by Morrison.[115] The inquiries—he suggested they should take place every seven years—would be on the lines of those held into the affairs of the B.B.C. before its Charter is renewed every ten years. But, in the same debate, the alternative—of setting up a Select Committee of the House—was urged by Molson[116] and supported by Members from both sides of the House. Molson's idea was that the Committee should report to the House from time to time, and that the House's annual debates on the nationalized industries should be founded on those reports.

The Select Committee which the House set up in 1951 to advise it on its future relationship with the industries decided, in their Second Report, that there was a case for a permanent Select Committee to act along the lines that Molson had suggested.[117] The Committee should, it thought, have the help of an officer of the calibre of the Comptroller and Auditor-General, at least one accountant, and any other specialized staff it found necessary.

When this Committee was duly set up in 1955, however, it was not given the use of any special staff, and its terms of reference were restricted to exclude matters of ministerial policy, as well as matters of day-to-day administration within the industry.[118] These terms of reference the Committee found altogether too restrictive, and they were able to make no progress.[119] Accordingly, when a new Committee was set up in 1956, its field of activity was left very general. However, by a piece of typical House of Commons practice, the Committee were given to understand that, while the former restrictions were not specified, the House hoped the Committee would keep off those subjects; and it was no surprise when the Committee, in one of their first reports, said: 'We have tried not to become involved as critics with the day-to-day administration of the Board on the one hand, and with matters of Government policy on the other.'[120]

The setting up of a Select Committee was accompanied by a number of gloomy forebodings. *The Times*, seeing the Committee as the creature of Parliament's distrust of the nationalized undertakings, thought that, under the new arrangement, long-range vigilance and wise forbearance would both wither.[121] The *Observer* 'could not see how (the Committee's) existence would appreciably alter the relations between Parliament and the Boards'.[122]

A vigorous critic of nationalization, R. Kelf-Cohen,[123] questioned the whole principle that the industries, as statutory bodies, could be accountable to Parliament at all. He quoted a former head of the B.B.C., Lord Reith, as saying that the Select Committee might end by controlling the industry. The plain simple fact is that Parliament could not cope with the problem unless the industries were converted into Departments of State; and if that happened, parliamentary business would be hopelessly overloaded.

However, the first Reports of the Select Committee brought about a change of heart, *The Times*, to some extent, retracting its earlier prognostications.[124] Kelf-Cohen, on the evidence of one Report for the Committee, said it was too early to judge the value of their work. They could only justify their existence if they provided a body of informed opinion in the House; to do so, they would have to work very hard. In its debates on the Reports, the House itself appeared to welcome them;[125] whilst one Member suggested that two Select Committees on the Nationalized Industries were needed—one dealing with transport, and the other with fuel and power.[126] The Committee's subsequent Reports continued to win golden opinions. 'Ostensibly reporting on the latest annual reports and accounts of the particular industry in question, it has managed to produce some of the most distinguished government reports of this century', wrote an academic observer[127]; and the Procedure Committee, in recommending a scheme of specialist Committees, hoped for no more than that they should take the Nationalized Industries Committee as their example.[128]

A general criticism of a Committee of this kind is that its members are 'amateurs, and experience has shown that a Parliamentary Committee cannot readily find out much more about a complex enterprise than its managers want to reveal'.[129] The Committee, it will be remembered, does not have the use of the technical staff which was recommended for it. That it may have been in need of such a staff can be inferred from one of its Reports, which says: 'In much of the enquiry, it was a case of laymen hearing technical evidence from one quarter only. Your Committee have been conscious of the absence of a yardstick by which to judge the performance of the Board.'[130]

In a Special Report,[131] the Committee considered the various kinds of specialized assistance which might make their work more effective. They had in mind no change in their general method of working, and they insisted that any special staff should be servants of Parliament, and not of the Executive. They recognized, furthermore, that they were on the edge of suggesting an innovation in the traditional way in which Select Committees have worked. After setting out the pros and cons of a number of different proposals, they left it to the House to decide whether the staff of the House should be augmented to include someone to offer them technical advice, or whether they should be allowed to call in an 'assessor', an expert adviser who would act in a special intimacy with the Committee.

The trumpet had given an uncertain sound; the House had no clear indication of what to do. The 1958/9 Special Report was not debated. After an interval, the Committee was set up again in the new Parliament, with the same terms of reference, and without the mention of any special assistance. Since then, however, the new Committee has been assisted by two Clerks, and not one as hitherto. His long study of the matter led Coombes to the conclusion that the Committee had no need of special expert assistance.[132]

A different proposal for breaking through the technical barrier and assessing the efficiency of a nationalized industry had been made by Morrison. He had been impressed by the work done by good industrial consultants, and suggested that the Boards should collectively create an industrial efficiency unit of their own, which would be available to investigate the troubles of any of them; it would report to the Board concerned. This idea which he put forward, when in office, to the nationalized Boards, did not meet with their approval. It was, they thought, a reflection on their ability and efficiency, and the idea was dropped.[133] Goodhart pointed out a deficiency in the idea—it did not make clear whether or not the recommendations of the unit should be binding on the Boards.[134] Advice might be valuable, but it was no substitute for dynamic and efficient management.

Writing in 1960, Professor Hanson thought that the existing relationship between Minister, Board and Parliament was unsatisfactory. The Select Committee had improved the situation, but not enough to cure the fundamental malaise. He reported a growing belief that the industries should, like the Post Office at that time,[135] return to a departmental form of administration. There would however have to be a new form of departmental control worked out, since the normal departmental practices would be fatal for them.

He turned to consider if there was not a halfway house between the Corporations as they then existed and government departments —a different halfway house from the unsatisfactory one in which the industries then found themselves. It was, he argued, unnecessary to protect the industries from political interference when they were doing well, and so impossible to protect them when they were doing badly. He argued that it should be possible to preserve the form and spirit of the public corporation and yet hold the industry entirely responsible to its Minister, thus abolishing the equivocal aspects of the present Board-Minister-Parliament relationship.

For this to work, what was needed was what the Webbs called 'Measurement and Publicity'. The Committee was very useful as a method of conveying information, but as a tool for investigating the industries it was less satisfactory. Sooner or later, we should have to establish some definite organ of measurement, similar to the French '*Commission de Verification*', a specific agency, independent of Ministry, Board and Parliament, exclusively devoted to producing high-quality information and the provision of reasoned advice.[136]

After making a detailed study of the Reports and Accounts which the nationalized industries are statutorily required to lay before Parliament, Raymond Nottage suggested in 1957 that the Select Committee on Nationalized Industries should see that a code of conventions is laid down, which would make for brevity and effectiveness in those Reports. This could lead to a greatly improved relationship between Parliament and the industries.[137]

This problem of the accountability of the nationalized industries, perhaps as much as any other discussed here, is still in flux; much of the recent writing on the subject has already been overtaken by events. Thus, Kelf-Cohen (writing in 1958) said that the persuasive and far-reaching influence of Ministers, acting outside their statutory powers, on the decision of the Board, was something Parliament hardly seemed to have noticed;[138] however, this is a subject of which, as a result of the reports of the Select Committee, Parliament is now very much aware. There is nevertheless essentially a paradox at the heart of the matter; how can you have a business free to fight its competitors in the commercial world, yet expected to behave as a public service under the control of a Minister answerable to Parliament? There is a chasm of difference between the politician saying 'We are trying to get the best of both worlds',[139] and the Coal Board's former Chairman referring to 'this kind of half world in which we live'.[140]

Recent proposals for a closer watch over the expenditure on nationalized industries have been mentioned above.[141] The emphatic way in which these proposals were put forward might seem to show that 'nationalization' is still sometimes treated very much as a political issue in the House.

Some progress is being made. It would have been unthinkable, during the nationalization debates of 1946/50, to suggest that ten years later a Select Committee would be able to publish reports, objectively assessing the performance of nationalized Boards, and showing precious few differences of opinion between the stoutest propounders of each party's views. It might be that we are approaching the time when a suggestion such as Morrison's efficiency unit could be considered, without its being taken automatically to be a reflection on the Board's ability. So far, the Select Committee has conceived its function to be 'to acquaint the House with the activities and problems of the nationalized industries, to question those industries on the matters about which Members are most perplexed, and to report to the House with such comments as are appropriate'.[142] The House would then be sufficiently well-informed to take objective decisions. But if it is true, as Goodhart says,[143] that 'it is more in the threat of what it may do than in what it actually does, that the force of Parliamentary control lies', it may be that in the existence of a Select Committee with wide general terms of reference, capable of summoning before it any of the Boards' members which it thinks fit, capable of sending for any information it requires, the House has now got the instrument it needs.

(f) A BRITISH OMBUDSMAN

Although there was a Justitieombudsman in Sweden as early as 1809, the Ombudsman who has recently attracted considerable attention is Professor Stephan Hurwitz of Denmark. The latter's office was created in 1953 under Section 55 of his country's new constitution, and Professor Hurwitz has himself written an account of his duties which aroused some interest in this country.[144] He further visited Britain in the spring of 1960, and broadcast on the subject. Donald Johnson, a former M.P. who has pleaded eloquently for a British Ombudsman, describes the Professor's functions thus: 'A Sir Andrew Clark in permanent session, inquiring and extracting papers, and commenting publicly upon the defects in the whole range of public administration—surprisingly, this is not far from what is happening in Denmark.'[145] The Ombudsman is not a Member of the Folketing—the essential point of his existence being that he is an impartial observer, or investigator, on behalf of the legislature.

The need for such an independent, high-ranking official in Britain was debated with mounting interest in the 1960s. Professor Wade has pointed out that parliamentary devices (such as Questions and Adjournment Motions) are a safety valve, not a control mechanism of the administrative system. It is thus unrealistic to say that the Minister is always accountable for what is done in his department; some quite different organization is needed, and some countries have created an Ombudsman with this in mind.[146] A report by Justice, for which Sir John Whyatt had been Director of Research, was published in 1961 and advocated the establishment of an Ombudsman in Britain;[147] such a post was established in New Zealand in the same year. Although the Whyatt proposal was rejected by the Government of the day,[148] debate on it continued; an article in *The Times* suggested that the Select Committee on Public Petitions could be adapted for the purpose,[149] an article in the *Economist* argued for a new and formal system of administrative law based on the French *conseil d'état*, rather than an Ombudsman.[150] In the event, the new Labour government decided to create a Parliamentary Commissioner who would be an officer of Parliament empowered to pursue such cases as M.P.s referred to him.[151] A Bill to give effect to this failed to make progress in the Session

1965/6, but was reintroduced after the General Election in 1966. The first British Parliamentary Commissioner was duly named in 1966.[152] Supporters of the idea argue that such a person will go some way towards restoring the balance between Parliament and Executive—a vital need in the opinion of many whose criticisms and constructive proposals have been discussed in the present chapter.

NOTES AND REFERENCES

[1] K. C. Wheare: 'The Machinery of Government' in *Public Administration*, Vol. XXIV, pp. 75–85 (Inaugural lecture at Oxford, 16th November 1945).

[2] Jennings: *Cabinet Government*, 3rd ed., 1959.

[3] Lord Salter in *Parliament: A Survey*, Chap. V.

[4] See, for example, an article by Strachey and Joad: 'Parliamentary Reform: The New Party's Proposals', in *Political Quarterly*, Vol. II, 1931, pp. 319–36. Parliament's role is here virtually restricted to that of placing in office a Government with full powers to govern.

[5] Muir discusses the 'ineffective' control of the Executive by Parliament at length (pp. 41–80), as well as the 'dictatorship' of the Cabinet (pp. 87–106).

[6] Fabian Tract 319; p. 2.

[7] Iwi: *Laws and Flaws: Lapses of the Legislators*, 1956, p. 107.

[8] Lord Campion and others, pp. 25–6.

[9] H.L. Deb. 167, c. 360.

[10] Crick: *Reform of the Commons*, 1959, p. 2. Wedgwood Benn made the same point in a Commons debate on Accommodation: H.C. Deb. 620. 31st March 1960.

[11] Professor Byrum E. Carter's book of that name was first published in 1956. It is a long account of the subject, both from the historical and the practical points of view. Wiseman, however, rightly observes that Carter's work contains certain errors and misleading generalizations (*Parliamentary Affairs*, Vol. XII, No. 2, 1959, p. 243).

[12] Introduction to Bagehot's *The English Constitution*, p. 51.

[13] Mackintosh, p. 451.

[14] Crick, *The Reform of Parliament*, p. 36.

[15] *ibid.* p. 30. In February 1966, there were 88 M.P.s holding office and 28 Parliamentary Private Secretaries.

[16] Broadcast on the Third Programme, 6th January 1960, and published in *Parliamentary Affairs*, Vol. XIII, No. 3, 1960, pp. 297–303.

Tom Clarke, in *My Northcliffe Diary*, 1931, p. 108, tells an anecdote which, whilst clearly exaggerated and not to be taken too seriously, brings out the extent to which this personal influence can be carried: 'The other day in Red Wharf Bay, Anglesey, I was looked upon as a heathen by a Welsh newsagent when I asked for the *Daily Mail*. . . . "Nobody in these parts reads that lying rag, look you," said the man, "except a silly old man in Pentraeth, indeed. Stick you to the *Daily News* and Lloyd George". He went on to protest so much about the virtues of Lloyd George that I interposed, "But he's not God, you know". "Ah, indeed, no, you are right", was the reply," but he is young yet, look you!" '

[16] (cont.) Winston Churchill himself said: 'In any sphere of action there can be no comparison between the positions of number one and number two, three, or four. The duties and the problems of all persons other than number one are quite different and in many ways more difficult. It is always a misfortune when number two or three has to initiate a dominant plan or policy.' (Cited by Carter, pp. 331–32.)

[17] Laski, pp. 116–17.

[18] ibid. p. 119.

[19] Amery, pp. 27–8.

[20] ibid. p. 28.

[21] cf. Manchester Guardian, 11th and 12th January 1957. A similar problem faced King George V in 1923 when Bonar Law retired: see Iwi, pp. 107–9. It is of course well known that the Queen sought the advice of Sir Winston Churchill and Lord Salisbury in 1957, but the ultimate decision lay none the less with the monarch.

[22] Curtis, p. 69. However, recent changes made by the Conservative Party organisation have reduced the likelihood of the Sovereign nominating as Prime Minister someone other than a leader chosen by the party in power.

[23] For a factual summary, see Carter, pp. 42ff.

[24] Laski, p. 112.

[25] ibid. p. 112. (Laski gave this lecture in 1950, i.e. before General de Gaulle became first President of the new Republic.)

[26] ibid. pp. 112–13.

[27] Marshall & Moodie: Some Problems of the Constitution, 1959, p. 62.

[28] Laski, pp. 113–14. This view is to some extent controverted by W. G. Andrews in an article in Parliamentary Affairs (Vol. XIV, pp. 178–88). He argues that the power of dissolution cannot be used effectively as a weapon for the maintenance of party unity.

[29] Carter, pp. 335–6.

[30] Laski, p. 115.

[31] ibid. p. 119.

[32] ibid. pp. 119–20.

[33] Amery, p. 86. In his proposed remedies for these defects (see the following pages) Amery was much influenced by Lloyd George's 'War Cabinet', composed at the outset of five members.

[34] ibid. pp. 86–7.

[35] Taken from Curtis, p. 77.

[36] Vol. CXIX, pp. 765–6.

[37] e.g. Hollis: Can Parliament Survive?, p. 94; and Lord Samuel, who thought many administrative mistakes had been made because Ministers had so little opportunity for thinking ahead (H.L. Deb. 171, cs. 1087–89). He favoured a 'policy Cabinet' of 10–12 Ministers.

[38] Curtis, p. 77.

[39] Laski, p. 126.

[40] ibid. p. 130.

[41] ibid. p. 131. The same point was made in the 1918 'Machinery of Government' Report: Cd. 9230, p. 5.

[42] ibid. p. 132; Carter, p. 340; Morrison, pp. 52–3.

[43] Laski, p. 134: Carter, p. 340.

[44] Morrison, pp. 34–5.

[45] That is, a Cabinet of about 23 Members such as Mr. Neville Chamberlain's Cabinet in the spring of 1939.

[46] Published by O.U.P., 1946.

[47] *op. cit.* p. 126. The committee which made these proposals included Lord Ridley, Lady Davidson, and Mr. K. W. M. (now Sir Kenneth) Pickthorn.

[48] Morrison, pp. 16–27.

[49] No secret was made, for example, of the existence of the Defence Committee, under the chairmanship of the Prime Minister, since it was the successor of the Committee of Imperial Defence.

[50] H.C. Deb. 493, cs. 66–7.

[51] These arguments are discussed at some length in Morrison, pp. 45–54.

[52] These views are set out in detail in Morrison, pp. 53–5.

[53] In *The Labour Party in Perspective*, 1949.

[54] *As it Happened*, 1954, p. 152.

[55] *ibid.* p. 153.

[56] Mackintosh, pp. 451–2 and *passim*.

[57] Introduction to Bagehot's *The English Constitution*, p. 56.

[58] In a letter to *The Times*, 14th December 1956, p. 11.

[59] H.L. Deb. 110, cs. 579–611.

[60] Cd. 9230 (1918), p. 6, para. 14.

[61] Laski, pp. 139–40.

[62] Cmd. 6404.

[63] *Crossbow*, Vol. 4, No. 10, pp. 13–14.

[64] Cd. 9230, p. 5.

[65] Muir, p. 113. The author envisaged a 'Supreme Cabinet' of 10, together with a series of 'Sub-Cabinets' for consideration of detailed routine.

[66] Laski, p. 153.

[67] Morrison, p. 56. Stewart in *op. cit.* pp. 45–6 also favours a more restricted Cabinet.

[68] *The Constitutional History of Modern Britain since 1485*, 6th ed., Adam and Charles Black, London 1960, p. 500.

[69] In practice, as is well known, the strong Party organization in Parliament considerably reduces such Ministerial risks.

[70] Cmd. 4060 of 1932.

[71] In Lord Campion and others, p. 233.

[72] D. Foot, H.C. Deb. 295, cs. 693ff.

[73] H. Strauss, H. C. Deb. 330, c. 1264.

[74] Holdsworth: *ibid.*, c. 1279.

[75] Pollard: *How to Reform Parliament*, p. 43.

[76] Carr's statistics. Lord Campion and others, p. 241.

[77] *Contemporary Review*, Vol. CXLIII, February 1933.

[78] *Political Quarterly*, Vol. V, 1934.

[79] H.C. 303 of 1964/5, p. 133.

[80] Lord Campion and others, p. 251.

[81] *Administrative Law*, O.U.P., 1961, p. 278.

[82] *Law and Orders*, 2nd ed., 1956. (3rd ed., 1965.)

[83] *Justice and Administrative Law*, 3rd. ed., 1951.

[84] *The Passing of Parliament*, 2nd ed., 1954.

[85] Lord Campion and others, Chap. XI.

[86] Curtis, p. 108.

[87] H.C. 189 of 1945/6, p. xlv.

[88] *ibid.* p. xli.

[89] H.C. 303 of 1964/5, p. 133.

[90] See section (*a*), Chapter III.

[91] *Speed up Law Reform*, pp. 24–5.
[92] H.C. 211 of 1956/7.
[93] Cmd. 4060, pp. 67–8.
[94] Lord Campion and others, p. 251.
[95] H.C. 310 of 1952/3, p. xxiv.
[96] Lord Campion and others, p. 233.
[97] *ibid.* p. 248.
[98] See Morrison, pp. 248–9.
[99] *ibid.* p. 251.
[100] For an analysis of the various nationalization measures, see Chester, *The Nationalized Industries, A Statutory Analysis*, Allen & Unwin Ltd., 1951.
[101] Morrison, p. 251.
[102] H.C. Deb. 478, cs. 2795–814 (Debate on the Socialized Industries, 25th October 1950).
[103] In Lord Campion and others, p. 266.
[104] H.C. Deb. 451, c. 1635.
[105] H.C. 332 of 1951/2.
[106] *Nationalised Industry I—Accountability to Parliament*, Acton Society Trust, 1950.
[107] H.C. 332 of 1951/2, Q. 458.
[108] Morrison, p. 262.
[109] *ibid.* p. 261.
[110] e.g. Motion, 10th July 1958.
[111] *The Times*, 26th February 1960.
[112] H.C. Deb. 682, cs. 449–55.
[113] H.C. Deb. 478, c. 2872.
[114] Curtis, p. 123.
[115] H.C. Deb. 478, c. 2806.
[116] H.C. Deb. 478, cs. 2842–3.
[117] H.C. 235 of 1952/3.
[118] H.C. 121 of 1954/5.
[119] H.C. 120 of 1955/6.
[120] H.C. 187 of 1957/8, para. 5.
[121] *The Times*, 13th August 1953.
[122] *Observer*, 16th August 1953.
[123] *Nationalisation in Britain. The End of a Dogma*, Macmillan & Co., Ltd. 1958, Chap. 8.
[124] *The Times*, 30th November 1957.
[125] H.C. Deb. 581, cs. 103–66; 591, cs. 825–946.
[126] H.C. Deb. 617, c. 113.
[127] *The British Economy in the 1950s*, ed. G. D. N. Worswick and P. H. Ady, p. 383.
[128] H.C. 303 of 1964/5, para. 9.
[129] *Observer*, 16th August 1953.
[130] H.C. 187 of 1957/8 para. 4.
[131] H.C. 276 of 1958/9.
[132] *The Member of Parliament and the Administration*, pp. 204–11. This book gives a very good account of the history of the Nationalized Industries Committee, and explains its value as a precedent for other specialist committees.
[133] Morrison, pp. 274–5.
[134] In Lord Campion and others, p. 270.

[135] Since then, something like the opposite has happened. The industries have not been brought more closely under Ministers, but the Post Office has achieved something of the same kind of autonomy as the other nationalized industries.

[136] *Parliament and Public Ownership*, pp. 208–37.

[137] *Reporting to Parliament on the Nationalised Industries*, published by the Royal Institute of Public Administration 1957.

[138] Kelf-Cohen, pp. 161–2.

[139] Morrison, H.C. Deb. 478, c. 2799.

[140] Sir James Bowman, H.C. 304 of 1956/7, p. 128.

[141] In Chapter III, under 'Financial Procedure', section (b).

[142] H.C. 187 of 1957–8, para. 5.

[143] Lord Campion and others, p. 263.

[144] *Parliamentary Affairs*, Vol. XII, pp. 199–208.

[145] *Spectator*, No. 6832, p. 800. There were also articles in the *Observer* of 31st May 1959 and 7th June 1959 on the functions of the Ombudsman.

[146] *Administrative Law*, p. 11.

[147] *The Citizen and the Administration.*

[148] On 8th November 1962; see H.C. Deb. 666, cs. 1124–6.

[149] *The Times*, 12th December 1960.

[150] 15th August, 1964, p. 623.

[151] Cmnd. 2767 or October 1965.

[152] For a brief discussion of his powers, see Menhennet and Palmer, p. 78.

VI

Parliament and Public Opinion

(a) PARLIAMENT AND THE PEOPLE

Parliamentary government involves, if not the agreement of the governed, at least their consent; and the preservation of parliamentary institutions rests finally upon the goodwill of the people. As Gilbert Murray once said, if we are to keep the parliamentary system the people must be in a parliamentary frame of mind, must have a respect for Parliament and an interest in public affairs.[1] 'The ultimate sanction of the British Constitution', asserted Carter, 'is found in public opinion.'[2] There is no doubt of the importance of public opinion. It has two aspects: it must not only accept parliamentary institutions if they are to be maintained, it can also exercise direct influence upon the course of Government. This second aspect is of less immediate concern here: it is one of the accepted characteristics and glories of parliamentary government.[3]

It is the first aspect of public opinion—its acceptance of parliamentary forms—which more concerns us here. In this, there is little doubt that the trend of opinion over the last thirty years or so has been one of the happiest features of our public life. It is often a strange experience to read articles and books on Parliament published in the 1930s. It is typical of the period that Murray should begin the article referred to above by saying that *if* we are to keep our parliamentary institutions certain conditions must be satisfied. The sense that there was a real doubt whether we would, should or could keep our parliamentary institutions runs through many publications of the time. That it should have been so then, and that the situation should have changed since, is understandable. In the 1930s Parliament was seemingly impotent

For Notes and References see pages 177–179

in the face of one overwhelming problem: economic depression, with its harsh consequences in unemployment, poverty, frustration, and waste. At the time it seemed to many that while Hitler, Mussolini and Stalin were showing the way with vigorous economic planning, it was the parliamentary system itself (the 'talking-shop') that hampered similar efforts here. The wane of parliamentary institutions in the Fascist states and, of course, the example of Soviet Russia which had always appealed strongly to people of very left-wing views, together led to insistent questioning of the adequacy of Parliament to cope with modern problems of government. Writing in the *Daily Mail* in April 1935, Winston Churchill said that the preceding decade had been 'disastrous' to parliamentary institutions in almost every part of the world, and he felt obliged to stress that there was no greater guarantee of this country's liberties than the House of Commons. The 'official statement of the proposals of Mosley's New Party' for parliamentary reform which appeared in an article in the *Political Quarterly* in 1931[4] makes strange reading today, as do Stafford Cripps' plan[5] for Government by Order in Council under an enabling Bill. Socialist writers were concerned about the difficult conditions which they would meet if they achieved power, and Cabinet dictatorship—at least for a temporary period—seems to have been widely envisaged as the only way of preventing economic collapse (the fall of the second Labour Government in 1931 was, naturally, always in mind). How different is the situation today! It has been said that the basic health of our parliamentary institutions was shown by the fact that they were adequate to the purpose of the Labour Party when it came to power in 1945, with an extremely extensive programme of legislation. No major changes were made or needed to be made.[6] There is no doubt that the experiences of the war[7] and post-war years have completely altered the climate of opinion: the indefinite suspension of parliamentary government is no longer seriously envisaged.

The difference in the attitude of the public towards Parliament in 1945, as compared with what it was in 1931, is summed up in the Third Report of the 1945–6 Select Committee on Procedure. Referring to the work of their predecessors in 1931–2, the Committee reported: 'The atmosphere in which your Committee approach their task is entirely different from that in which the former Committee found themselves. The country was then under-going a period of severe economic stress ... and there was a tend-ency to criticize all the institutions of government, including Parliament itself. ... Your Committee have been appointed at a time when the country has recently emerged from a war in which parliamentary activity was maintained and contributed in large measure to its successful prosecution. Consequently, there is not at the present time any strong or wide-spread desire for changes in the essential character of the institution. Indeed, the prestige of Parliament has probably never been higher.'[8]

It seems that in the 1930s the continued viability of parliamentary institutions was not only in doubt among politicians themselves, writers to *The Times*, and so on, but among many ordinary people as well. Today it is probably true to say that the British Parliament as an institution is generally believed to be well able to discharge its functions. There are few signs of hostility to Parliament as a system, or of dissatisfaction with it, however much its particular actions may be criticized. Nor would it be true to say that there is apathy: Parliament is something that is accepted—often accepted, perhaps, with nearly complete ignorance of what it really is or how it works—but accepted along with our system of driving on the left. Support for movements which would involve changing parlia-mentary government radically—Communism, Fascism—has always been minute.[9]

It is against this reassuring background that the question of possible reforms regarding the relationship between Parliament and the public may be discussed.

(b) PUBLICITY FOR PARLIAMENT

The understanding and informed acceptance of Parliament are aims never finally achieved: for one thing, there is always a new generation. There is no need to rehearse here the achievements of the Hansard Society for Parliamentary Government. But the work of such a body can only reach a comparatively small pro-portion of the people (though the influence of its publications in universities, schools, W.E.A. classes, etc., may be more extensive), and the twelve Members who contributed an article to *Socialist Commentary* in July 1964 advocated a Council for Education in

Citizenship, to be independent but publicly-financed. They also thought there should be an Information Bureau set up inside the Palace of Westminster. For most people, what they know and understand of Parliament—and the esteem in which they hold it—depend largely on the organs of mass communication: particularly the radio, television, and the Press.

The effect of radio and television has probably been almost entirely beneficial, so far as spreading a knowledge and understanding of Parliament is concerned. Such popular programmes as 'Any Questions?' in which Members and others discuss informally serious and frivolous topics of the day, generally do an immense amount of good in bringing a fairly wide selection of Members in close contact with millions of people; the same is true of similar television programmes. But there have been problems, some of which remain.

A source of friction in the past in the relation between Parliament and the broadcasting mediums was the 'Fourteen-Day Rule'. A skeleton account of this affair may be in place here. In 1944, the Governors of the B.B.C. considered the situation which had arisen from a broadcast by the President of the Board of Education on the eve of the Second Reading of the Education Bill in the House of Commons. They resolved that the broadcasting of *ex parte* statements was undesirable at a time when debates on major matters of policy were imminent, and thus brought into play, of their own volition, what came to be known as the Fourteen-Day Rule. After the war, a number of meetings were held in order to re-define the Rule. In the course of these, in 1948, the B.B.C. were prepared to give the assurances:

(i) that they had no intention of becoming an alternative, simultaneous debating forum to Parliament;
(ii) that they would not have discussions on any issues which were to be debated in either House within a fortnight; and
(iii) that while matters were subjects of legislation, M.P.s would not be used in such discussions.

The Rule, however, began to impose some difficulties on the Governors, and the 1949 Broadcasting Committee, reporting in January 1951 (Cmd. 8116), felt that it should be reconsidered. In May 1952, the Government said they would initiate discussions on the point; in March 1953, the B.B.C. definitely sought to disengage themselves from the Rule which, they said, imposed great administrative difficulties, and which the public thought absurd. Government and Opposition representatives, on the other hand, attached importance to the Rule being retained; it was desirable to protect M.P.s from undue pressure before a debate from the loud, but single, voice of the B.B.C.

After a debate in the House on 30th November 1955, a Select Committee was set up, which recommended[10] that in future the limitation should be, at the most, one of seven days only, and that the ban on discussion of proposed legislation should be altogether removed after a bill had been read the second time. In December 1956, the Prime Minister was able to announce that the B.B.C. and I.T.A. had agreed that, if the Fourteen-Day Rule was suspended, they would continue to act in a way which would not derogate from the primacy of Parliament as the forum for debating the affairs of the nation.[11] In the light of this, the Fourteen-Day Rule was suspended—at first, for an experimental period, and, later, indefinitely.[12]

There have been, from time to time, several suggestions for the direct broadcasting of Parliament itself. Amery has summarized the aims of one school of thought: 'The real opportunity to my mind of rekindling interest in Parliament . . . is to have Parliament broadcast on a special wavelength throughout the session. . . . I do not believe that this would lead to "talking to the gallery". . . . On the contrary, broadcasting audiences are very critical of anything but sober good sense, and I believe the effect would be definitely to raise the standards of debates and to create an ever-increasing body of parliamentary fans following the proceedings.'[13] Aneurin Bevan advocated sound broadcasting of the complete proceedings in the House on 30th June 1944. However, the broadcasting of debates was rejected by the Commons on 21st August 1945. A slightly different suggestion—that all proceedings should be recorded—was advanced by King-Hall on 30th June 1944.[14] This also was refused (11th December 1945)—it had been considered 'over and over again' and there was said to be no substantial support for it.[15] Permission to broadcast or record can, of course, come only from the whole House. It is well known that during the war the Prime Minister asked the House to allow his own speeches to be recorded so that they could later be broadcast, thus saving himself precious time and energy. However, he found that the motion to implement the suggestion aroused so much difference of opinion in the House that it was never moved.

The campaign for televising the proceedings of the Commons received support from Aneurin Bevan at the beginning of the 1959 Parliament. Referring to 'a considerable gulf growing between this House and the nation', and to a general lessening of interest in Parliament, he called for a serious investigation into the technical possibilities of televising parliamentary proceedings. A special channel would be required: viewers should be able to switch over to a debate when they wished to do so.[16] R. A. Butler, replying, confirmed that if this 'revolutionary suggestion' were adopted then a special channel might well be imperative—since the problem of 'editing' debates would otherwise be bound to arise.[17] The Prime Minister subsequently announced on 1st March 1960 that from inquiries made by the Government it appeared that the proposal to televise debates did not yet command the support necessary to justify 'so radical a departure from our traditions'.

This support, however, continued to grow; it was reflected in debates in the House[18] and in the flood of pamphlets[19] and articles in the newspapers. A Select Committee of the House began to consider the matter in the Session of 1964/5; its deliberations continued until August 1966, and, after collecting a considerable amount of oral and written evidence, it reported that continuous live broadcasting of all the proceedings of the House was impracticable and undesirable; but that the House could make available to interested parties a continuous 'feed' of all its proceedings; and that a closed-circuit experiment should be conducted for M.P.s only, after which the House should decide whether or not to make permanent arrangements.[20] On 24th November 1966, however, by a single vote, the House rejected a proposal to start such an experiment.

Television and radio in any case have already been admitted to the Palace of Westminster to cover the State Opening of Parliament, and certain important ceremonies such as the visit of President de Gaulle in the spring of 1960; they also play an increasingly prominent part in elections. After the first television by-election in 1958,[21] an article by the political correspondent of *The Times* discussed issues which might arise in the future:[22]

> There is little doubt what the television authorities want. They are going to press for the right to treat a General Election as they treat other first-class news, and to arrange discussion programmes during an election campaign in which the speakers will be something more than the puppets and voices of the Party caucuses. The television authorities, in fact, must be expected to found themselves upon the principle that a General Election cannot be a closed shop for politicians, and that the electorate at large and the commentators have as good a claim to settle what the issues shall be as the politicians. But this large proposition has only to be mentioned to many professional politicians to make them behave like a nervous matron cycling in a high wind, never sure how only two hands may be used to grip the handlebars, hold on to a hat, and keep down a hemline. One calamity or the other is almost certain.

Other suggestions for making Parliament better known to the public have concerned facilities for visitors within the Palace. The Public Gallery in the new House of Commons is considerably larger than that in the old. King-Hall suggested to the Select Committee on House of Commons Rebuilding that one side-gallery should be enclosed in glass and soundproofed.[23] Such a gallery would be particularly useful for organized parties, with an official present to explain proceedings. A further suggestion was that there should be a 'Look-Listen' room accommodating 500 people near the Chamber, where proceedings could be watched on television.

Diana Spearman has pointed to a possible danger in the effect of the use of radio, television, etc., in politics.[24] She says that 'the back-bencher remains a back-bencher even in his own constituency' —the Press, radio and television enable the Party leaders to address the public over the heads of local Members. At the moment, the complaint can to some extent be borne out by the fact that we have, in this country, no network of local radio stations as there is in America. But a network of local television stations is being developed and these may well go some way towards restoring a fairer balance. The local candidates, and not the Party leaders, had the limelight at the first televised by-election in Rochdale, and Granada TV's 'Election Marathon' of 1959 was an experiment in *constituency* television: 229 candidates contesting 100 northern constituencies appeared. Ed Murrow said of this 'operation' that it had the laudable aim of *not* concentrating too much on the national political figures. We may one day reach a situation similar to that in America, where local political issues and personalities are reported at length by the different local stations, with occasional 'national' programmes by the Party leaders relayed by every station.

The Select Committee on Broadcasting in 1956 brought to light another aspect of the relationship between Parliament and the public. Sir Robert (now Lord) Boothby averred that the Party machines interfered with the ordinary programmes of the B.B.C. and I.T.V., and that this was undesirable.[25] He quoted a statement in a book by a former Chairman of the B.B.C., in which it is said that the leaders of the political Parties objected to the employment in B.B.C. programmes of Members who were not 'reliable' Party men;[26] the B.B.C.'s dilemma came from the fact that many of the 'extreme' politicians made the best broadcasters. It was also claimed that a particular M.P. was debarred from appearing in a sports broadcast because, in any radio programme, each M.P. had to be balanced by a member of the other main party.[27] The spokesmen for the political parties and the B.B.C. denied that there had been any improper dealings on the subject.[28] The Director-General of the B.B.C. explained that it was not in any way their policy to build up political personalities and give them a spurious standing.[29] The party spokesman said that the pressure they exerted was solely designed towards ensuring a reasonable balance of political views.[30] The Committee were satisfied that the charges were unfounded, and that the B.B.C. was quite able to defend itself from political interference.[31]

The Press is still a vitally important medium for the dissemination of information and comment about Parliament, despite the growing significance of television, and even allowing for the fact that popular newspapers can normally afford but a modest space for parliamentary and political matters. Grimond has distinguished three essential roles played by the Press in relation to Parliament: it interprets the country to Parliament: it interprets Parliament to the country; and it is itself a 'third Chamber' by virtue of its own discussions. Grimond points to the value of the independent, reasoned reports and articles in *The Times*, the *Guardian* and certain other newspapers which tend to treat problems from a national point of view; at the same time, he deplores our present dearth of political commentators of high standing.[32] Later, Bevan castigated much newspaper reporting as 'sheer travesty'; but this seems to be an extreme view.[33]

Relations between Parliament and the Press are not always happy, as the last remark shows. There is a long, well-known history of jealousy between these two institutions, both competing for the claim to be the decisive *vox populi*. Even today, the reporting of Parliament is technically a breach of privilege and, according to *The Times* political correspondent, there is controversy amongst pressmen as to the desirability of repealing this ancient technicality; some reporters, it seems, argue that the freedom to do their job rests on a rule that they have no basic right to do the job at all.[34]

There are other dissensions amongst journalists about the way in which the Lobby operates. Charges are made that the standard of lobby reporting in London is lower than in Washington, that it surrounds itself with unnecessary mystique and secrecy, and that foreign and Commonwealth reporters do not get a fair deal.[35] There is, however, widespread agreement among the journalists concerned that Parliament acts with unnecessary secrecy in withholding from the Press details of Division Lists, Early Day Motions etc., until they have been published in the official *Votes and Proceedings*.[36] There is, too, agreement that the conditions under which the Press operates in the House of Commons need considerable improvement.

A particular cause of friction between Parliament and the Press has been the reporting of 'secret' Party meetings. The subject was gone into at length by the Committee of Privileges with reference to the Garry Allighan Case.[37] In an article, 'Parliament and Press', H. G. Nicholas pointed out the 'impossibility' of the situation:[38] journalists can only print news of such Party meetings when what is supposed to be secret information is divulged to them. Nicholas proposed, as a remedy, that Party meetings should no longer be secret—at least not all of them.[39] An instance of similar friction occurred in March 1958. Arthur Lewis then raised the question of a report in certain newspapers—which claimed that two rooms in the Palace where Party meetings were held had been searched for hidden microphones—as part of an intensive effort to solve the mystery of how 'accurate verbatim accounts' of 'secret' meetings had reached the Press.[40] The whole question of such 'secret' meetings cannot be said to have been happily solved to date.

(c) THE MEMBER AND HIS CONSTITUENTS

The relationship between an M.P. and his constituents has already been partly considered in Chapters I and IV. Nigel Nicolson has pointed out how contradictory are the demands made on M.P.s by their constituents.[41] The Member is constantly being pressed to voice the views or needs of special interests, and these may easily be in conflict with his own conception of the national interest and of his duties as someone who is more than the 'delegate' of his constituents.

It is occasionally argued that one reason why, if practicable, the Commons should sit for a lesser part of the year is that Members would then have improved opportunities to develop their contacts with the people—above all, of course, with their constituents. The extent to which an M.P. should devote himself to 'constituency interests' has attracted much attention of late. The term does not apply so much to the major, collective problems of any given area—a Member must (and invariably does) devote his time selflessly to such things as growing local unemployment, general lack of housing, flood disasters, etc.—as to the countless *individual* worries of the constituents. In other words, how far should the Member regard himself as a welfare officer? Should he spend much time investigating whether Mrs. X's son was dismissed from his job without proper notice, or whether Mr. Y's daughter's adverse school report was fair comment on the latter's abilities? A distinguished opponent of excessive 'surgery' work was Lord Attlee, who contended that in these days of legal aid, Citizens' Advice Bureaux and similar institutions, a Member should not be bothered with such a mass of detailed work—to

171

the detriment of his duties in Parliament.[42] Lord Winterton voiced similar comments.[43] The idea that M.P.s should be paid 'a whacking salary and then become full-time constituency welfare officers' does not appeal to Philip Goodhart.[44] Yet there is a strong current of informed opinion that it would be undesirable for a Member to cut himself off from this work—however weary, stale and unprofitable it may sometimes be.[45] To whom is the constituent with a genuine personal grievance to turn, if not to his Member? Moreover, the latter can, should and does refer many of such inquiries and complaints to the 'appropriate authorities'. There is no doubt that an M.P.'s 'welfare' services are sometimes abused, and precious time wasted in consequence; yet to many the alternative seems even less acceptable, and would scarely improve relations between Parliament and the public.

This responsibility to his constituents adds heavily to an already busy man's work, and it is small wonder that there has been substantial agreement that at the very least 250 full-time Members are required in the House.[46] For, apart from constituency responsibilities, the duties of Members at Westminster *outside* the actual Chamber have multiplied with the increase in Committee work (and in other work besides)—to an extent which only the Members concerned are in a position to assess accurately. At the same time, it must be conceded that critics of 'too many professional politicians' have not been slow to speak up. In some quarters there undoubtedly exists an apparently innate preference for the man who combines his duties at Westminster with an outside profession. There are, of course, certain serious motives for this preference. It is felt that the Member entirely dependent on his parliamentary salary may feel disinclined to speak against his Party's policy, since expulsion from the Party could easily entail the loss of his seat. The other reason is the desirability of keeping Parliament in close touch with the country as a whole; it is argued, very plausibly, that to achieve this contact at least a proportion of Members must not be full-time politicians. Otherwise, asked *The Times*, how can the House of Commons remain the microcosm of the nation?[47] The ideal, widely accepted solution, of course, is that the composition of the House should strike a happy balance between full-time Members and those who are able to combine their parliamentary duties with an outside profession. Both forms

172

of service are essential to the modern parliamentary machine; and public opinion, generally speaking, accepts the fact.[48]

The major contentious issue of recent times, in this particular context, has been the extent to which a Member is bound to follow the known wishes of his constituents and, in particular, of his local association. The reader is referred to Chapter IV for consideration of this question.

(d) PARLIAMENTARY PRIVILEGE

The assertion of parliamentary privilege seems to run increases in Members' pay a close second in its ability to render public opinion towards Parliament hostile. A note on the subject is therefore in place here.

The notion that parliamentary privilege works for the benefit of the common people is perhaps rather too difficult for many people to grasp.[49] There have also been some cases in recent years in which the claims of Members for protection have appeared, to many, to border on the absurd; these claims may have caught the public attention, while the decisive rejection of them by the House may have gone unnoticed. The sensible position on this matter has been stated by the Committee of Privileges itself:[50]

> Your Committee are of the opinion that it is not consistent with the dignity of the House that penal proceedings for breach of privilege should be taken in the case of every defamatory statement which, strictly, may constitute a contempt of Parliament. Whilst recognizing that it is the duty of Parliament to intervene in the case of attacks which may tend to undermine public confidence in and support of the institution of Parliament itself, your Committee think it important that, on the one hand, the law of Parliamentary Privilege should not be administered in a way which would fetter or discourage the free expression of opinion or criticisms, however prejudiced or exaggerated such opinions or criticisms may be; and that, on the other hand, the process of Parliamentary investigation should not be used in a way which would give importance to impossible statements.[51]

The question of whether the Committee of Privileges has been right or wrong in its assessment of particular cases is not relevant here. There have been, however, some suggestions recently for reform of the way in which alleged breaches of privileges are dealt with. An unsigned article appearing in *The Times* of 27th March 1957 stated an opinion which has since received a good deal of support. The writer pointed out that the House of Commons is not, in law, a court, and is not, in practice, adapted to the exercise of functions of a judicial nature. A recognition of this fact led in 1868 to the transfer from the House to the courts of jurisdiction over disputed elections. The writer goes on to suggest that this course could be followed in matters of privilege also. The basis of the rules which relate to breach of privilege is clear enough—whether an alleged breach tends to obstruct the functioning of the House. This is a question with which the courts could well cope. The writer suggested that it would be better for the dignity of Parliament if affronts to its authority were either clearly seen to be assessed in accordance with judicial standards, or else ignored as unworthy of notice.

In the ensuing correspondence, O. Hood Phillips suggested a distinction between cases of privilege, with which the House is necessarily concerned, which are recognized by the courts, and which may not be extended, and cases of contempt which are incapable of enumeration, and which might well be triable only in the courts.[52] B. E. H. Amps pointed out that those investigated by the Committee of Privileges had no right to defend themselves, or to be heard, or to make public their defence.[53] He suggested that procedure could be devised similar to that of courts by which the accused had the right of hearing by the Committee, and by which the House and the public should hear both sides of the case. Clearly, public interest had been aroused. On 10th April 1957, six Conservative Members tabled a motion which read: 'That it be an instruction to the Committee of Privileges, *in view of the prevailing public uncertainty and anxiety on the matter*, to prepare and submit to the House a report which shall define the nature and clarify the purpose of parliamentary privilege; and recommend a procedure designed to secure its equitable protection.'

The later stages of the 'Strauss' case have led to several repetitions of the suggestion that jurisdiction in matters of privilege should be transferred to the courts.[54] The outcome of the question of privilege raised by G. R. Strauss, M.P. for Vauxhall, caused some anxiety to a number of Members. If the 'Strauss'[55] letter was *not* covered by privilege (as the House decided by a small majority), were Members likely to be involved in libel actions if they followed up constituency grievances? A group of Labour Members subsequently asked for an extension of Question Time, to accommodate business that was conducted formerly by correspondence. It has been suggested that the proper means of dealing with grievances which might involve libel action is for the Member to forward them to the Minister with the simple addition of a 'compliments' slip. The matter was raised on 16th March 1954, when Winston Churchill added that the M.P. might be well advised to ask his correspondent whether he would be willing for the letter to be disclosed to a wider circle.[56] Sir H. Lucas-Tooth has proposed that the Member should ask the complainant whether he would object to his letter being forwarded to the person against whom the charge is made.[57] All this takes us some way from the specific question of privilege, as it affects Parliament's relations with the public, but it serves to show the importance and the complexity of the issues raised by the 'Strauss' case. As had been pointed out, the threat of the London Electricity Board to proceed against Mr. Strauss came as a shock to a wide body of parliamentary opinion.[58]

Many of those who have recently argued that procedure in dealing with alleged breaches of privilege should be amended, have explicitly advanced the point that the present system—in which the House is at once (so it is said) prosecutor, judge and jury—has lowered the esteem in which Parliament is held; and the House has shown enough sensitivity to this charge to set up, in 1966, a Select Committee to review the law of privilege and the procedure adopted in cases of privilege. Yet, despite the criticisms that have been made, it seems that the principle of privilege in itself has not been attacked by those informed observers (few though they may be) who grasp its true significance and function.

Conclusions

In a debate on the matter of privilege which he had raised, Strauss said:[59] 'While there is a deep respect in this country for

Parliament as an institution there is, unfortunately, not the same respect for the Members who compose it.'

It is true that public opinion does not accord automatically an exaggerated degree of respect to Members. This is, perhaps, not a matter for regret, and those who argue that things were different in earlier days produce little evidence to support their case. The idea that harsh, often unfair criticisms were *not* levelled at Members in 'the good old days' is in fact completely erroneous.[60] 'As the franchise became more democratic', observed Winston Churchill in the Commons on 27th February 1941, 'it grew to be the fashion in certain social circles to speak with contempt about Members as a class and as a type. They were represented as mere spouters and chatterboxes, the putters of awkward questions and the raisers of small points of procedure.' Members can at best expect to win the general public's respect according to their abilities and merits, and cannot count on receiving respect merely, as it were, *ex officio*. There is a genuine distinction, however, between Parliament, and the Members who at any one time compose it; and Strauss is surely right in saying that there is in this country today a deep respect for Parliament itself. The continuance of this respect, a prerequisite of parliamentary government, is not an end and aim that can be pursued by itself. It is a by-product: something that must depend on the ability of Parliament to discharge its traditional functions in continually changing circumstances. The problems raised by these changes have been discussed in the present and preceding chapters; the attitude of public opinion towards Parliament may well depend upon the efficacy of the solutions adopted.

The chances are, however, that Parliament will long remain the people's hope. Professor André Mathiot has written an interesting, sympathetic account of *The British Political System*.[61] In it, he deals with the various aspects of our Constitution. His conclusion reveals how he, a foreigner, appreciates the vital, intimate interrelation between that Constitution and the British people at large: describing the system as 'an enviable model of democratic government', he adds that 'one can only regret that it could not possibly be transplanted to any other country.'[62] 'Only if the character of the British people changes radically,' according to Menhennet and

Palmer, 'will Parliament decline and disappear.'[63] Could it be that Winston Churchill summed up the whole situation in 1908 when he described the British Constitution (of which Parliament is the centre-point) as 'mainly British common sense'?[64]

NOTES AND REFERENCES

[1] *Contemporary Review*, Vol. CXLI, 1932, pp. 296–308.

[2] Carter, p. 198.

[3] Of course, the exercise of public opinion is no simple matter in a highly organized country of 56 million people with centralized organs of mass communication such as the Press, radio, television, political parties, trades unions, and so on. Everything from a letter to the *Guardian* signed by, say, 200 members of the academic staff of London University, to a report of a resolution by a local branch of the T. and G.W.U., plays its part in the whole complicated story. The organs of communication play a double part in both expressing, and helping to form, opinion.

[4] Vol. II, pp. 319–36.

[5] *Political Quarterly*, Vol. IV, 1933, pp. 467–81.

[6] R. Bassett, 'British Parliamentary Government today', in *Political Quarterly*, Vol. XXIII, 1952, pp. 380–89; cf. also Crick, *Reform of the Commons*, p.1.

[7] It is true that Governments had exceptional powers in these years—but these powers were granted by Parliament, were subject to parliamentary scrutiny and questioning, and were gradually diminished. The extent of these powers was a legitimate subject for Party differences, but it was seldom suggested that they were necessarily inimical to the parliamentary system. Ed Murrow, in a famous broadcast, said: 'Do you remember that while London was being bombed in daylight, the House devoted two days to discussing conditions under which enemy aliens were detained on the Isle of Man?' (Quoted by K. R. Mackenzie in *The English Parliament*, revised and reprinted, Penguin Books, 1959).

[8] H.C. 189–I of 1945/6, p.v.

[9] A subject that is raised from time to time is how much better things would be if we could have a government of wise men, instead of the parliamentary battle. Sir Hartley (now Lord) Shawcross gave the subject an airing when he said that a committee of ten sensible men of goodwill could accomplish in a couple of hours what may occupy the time of Parliament for a couple of days. (*The Times*, 23rd December 1957, p. 4.) He might have said 'a couple of years' and the remark could still have been perfectly true. Remarks such as these, which when considered are seen to challenge the roots of the parliamentary system, seldom receive wide support. And, after all, the parliamentary system already contains within it a committee of ten (or twenty) sensible men of goodwill—the Cabinet. The men of goodwill envisaged by Lord Shawcross could only achieve more than the Cabinet if they were unfettered by parliamentary control—if they had, in fact, dictatorial and not parliamentary power.

[10] H.C. 288 of 1955/6: Broadcasting (Anticipation of Debates) Select Committee Report.

[11] H.C. Deb. 562, cs. 1095–7.

[12] H.C. Deb. 574, cs. 91–2W. (25th July 1957).

[13] Amery, p. 56.

[14] H.C. Deb. 401, c. 976.

[15] H.C. Deb. 417, cs. 213–4.

[16] H.C. Deb. 612, cs. 865–67.

[17] H.C. Deb. 612, c. 972.

[18] H.C. Deb. 673, cs. 1715–1820; 713, cs. 1033–1133.

[19] See, for instance, Robin Day, *The Case for Televising Parliament*, published by the Hansard Society; Allan Segal's article published as an Appendix to Crick's *The Reform of Parliament*; article by Colin Seymour-Ure, *Parliamentary Affairs*, Spring 1964, pp. 172–81.

[20] H.C. 146 of 1966/7.

[21] Ably documented in the pamphlet *Granada goes to Rochdale* published, by Granada Television, 1958.

[22] 23rd June 1958, p. 6.

[23] H.C. 109–I of 1943/4, p. 139.

[24] Spearman, p. 167.

[25] H.C. 288 of 1955/6.

[26] The late Lord Simon of Wythenshawe: *The B.B.C. from Within*, Gollancz Ltd., 1956, p. 133.

[27] H.C. 288 of 1955/6, p. 165.

[28] For some statistics of M.P.s' television appearances see H.C. Deb. 588, cs. 394–6; and 546, c. 174.

[29] *ibid*. Q. 184.

[30] *ibid*. p. iv.

[31] *ibid*.

[32] In Watson, pp. 47–8.

[33] H.C. Deb. 612, c. 865.

[34] *Political Quarterly*, Vol. 36, No. 3, pp. 309–322.

[35] *ibid*. See also *Listener*, 15th August 1963 and 21st January 1965; *New Statesman*, 22nd January 1965, and *Encounter*, June 1965.

[36] See *Partners in Parliament*, published by the Press Gallery in 1965.

[37] H.C. 138 of 1946/7. Allighan's 'contempt' was based on an article in which he said that some M.P.s disclosed confidential information to newspapers in return for financial reward or personal publicity.

[38] *Nineteenth Century and After*, Vol. CXLIII, pp. 249–55.

[39] The case against the secrecy of Party meetings is also argued on other grounds: see Chapter IV, section (*b*).

[40] H.C. Deb. 584, cs. 924–6.

[41] *People and Parliament*, Chap. I.

[42] *Fabian Journal*, November 1958, p. 6.

[43] In a letter to *The Times*, 15th April 1957, p. 11.

[44] *Crossbow*, Vol. III, No. 10, pp. 10–11.

[45] e.g. Crick, *Reform of the Commons*, pp. 9–11 ('The Constituency Case'); and Donnelly, *The Times*, 17th April 1957, p. 11.

[46] From 250 to 300, according to Lord Attlee: *The Times*, 11th April 1957, p. 11. The Select Committee on Procedure (H.C. 92 of 1958/9: Proceedings, p. lii) recognized the growing tendency in recent years 'to divide Members into what are called "whole-time parliamentarians" and those "with outside interests".'

[47] 17th January 1958, p. 11.

[48] The distinction between these two 'forms' of Membership, as has been rightly emphasized, is artificial, and is made in the present context purely for convenience of discussion. For a categorical rejection of this distinction, see

the (narrowly defeated) paragraph brought up and read before the 1958/9 Procedure Committee: H.C. 92 of 1958/9, pp. lii–liii. For a summary of the position (in 1966) see Menhennet and Palmer, Chapter 5, pp. 70–77.

[49] 'In its famous protestation ... in 1621, the Commons declared the Privileges of Parliament to be the birthright and inheritance of the subject. In principle, the Privilege of Parliament is designed to protect a Member's constituents, since without Privilege grievances would be harder to remedy and abuses less likely to be uncovered.' R. A. Butler, H.C. Deb. 591, c. 217.

[50] A statement that compares very favourably with the comments of *The Times* (leader of 23rd December 1957): 'Members' fussiness about their privilege may well be a reflex action. They know that the standing of Parliament in the nation is not what it ought to be and they seek to enforce respect for it. A different mental deportment ... would be far more effective.'

[51] H.C. 112 of 1947/8, p. iv.

[52] *The Times*, 1st April 1957.

[53] *ibid.* 16th April 1957.

[54] For example, the *Spectator*, 16th May 1958, pp. 611–12. There was a considerable correspondence in *The Times* in July 1958 arising from the debate on the Strauss case.

[55] Richards has summarized the main issues involved in *op. cit.* pp. 262–7. The House debated the matter on 8th July 1958. (H.C. Deb. 591, cs. 208–346.)

[56] H.C. Deb. 525, cs. 210–11.

[57] In a letter to *The Times*, 10th July 1958.

[58] Richards, p. 267.

[59] H.C. Deb. 591, c. 246.

[60] Charles Pannell has brought out this point on a number of occasions; e.g. his letter to *The Times*, 3rd January 1958.

[61] Translated by Jennifer S. Hines, Hogarth Press, 1958.

[62] *ibid.*, p. 335.

[63] Menhennet and Palmer, p. 34.

[64] At the Kinnaird Hall, Dundee, 14th May 1908; cf. G. M. Trevelyan, quoted by Lord Elton (Ramsay Muir Memorial Lecture, 1959): 'The English Parliament ... was the natural outcome, through long centuries, of the commonsense and the good nature of the English people. ...'

VII

Parliamentary Life

INTRODUCTION

Criticism of the amenities offered by the Palace of Westminster, and of the way such amenities are controlled, has increased very considerably since the war; and this despite the fact that opportunity was taken, at the time of the re-building of the House of Commons, to provide more accommodation than the pre-war House had allowed.[1] It is still sometimes said that the poor accommodation detracts from the efficiency of Parliament's work; there is also the wider implication that able people are deterred from seeking a career in Parliament because the conditions of life there are so unattractive.

The chief criticisms have concerned lack of accommodation, and the method in which rooms are allocated for use; the lack of those amenities which would make life more tolerable and Members' labours more productive; the unavoidable expenses of being a Member, and the insufficient salary.

The remedy proposed by Maxton—that Parliament should move to Hampstead—does not seem to have been weightily considered, although Mr. W. W. Hamilton, in a debate on House of Commons Accommodation of 1st August 1963, strongly supported the idea of 'a new administrative city' in northern England.

(a) ACCOMMODATION

Mrs. Barbara Castle has called the Palace of Westminster a 'neo-Gothic monstrosity',[2] and it is incontestable that the inadequate nature of the accommodation provided for individual Members within its walls has been constantly adverted to in the post-war years.[3] At first, Government spokesmen countered these complaints

For Notes and References see pages 191–192

by referring to the increased space that would be available when
the new Chamber of the House of Commons was built.[4] A Joint
Committee, sitting in 1945, had recommended that Sir Charles
Barry's original proposal for buildings around New Palace Yard
should be reconsidered as a long-term project.[5] The attractions
and advantages of realizing the 'great and grandiose' Barry scheme,
together with a claim that the names of at least one hundred M.P.s
in support of such a plan could soon be collected, were again
voiced in the Accommodation debate of 31st March 1960, and
were re-echoed in the Report of the Speaker's Committee on
Accommodation of 1964.[6] In this important Report, according to
the Study of Parliament Group in their pamphlet *Reforming the
Commons*, recommendations for improved accommodation and
facilities 'got obscured in the debate about "the Gothic style"
recommended for the proposed new Bridge Street extension'.

A Select Committee of the Commons, set up in 1953 to meet
criticisms of lack of space, recommended that a long waiting-room
should be built over the arcade on the east side of New Palace
Yard.[7] Desks should be provided for a limited number of Members.
The Speaker's Library (one large room) should be made available
to Members, thus reducing over-crowding in the Commons
Library itself. It was clear to the Committee, however, that whilst
minor improvements could be carried out at once, no substantial
progress could be made except by large building operations.

These two Reports of the 'Stokes' Committee, and the extensive
evidence given by witnesses, make a fascinating picture of the
inconvenience of life in the Palace of Westminster in the 1950s.
(This was perhaps the only Select Committee that has ever
discussed, *inter alia*, the shortcomings of the accommodation provided by the House of Commons' mortuary.)[8] The picture afforded
by the above Reports has since been very fully supplemented by
debates and Questions in the House of Commons, and by a
number of important Reports from unofficial and from Select
Committees of Members. Throughout, the emphasis has been on
the need for better working space and conditions for Members.
But it was not until July 1965 that the crux of the vexed problem—
that of the *control* of accommodation—was tackled and settled
in a Report from a Select Committee set up primarily for that
purpose.[9]

(b) THE CONTROL OF ACCOMMODATION

Until recently, the Palace of Westminster was in the charge of the Lord Great Chamberlain, and he allocated the accommodation in it by warrant to the different users, who made their own detailed distributions. For the House of Lords, this was done by the Lord Great Chamberlain through the Yeoman Usher of the Black Rod. For the Commons it was done on behalf of the Speaker (a) by the Ministry of Works in respect of Ministers' Rooms, and (b) by the Serjeant at Arms in respect of other rooms.

The 1945 Joint Committee rejected the suggestion that this system should be drastically altered;[10] but over a hundred members subsequently supported a motion that the Lord Great Chamberlain's powers should be transferred to a Joint Committee of both Houses,[11] whilst the Commons Select Committee in 1953 expressed the belief that the existing system tended to frustrate or delay desirable changes.[12] As a first step, the Stokes Committee supported the suggestion made by the Joint Committee eight years before, that a sessional 'House' Committee should be appointed to advise the Speaker on the allocation of the rooms at his disposal.[13] The House of Lords already had such a Committee, and it was thought that the two Committees could sit together when it was necessary to discuss matters of mutual concern. It was desirable, the Committee believed, that a unified control of the whole Palace could be exercised. An amendment, repeating this point, to the draft Report of the Select Committee on Procedure in 1958/9 was narrowly defeated.[14] The subject was yet again discussed in the Accommodation debate of 31st March 1960 when Mrs. Barbara Castle, speaking from the Opposition front bench, begged to move that 'this House . . . believes that the time has come to implement the proposal of the Select Committee on House of Commons Accommodation, 1953/4, for the establishment of a unified control of the Palace of Westminster under this House; and is, therefore, of the opinion that a House of Commons Commission should be appointed forthwith with the powers and duties proposed in the Select Committee Report, including the consideration of the machinery required to establish such unified control.' Charles Pannell went further; he questioned the whole right of a Court official to operate at Westminster at all, and drew attention to the inefficiency which had sprung from 'the amiable fiction that the workshop at Westminster is a royal palace'.[15]

The repeated demands made for internal reforms of this type were to a large extent vindicated and satisfied when the Prime Minister announced that control of those parts of the Palace occupied by or on behalf of the House of Commons was in future to be vested in the Speaker *on behalf of the House* at all times. The announcement was made in the House on 23rd March 1965.[16] In July of that year the Report of the Select Committee on the Palace of Westminster recommended the setting up of a sessional Select Committee—to be known as the House of Commons (Services) Committee—to advise the Speaker on the control of the Commons' services and accommodation. Four Sub-Committees (on Catering, Administration, the Library, and Accommodation and Housekeeping respectively) were initially proposed;[17] and the powerful new 'Services Committee' duly came into being in the Autumn of 1965. An important reform was thus accomplished, and a potential major instrument of domestic change and progress forged on behalf of Members.

(c) THE LIBRARY OF THE HOUSE OF COMMONS[18]

In their First Report of Session 1966/7, the Services Committee had this to say of the Library which, since 1818, has existed to serve impartially Members of all parties:

> Before the last war the atmosphere of the Library tended to be that of a private library, and it was not until the first post-war Parliament, in 1945, that a thorough re-appraisal of policy was undertaken. The Select Committee of 1945/6 concluded that '... the essential purpose of the House of Commons Library is to supply Members with information rapidly on any of the multifarious matters which come before the House or to which their attentions are drawn by their Parliamentary duties.' Since then the emphasis has been on the development of the research and reference side of the Library's work which has proceeded apace. Your Committee agree with the post-war policy which has been followed and are satisfied that, within the enforced limitations, the objectives of the Select Committee of 1945/6 have been followed. Their

only doubt is whether the services provided have gone far enough to meet Members' reasonable demands.[19]

Though still modest by some foreign standards—those of Bonn, Tokyo, Ottawa and Washington, for instance—the House of Commons Library has expanded and developed its services noticeably since 1946. Its busy Research Division answers general and statistical enquiries, and prepares annotated bibliographies (with occasional statistical memoranda) in anticipation of most major debates. A new Scientific Section has been established. And the increasingly complex processes of information retrieval have been developed and reinforced by specialist indexes, press cuttings services and similar aids in the main Library.[20]

Facilities need to be related to function. What can and should a legislative library do? In their pamphlet, *Reforming the Commons*, the Study of Parliament Group suggested:

> Basically the (House of Commons) Library can do no more than make use of every possible source of already published information on governmental activities: but these sources are by no means negligible as weapons of Parliamentary control or sources for public information constantly in need of repointing and digesting. And if the Library cannot institute original research, Departments of State and other public bodies are usually fairly helpful in sharing what information they have.[21]

For a considerable number of years, and particularly since about 1960, there have been pressures both within and outside the House for 'a quite different approach' to the range and type of official research and briefing facilities which the modern Member should have. Mrs. Castle's question during the debate of 31st March 1960 on House of Commons Accommodation: 'Are we not setting our sights too low?'[22] was to some extent echoed in the Lawrence Committee's Report on Members' Pay in 1964:

> We desire to place on record the fact that Members referred with gratitude to the assistance which they receive from the staff of the Library of the House, while suggesting that a further strengthening of this staff would be a great assistance to them.[23]

Members' opinions concerning their Library cover an astonishingly wide spectrum, and unanimity would appear to be impracticable—if, indeed, it is desirable or necessary at all. Whilst there is strong support for the idea that opposition to 'bigger research staffs' is as unreasonable as opposition to 'motherhood or virtue',[24] others both inside and outside the House take a more cautious view on the grounds that Parliament has obtained, and will continue to obtain, a great deal of information from Ministers of the Crown and their Departments. But the influx of many new and younger Members since 1964, on both sides of the House, and a general awareness of the need for the House of Commons Library to keep pace with the growing complexity and volume of the information explosion which has expanded and increased the post-war responsibilities of all libraries, have combined to produce a broad consensus of opinion that the Library's present budget and staff structure are the minimum required for its efficient functioning as a 'legislative reference service'. Already the suggestion that the Library should provide subject specialists—in such fields of research as Economics, Science and Technology and the Social Services—has been discussed by Members and others, and implemented in part.[25] And the whole question of the provision of information for M.P.s, which is of course a much wider subject than that of the official services provided within the House, is at present being investigated independently of Parliament by a small study group under the auspices of Political and Economic Planning. Their report, when published, is likely to be of considerable interest.

(d) AMENITIES

(i) *Secretaries.* The provision of free secretarial assistance to Members of Parliament has been often suggested. Acland[26] and Pollard[27] both supported the idea during the war. It was considered by the Select Committee on Members' Expenses in 1954,[28] who, however, recommended that there should be a straight increase in salary, rather than an allowance, disguised or open, to cover secretarial assistance; *The Times* criticized this decision in an article headlined 'A Bad Business'.[29] Since then, the provision of free secretarial facilities has been adverted to by Crick,[30] Nicolson,[31] and many others. In 1960 Mrs. Castle asked that a central remote-control dictation system should be provided for Members; Members would record letters over the telephone, and secretaries would subsequently type them at their convenience. This would afford 'a continuous flow of efficient office output for very little expense'.[32]

(ii) *Post Office Charges*. A suggestion that Members should be allowed to frank their letters (in view of the increasing interest taken by citizens in the work of Parliament, and hence of Members' considerably augmented correspondence), was turned down in 1936.[33] But the proposal has been repeated since on various occasions—for example, to a Select Committee in 1954.[34] In 1964, the Lawrence Committee on Members' Pay recommended (paragraph 69) that M.P.s' letters to local authorities should be exempt from postal charges: a suggestion which the House of Commons (Services) Select Committee endorsed in February 1966.[35]

(iii) *Other Suggested Amenities*. Amongst other suggestions of detail made to the 1954 Select Committee on Members' Expenses and to the Lawrence Committee ten years later (too numerous to consider here at length) were the provision of free stationery, of living accommodation for Members at a reasonable cost, and of a limited number of free travel-vouchers for a Member's wife (or husband). An information service, for the speedy answering of smaller technical problems put by constituents to Members, has also been suggested;[36] Leslie Hale thought that a teleprinter service direct to the various Departments might contribute to that end.[37] Mrs. Castle, amongst others, has said that each Member ought to have his own telephone on his own desk.[38] Various proposals have been made, too, for improving and simplifying the car allowance for Members: the Lawrence Committee suggested that this allowance should be 4½d. per mile (paragraph 167 (2)).

With the setting up of the new Commons' Services Committee in 1965, the provision and control of many such amenities and facilities have become the responsibility of the House—or rather, of the Speaker acting on the advice of that Committee. Changes and improvements, some of them noted above, have already been made, although it is clear from comment inside and outside the House that a good number of Members would like to see faster and more radical improvements effected.

(e) MEMBERS' PAY, ETC.

Members' pay is not a subject about which much objective thinking takes place; it periodically lurches into the public's attention, generally when Members themselves have been forced to raise the matter (as a result, normally, of some privation in their midst). Hence, few long-term proposals are made on the subject; and argument, both inside and outside the House, is generally confined to the circumstances of a particular time, and the merits of a particular proposed increase. The situation is complicated by the fact that the issue has to be decided, publicly, by Members themselves; the decisions are taken subject to personal pressures and inhibitions.

Even the appointment in 1963 of an independent Committee under the chairmanship of Sir Geoffrey Lawrence,[39] and the full, carefully reasoned Report of that Committee in November 1964,[40] did not avoid all the difficulties and pitfalls inherent in such a delicate and important situation. However, their Report on the Remuneration of Ministers and Members of Parliament does provide a convenient, impartial and authoritative statement of the situation in 1964, and it did result in an increase in Members' salaries from £1,750 to £3,250 per annum.[41] The following brief notes are therefore concerned only with those main issues left wholly or partly unanswered by the Lawrence Committee of 1963/4.

Suggestions that 'whole-time' Members should receive higher pay than the others, or that a fee should be paid to Members attending Committees of the House, have been heard.[42] Philip Goodhart has said that chairmen of committees ought to be paid at least £500 a year over and above their parliamentary salaries.[43] The difficult—perhaps insuperable—question as to whether Members should be in the first instance 'professional' and full-time in their parliamentary duties is involved here. The Lawrence Committee accepted 'lack of homogeneity' as a central feature of Membership,[44] rejected a system of differential remuneration,[45] and recommended that the basic salary should be sufficient to

187

enable Members *without* alternative sources of income to discharge their duties efficiently and to maintain themselves and their families at a 'modest but honourable level'.[46]

One point of general principle which the House has had to decide has been whether it would be better to have a certain fixed salary, or to have a lower salary with an expense allowance claimable in addition. Here the House decided, as the Select Committee had done in 1954,[47] that a flat salary was better.[48] In this respect, they ran counter to the views of several writers to *The Times*, who felt it would be more equitable if their legislators received a small fixed sum, above which they would have to argue with the Inland Revenue in order to establish whether their expenses had been wholly and necessarily incurred in their parliamentary duties.[49] *The Times* itself said, in a leader,[50] that an allowance for secretarial help and postage, on top of a small fixed salary, was the better arrangement; Crick agreed that the first thing to be done was to separate the question of salary from that of expenses.[51] But, as stated above, the 1954 Committee recommended a flat, inclusive salary, and both the Lawrence Committee and the House have since endorsed this principle.

It is often suggested that an increase in salary should be paid to Members only when they can establish that they are in need of it;[52] but the employment of a means test of this kind has never seemed as popular inside the House as outside it. Other ideas voiced have proposed that parliamentary salaries should be fixed by referendum,[53] and that Members should not be allowed any increase in salary until they had presented themselves to the electorate for re-election.[54]

Argument is often caused by the reasons which Members of Parliament advance to justify a particular salary increase. In 1954, the rise in the cost of living was said to require reflection in Members' salaries; but *The Times* objected to this. If the increased cost of living was to be the precedent for raising salaries, it was said, 'the gulf between "we" and "they", which is one of the constant dangers of democracy, will grow'.[55]

Perhaps the most discreet method of adjusting Members' salaries, as and when necessary, was advocated in 1954 in a letter to *The Times* by W. Pickles.[56] He stressed the virtues of the French system, which he believed should be mirrored here, under which

Members would be tied to the salary level of a particular category of Civil Servants. In this country the Whitley Council would decide when a change in Members' salary was needed; changes would take place without fuss or publicity, though the facts would be ascertainable by the public. The Lawrence Committee firmly rejected any such idea of a link between Members' and Civil Servants' remuneration.[57] They gave their reasons clearly and succinctly; but in so doing, the Committee laid themselves open to the criticism that their proposals could not be permanent in nature and scope.

Finally, the point has often been made that the amount of a Member's parliamentary salary ought to be assessed in the light of those services and facilities which he can enjoy, freely and as of right, in his official capacity. The Lawrence Committee considered that the issue of Members' facilities lay *outside* their terms of reference,[58] a decision which the Study of Parliament Group considered to be 'a small mystery' and 'an opportunity lost'.[59] Certainly, a number of Members have stated publicly their readiness to accept a more modest salary in return for expanded secretarial, procedural and research assistance. For the present, however, the 'lack of homogeneity' amongst Members' preferences seems to rule out the practical possibility of such a scheme.

Conclusion

Life in the Palace of Westminster is still partly based on standards existing in the West End clubs of the nineteenth century. But, says a former Independent Member of Parliament, 'when it is said of the House of Commons that "it is the best club in the world", this must be taken as referring to the company, and not the comfort, of the club.'[60] Is this 'club' atmosphere desirable?

To be fair, many of the things that make life at Westminster less intolerable are due to its 'club' origin. Certainly, the principle that Members should share the House's facilities as a community, and not as a collection of factions or cliques—a principle which has had untold influence on the comparative calm of the British Parliament—stems directly from it.

The criticisms, nevertheless, remain. Many of them are caused by the physical difficulty of adapting a large and, in some ways, inefficient fabric to the needs of today. It is hard to say how wide-spread, and how deep, are these criticisms, and whether in fact they are enough to deter the best people from aiming to become Members of Parliament, or to hamper Parliament in the perform-ance of its proper functions. It seems, on the whole, unlikely that serious complaints from a majority of the House would not now be sooner or later remedied. Frequent reference has been made to the Select Committee on House of Commons (Services) first set up in 1965: the House now has the official means of expressing its views on domestic matters such as accommodation and amenities, and time will tell how far and in which direction these matters will be developed.

If the House is still affected by a nineteenth-century milieu, in one major respect at least things have changed during this century. Until the early years of this century, Members came to Westmin-ster, having spent great sums of money in election expenses, and prepared to live as M.P.s on their private income. Today, a Member's election expenses are rigorously controlled, and for his service in the House he receives a salary. Is this salary enough? On the one hand, a correspondent to *The Times* could say, 'Leaders in all walks of life (Burke's natural aristocrats) ... are excluded from Parliament ... because the present salary does not permit them to live or preserve their families from penury.'[61] That was in 1954, when the salary stood at £1,000. Although present remuneration is three times as much, opinion is still divided as to its adequacy. Since the House has to act as the final judge in this matter (and perhaps feels it has to show some measure of restraint in the matter of wage advances), it clearly finds it embarrassing to grant itself an increase in pay. The process by which the Lawrence Committee's recommendations were put forward and subsequently adopted by the House provided only a partial solution to the problem, which must recur at some point in the future.

Yet, important though these factors of salary and amenities may seem to be, they should not be viewed in isolation. Today's Member of Parliament is , says *The Times*, 'overtaxed by inexorable and growing demands upon both his money and his time'.[62] It is probably this latter commodity, time, which the Member can least afford. If the character of Parliament is changing, then it is hard to disagree with the same article when it says: 'It is the pressure of business on the ordinary Member which is the fundamental cause of the change.' If this change is felt to be for the worse, then the remedy could lie in a relaxation of that pressure.

NOTES AND REFERENCES

[1] H.C. 109 of 1943/4.
[2] H.C. Deb. 620, c. 1546, 31st March 1960.
[3] e.g. an article by A. Junz on 'Accommodation at Westminster' in *Parliamentary Affairs*, Vol. XIII, No. 1, pp. 100–13.
[4] H.C. Deb. 414, cs. 181–94; 477, 931ff.
[5] H.C. 64 of 1944/5.
[6] H.C. Deb. 698, cs. 849–981 (Debate on Report).
[7] H.C. 309 of 1952/3, and H.C. 184 of 1953/4.
[8] H.C. 184 of 1953/4, Q. 35.
[9] Report from the Select Committee on the Palace of Westminster; H.C. 285 of 1964/5.
[10] H.C. 64 of 1944/5, para. 2.
[11] Motion, 20th July 1951.
[12] H.C. 309 of 1952/3, para. 18.
[13] *Ibid.* paras. 18–19.
[14] H.C. 92 of 1958/9, p. liii.
[15] *The Times*, 3rd January 1958.
[16] H.C. Deb. 709, cs. 328–33.
[17] H.C. 27 of 1965/6.
[18] See also D. Menhennet, 'The Library of the House of Commons', in *Political Quarterly*, July/September 1965.
[19] H.C. 76 of 1966/7, para. 1.
[20] See D. Menhennet, *art. cit.*
[21] *Reforming the Commons*, P.E.P., October 1965, p. 283.
[22] H.C. Deb. 620, c. 1538.
[23] Cmnd. 2516, para. 68.
[24] *Crossbow*, Vol. 4, No. 10, p. 14.
[25] See D. Menhennet and J. Pook in *New Scientist*, 7th Sept. 1967, p. 502.
[26] Acland, p. 170.
[27] *How to Reform Parliament*, p. 43.
[28] H.C. 72 of 1953/4.
[29] *The Times*, 9th July 1954.
[30] *Reform of the Commons*, p. 8.
[31] *Crossbow*, Vol. 4, No. 10, p. 20.
[32] H.C. Deb. c. 1546, 31st March 1960. See also the plea for secretarial assistance by Mrs. White: *ibid.* cs. 1621–2.
[33] H.C. Deb. 310, c. 2407.
[34] H.C. 72 of 1953/4.
[35] H.C. 107 of 1965/6, para. 4.
[36] H.C. 92 of 1958/9, p. liii; Q. 564.
[37] H.C. Deb. 617, c. 132.
[38] H.C. Deb. 620, c. 1536, 31st March 1960.
[39] H.C. Deb. 686, cs. 1441–45.

[40] Cmnd. 2516 of November 1964. See also for comparative purposes, Grey and Marriott's study for the Commonwealth Parliamentary Association of *Payments and Privileges* (in 1965) *of Commonwealth Parliamentarians.*

[41] *ibid.* para. 167(1).

[42] H.C. 92 of 1958/9, Q. 518–19.

[43] *Crossbow*, Vol. 4, No. 10, p. 11.

[44] Cmnd. 2516, para. 34.

[45] *ibid.* para. 36.

[46] *ibid.* paras. 35 and 37.

[47] H.C. 72 of 1953/4.

[48] H.C. Deb., 528, cs. 30–158.

[49] The expenses generally spoken of in this context are those for secretarial help, correspondence and the running of a car. (H.C. 72 of 1953/4.)

[50] *The Times*, 9th July 1954.

[51] *Reform of the Commons*, pp. 7–8.

[52] e.g. *The Times*, 22nd February 1954. (Letter from H. V. Wiseman.)

[53] *The Times*, 1st March 1954. (Letter from J. Foley.)

[54] *The Times*, 28th May 1954. (Letter from Sir A. Herbert.)

[55] *The Times*, 8th March 1954.

[56] *The Times*, 28th May 1954.

[57] Cmnd. 2516, para. 39.

[58] *ibid.* para. 66.

[59] *Reforming the Commons*, October 1965, p. 284.

[60] W. J. Brown: *Everybody's Guide to Parliament*, 1945, p. 80.

[61] H. Maddick, *The Times*, 24th February 1954.

[62] *The Times*, 8th March 1954. For an account of the possible scope, variety and pressure of an 'average' M.P.'s day, see 'A Day in the Life of an M.P.' in Menhennet and Palmer, *Parliament in Perspective* (Bodley Head, 1967).

Select Bibliography

Books and pamphlets only are listed below. References to *Hansard*, Parliamentary Papers and other *official* publications, and to articles, newspaper reports, etc., are given in the notes to the text. The books listed below do *not* constitute a bibliography of Parliament: they are essentially the main sources (other than official publications) from which the preceding study on *Parliamentary Reform* has been compiled. A good recent bibliography on Parliament has been compiled for the Hansard Society by John Palmer: *Government and Parliament in Britain* (2nd ed. revised and enlarged, 1964). The reader is also referred to Anthony Barker's useful and detailed Bibliography of *Parliamentary Studies 1961–65*, published in *Political Quarterly*, July/September 1965.

Where a book included in the list below is referred to frequently in the text, the footnote reference is often given in shortened form, thus: Acland, p. 157. Shortened forms of this type are avoided in cases where more than one book by a particular author is listed below. It should be noted that the text, which reflects proposals for reform made over the last 30 years or so, often refers to an early edition of a work (cf., e.g., Richards, P. G., below). Later editions are noted in brackets below, where appropriate, but footnotes in the text refer to the earlier editions unless otherwise stated.

Acland, Sir R., *What It Will be Like in the New Britain*. Gollancz Ltd., 1942.

Acton Society Trust. *Nationalised Industry*. (*1*) *Accountability to Parliament*. (*2*) *Powers of the Minister*. Acton Society Trust, 1950.

Allen, Sir C. K., *Law and Orders*. 2nd ed. Stevens & Sons Ltd., 1956. (3rd ed. 1965.)

Amery, L. S., *Thoughts on the Constitution*. O.U.P., 1947.

Attlee, C. R. (Lord Attlee), *As It Happened*. Heinemann Ltd., 1954.

Bailey, S. D. (ed.), *The British Party System: A Symposium*. Hansard Society, 1952.

Bailey, S. D. (ed.), *The Future of the House of Lords: A Symposium*. Hansard Society, 1954.

Barker, Sir E., *Reflections on Government*. O.U.P., 1953 [1942].

Benn, A. Wedgwood, *The Privy Council as a Second Chamber*. Fabian Tract, 305, 1957.

Black, D., *The Theory of Committees and Elections*. C.U.P., 1958.

Bromhead, P. A., *Private Members' Bills in the British Parliament*. Routledge & Kegan Paul Ltd., 1956.

Bulmer-Thomas, I., *The Party System in Great Britain*. Phoenix House Ltd., 1953. (*The Growth of the British Party System*, 2 vols., 1965.)

Butler, D. E., *The Electoral System in Britain 1918–1951*. O.U.P., 1953. (*The Electoral System in Britain since 1918*. 2nd ed., 1963.)

Butler, D. E. and others. *Elections Abroad*. Macmillan & Co. Ltd., 1959.

Butler, D. E. & Rose, R., *The British General Election of 1959*. Macmillan & Co. Ltd., 1960. (Butler & Anthony King have produced similar studies for the General Elections of 1964 and 1966 (Macmillan, 1965 and 1966 respectively).)

Campion, Lord. *An Introduction to the Procedure of the House of Commons*. 3rd ed. Macmillan & Co. Ltd., 1958.

Campion, Lord, and others. *Parliament: A Survey*. G. Allen & Unwin Ltd., 1952.

Carter, B. E., *The Office of Prime Minister*. Faber & Faber Ltd., 1956.

Change or Decay, Parliament and Government in our Industrial Society, by a Group of Conservative M.P.s. C.P.C., 1963.

Chester, D. N. & Bowring, N., *Questions in Parliament*. O.U.P., 1962.

Chorley, Lord, and others. *Reform of the Lords*. Fabian Research Series, 169, 1954.

Chubb, B., *The Control of Public Expenditure*. O.U.P., 1952.

Constitutional Reform. Some Proposals for Constitutional Reform: being the Recommendations of a Group of Conservatives. Eyre & Spottiswoode Ltd., 1946.

Coombes, D., *The Member of Parliament and the Administration*. G. Allen & Unwin Ltd., 1966.

Crick, B., *Reform of the Commons*. Fabian Tract, 319, 1959.

Crick, B., *The Reform of Parliament: The Crisis of British Government in the 1960s*. Weidenfeld & Nicolson Ltd., 1964.

Crossman, R. H. S., *Introduction to Bagehot*. Fontana, 1963.

Curtis, M. R., *Central Government: An Introduction*. Pitman & Sons Ltd., 1956. (Rev. ed., 1962.)

Day, R., *The Case for Televising Parliament*. Hansard Society, 1963.

Duverger, M., *Political Parties: Their Organisation and Activity in the Modern State*. (Translated by B. & R. North), 2nd ed. rev. Methuen & Co. Ltd., 1959.

Einzig, P., *The Control of the Purse: progress and decline of Parliament's Financial Control*. Secker & Warburg Ltd., 1959.

Finer, H., *The Theory and Practice of Modern Government*. Methuen & Co. Ltd., 1954.

Finer, S. E., *Anonymous Empire: A Study of the 'Lobby' in Great Britain*. Pall Mall Press, 1958. (Rev. ed., 1966.)

Foot, M., *Parliament in Danger!* Pall Mall Press, 1959.

Gaitskell, H., *In Defence of Politics*. Birkbeck College, 1954.

Gordon, S., *Our Parliament*. 5th ed. Hansard Society, 1958. (6th ed. Cassell, 1964.)

Granada TV. *A First Report on Constituency Television in a General Election*. Granada TV Network, 1959.

Greaves, H. R. G., *The British Constitution*. 2nd ed., G. Allen & Unwin Ltd., 1948.

Hanson, A. H., *Parliament and Public Ownership*. Cassell for the Hansard Society, 1961.

Hanson, A. H. & Wiseman, H. V., *Parliament at Work: a Casebook of Parliamentary Procedure*. Stevens, 1962.

Harrison, W., *The Government of Britain*. Hutchinson & Co. Ltd., 1948.

Herbert, Sir A. P., *Independent Member*. Methuen & Co. Ltd., 1950.

Herbert, Sir A. P., *I Object: Letter to the Electors of East Harrow*. Bodley Head Ltd., 1958.

Hill, A. & Whichelow, A., *What's Wrong with Parliament?* Penguin, 1964.

Hollis, C., *Can Parliament Survive?* Hollis & Carter, 1949.

Hollis, C., *Has Parliament a Future?* Unservile State Papers No. 1, 1960.

Howarth, P., *Questions in the House*. Bodley Head Ltd., 1956.

Hughes, E., *Parliament and Mumbo-Jumbo*. G. Allen & Unwin Ltd., 1966.

Institute of Electoral Research. *A Review of Elections 1954–1958*. Inst. of Electoral Research, 1960.

Iwi, E. F., *Laws and Flaws: Lapses of the Legislators*. Odhams Press Ltd., 1956.

James, R. V. R., *An Introduction to the House of Commons*. Collins, 1961.

Jennings, Sir W. I., *Cabinet Government*. 3rd ed., C.U.P., 1959.

Jennings, Sir W. I., *Parliament*. 2nd ed., C.U.P., 1957.

Jennings, Sir W. I., *Parliament Must be Reformed: A Programme for Democratic Government*. Kegan Paul, Trench, Trubner & Co. Ltd., 1941.

Jennings, Sir W. I., *Parliamentary Reform*. Gollancz Ltd. (for the New Fabian Research Bureau), 1934.

Jennings, Sir W. I., *Party Politics I: Appeal to the People*. C.U.P., 1960; II: *Growth of Parties*. C.U.P., 1961; III: *The Stuff of Politics*. C.U.P., 1962.

Keeton, G. W., *The Passing of Parliament*. 2nd ed., Ernest Benn Ltd., 1954.

Kelf-Cohen, R., *Nationalisation in Britain: The End of a Dogma*. Macmillan & Co. Ltd., 1958.

Lakeman, E. & Lambert, J. D., *Voting in Democracies*. Faber & Faber Ltd., 1955.

Laski, H. J., *Reflections on the Constitution*. M.U.P., 1951.

Le May, G. H. L., *British Government 1914–1953: Select Documents*. Methuen & Co. Ltd., 1955.

Mackay, R. W. G., *Coupon or Free? Being a Study in Electoral Reform and Representative Government*. Secker & Warburg Ltd., 1943.

McKenzie, R. T., *British Political Parties*. Heinemann Ltd., 1955. (2nd ed., 1963.)

Mackintosh, J. P., *The British Cabinet*. Stevens & Sons Ltd., 1962.

Marshall, G. & Moodie, G. C., *Some Problems of the Constitution*. Hutchinson & Co. Ltd., 1959. (3rd ed., 1964.)

Mathiot, A., *The British Political System*. Trans. by J. S. Hines. Hogarth Press Ltd., 1958.

Menhennet, D. & Palmer, J., *Parliament in Perspective*. Bodley Head, 1967.

Morrison, H. S. (Lord Morrison of Lambeth). *Government and Parliament: A Survey from the Inside*. O.U.P., 1954 (3rd ed., 1964.)

SELECT BIBLIOGRAPHY

Muir, R., *How Britain is Governed: A Critical Analysis of Modern Developments in the British System of Government.* 2nd ed. Constable & Co. Ltd., 1930.

Nicolson, N., *People and Parliament.* Weidenfeld & Nicolson Ltd., 1958.

Political Quarterly, *Special Number on Parliament.* July/September 1965.

Pollard, R. S. W., *How to Reform Parliament.* Forum Press, 1944. *Speed-Up Law Reform.* Fabian Research Series, 194, 1958.

Ranney, A. *Pathways to Parliament.* Macmillan, 1965.

Richards, P. G., *Honourable Members: A Study of the British Backbencher.* Faber & Faber Ltd., 1959 (2nd ed., 1963.)

Ross, J. F. S., *The Achievement of Representative Democracy.* Bowes & Bowes Ltd., 1952.

Ross, J. F. S., *Elections and Electors: Studies in Democratic Representation.* Eyre & Spottiswoode Ltd., 1955.

Ross, J. F. S., *Parliamentary Representation.* 2nd. ed., Eyre & Spottiswoode Ltd., 1948.

Shinwell, E., *The Britain I Want.* (Chapt. XV: Parliament and Democracy), Macdonald & Co. Ltd., 1943.

Socialist Commentary, *Three Dozen Parliamentary Reforms,* by one dozen Parliamentary Socialists. July 1964.

Spearman, D., *Democracy in England.* Barrie & Rockliff, 1957.

Stewart, J. D., *British Pressure Groups: Their Role in Relation to the House of Commons.* O.U.P., 1958.

Stewart, M., *The British Approach to Politics.* 3rd ed. rev., G. Allen & Unwin Ltd., 1955. (5th ed. rev., 1965.)

Study of Parliament Group, *Reforming the Commons.* PEP, 1965.

Thomas, H. (ed.), *The Establishment: A Symposium.* Anthony Blond Ltd., 1959.

Wade, H. W. R., *Administrative Law.* O.U.P., 1961.

Watson, G. (ed.), *The Unservile State: Essays in Liberty and Welfare.* G. Allen & Unwin Ltd., 1957.

Wiseman, H. V. (comp.), *Parliament and the Executive.* Routledge, 1966.

197

Index

199

INDEX

Wilkinson, Ellen, 141
Williams, Sir Herbert
  Divisions, 91
Wilson, Harold
  Cabinet, 143
Winterton, Lord
  legislation, 76
  M.P.s and constituents, 172

Wiseman, Victor, 38, 51
Woolton, Lord, 140

Young, G. M., 45, 46